LITERATURE AND REVOLUTION
IN SOVIET RUSSIA
1917-62

Literature and Revolution
in Soviet Russia
1917–62

A Symposium Edited by
MAX HAYWARD
and
LEOPOLD LABEDZ

LONDON
OXFORD UNIVERSITY PRESS
NEW YORK   TORONTO
1963

Oxford University Press, Amen House, London E.C.4

GLASGOW NEW YORK TORONTO MELBOURNE WELLINGTON
BOMBAY CALCUTTA MADRAS KARACHI LAHORE DACCA
CAPE TOWN SALISBURY NAIROBI IBADAN ACCRA
KUALA LUMPUR HONG KONG

PRINTED IN GREAT BRITAIN
BY HAZELL WATSON & VINEY LTD
AYLESBURY, BUCKS

CONTENTS

These papers were given at a Conference, held under the joint auspices of St Antony's College and *Survey*, in Oxford, July 1962.

INTRODUCTION

In recent years Soviet literature has forced itself, often in a dramatic way, on the attention of the outside world, as probably no other literature has ever done before. It is hoped that the essays in this symposium will give historical perspective to recent events and bring into focus the unique problems of Soviet writers.

A study of the Party's attempt to impose its will on literature and the arts is interesting in a general sense for students of totalitarian politics. In this field, as also notoriously in agriculture, it has been a question of trying to impose total doctrinal and administrative discipline on a form of human activity which depends entirely on highly individual skills. It is not surprising to find that the object of this attempted control has proved to be recalcitrant and that the aims envisaged have almost always been defeated by the methods employed. The record has, broadly speaking, been one of failure: in contrast to other fields, such as industry, where production techniques may even benefit from a high degree of control and co-ordination by a monolithic political party.

It is sometimes forgotten that in its first decade the Bolshevik Party in Russia was extremely modest in its claims to control all aspects of social activity, and was equally conscious of its inability to do so. Furthermore, there was a certain scale of priorities. Political and economic control obviously came first, but even this was partially abandoned with the inauguration of the New Economic Policy (NEP). Cultural matters were the least of the Party's concern in a period when it was still numerically weak and bent above all on maintaining its hegemony as the 'vanguard of the proletariat'. At that time in fact the Party modestly contented itself with securing in all fields what it called the 'commanding positions'. It did not yet dispose of cadres sufficiently strong, loyal, and well-organized to infiltrate and set its image on the whole of society. In the economy, in the administration, and particularly in the cultural field it had to rely on so-called 'bourgeois specialists' bequeathed from the past. This meant that until about 1928 there were several autonomous literary and artistic organizations which were not under direct

Party control. During NEP there was furthermore a number of quasi-independent publishing firms, often organized on co-operative lines, which were relatively free of direct state control.

The literary organizations in the first decade of Soviet rule included small groups claiming to be proletarian, various *avant-garde* cliques such as the Futurists and the Constructivists, and the numerically predominant fellow-travellers. The last-named were bourgeois specialists in literature. They were for the most part *ancien régime* intellectuals who were already professional writers at the moment of the Revolution. Politically they ranged from sympathy, through luke-warm acceptance, to downright rejection of the new regime. The instability of their attitudes, their individualism, even more than their bourgeois intellectual origins, naturally made them suspect, and they were tolerated mainly on account of their indispensable professional expertise. The frankly expressed policy of the Party towards them was eventually to 'win them over' and fuse them with the so-called proletarian writers when these had developed sufficient technical competence. In the meantime, paradoxically, the main concern of the Party was to protect the fellow-travellers from premature attempts on the part of the 'proletarians' and the avant-gardists to assimilate them politically by coercive methods, thereby antagonizing them and making more difficult the ultimate aim of winning them over.

The Party at this stage thus found itself in the odd position of restraining its most vociferous allies in the cultural field and of refusing to arbitrate in their favour. The first major declaration of the Party on literature came in 1925, and it was essentially a declaration of neutrality as between the contending groups. This resolution, entitled 'The Policy of the Party in the Field of Artistic Literature', noted the existence of a considerable variety of literary trends, which, as it rightly pointed out, corresponded to the social, economic, and class complexity of the NEP period. Its policy of non-intervention was formulated in the following way:

. . . the Party absolutely cannot commit itself to any one trend in the sphere of literary form. While controlling literature in a general way, the Party can no more give support to any one fraction (fractions being classified according to differences of view about *style* and *form*) than it can decide by resolution questions of family life . . . .

There is every reason to believe that a style consonant with the new era will be created, but it will be created by different methods, and so far there is no sign of a solution of this question. *Any attempt to tie the Party down in this respect at the present stage of cultural development must be rejected.* [My italics.]

Therefore, the Party must declare itself for free competition between the various groups and trends in this field. Any other solution of the question would be a bureaucratic pseudo-solution. In exactly the same way it would be inadmissible to ordain by Party decree the *legalized monopoly* of literature and publishing by any one group or literary organization....

In speaking of 'control in a general way' this resolution was no doubt referring to the purely negative control exercised through the censorship organization set up by decree in 1922. This organization was known as *Glavlit* (standing for 'Chief Administration for Literary Affairs'), and its main function was to prevent the publication of overtly counter-revolutionary works. Like the tsarist censorship, its functions were preventive rather than prescriptive, and it did not interfere with basic literary freedom in matters of form and content as long as the political interests of the new regime were not adversely affected.

One important element in the comparative licence allowed to writers during the NEP period must be mentioned, namely that many of the old Bolsheviks then in power were themselves men of broad culture, intellectuals in the true sense of the word, who understood very well that cultural processes could not be artificially accelerated by doctrinaire interference, and that any attempt to force the pace, as demanded by left-wing hotheads, could only be disastrous. During the whole of the NEP period the direct responsibility for cultural policy was in the hands of Lunacharsky, who was himself an accomplished writer and well understood the need for tact in the handling of the postrevolutionary intelligentsia.

This relatively mild, in retrospect almost idyllic, period ended abruptly in 1929 (a year aptly described by Stalin as 'the year of the great turning point'), with the end of the New Economic Policy and Stalin's decision to make the Party, now under his undisputed personal control, into an instrument for the revolutionary transformation of society and an apparatus for the minute regulation of all aspects of life. Hence, just as the peasants were to be collectivized, so the writers and intellectuals in general were to be 'bolshevized', according to the slogan of the day. The policy of artificially stimulated class-warfare in the countryside was carried over into the cultural sphere. Needless to say, the main victims in the campaign were the fellow-travellers, from whom protection was now withdrawn. The relatively mild stewardship of Lunacharsky came to an end, and the so-called proletarian writers were deliberately let off the leash at which they had been straining for a number of years.

In 1929 there existed two main literary organizations: the All-Russian Union of Writers, and the so-called Association of Proletarian Writers, known in abbreviation as RAPP. The Union was the organization of the fellow-travellers and included most writers of any standing, among them many of the best-known of the old generation who have survived until the present day, such as Leonov, Kaverin and Fedin. It was a non-political organization, not dissimilar in its general structure and functions from, say, the PEN Club. It was concerned primarily with the welfare of its members, not with their ideology or their attitude to the regime, and it demanded no adherence to any particular aesthetic programme.

RAPP on the other hand was a militant organization of writers claiming proletarian origin, or at least spiritual kinship with the workers and peasants, and asserting the 'hegemony of the protelariat' in literature. They regarded themselves as the politically conscious vanguard, whose mission was the creation of a genuinely new, revolutionary culture. Up till now, the fellow-travellers had existed for them only on sufferance, and were regarded, according to the degree of their willingness to re-educate themselves, either as bourgeois specialists in literature, from whom something might be learnt in matters of technique, or at best as potential recruits to the 'proletarian' ranks. This desirable status could only be achieved, they maintained, by wholehearted inner submission to the will of the proletariat and its self appointed *avant-garde*, the Party. It should be stressed that the leaders of RAPP were able to exploit at this period a genuine feeling on the part of certain individuals that mystical union with the proletariat could lead to the blissful liberation from his miseries of the lone hag-ridden intellectual, who could sometimes be induced to believe that the intolerable burdens of individual responsibility might be miraculously resolved by total submission to the collective. RAPP's quasi-religious fervour was undoubtedly effective in the case of some fellow-travellers, but with the usual impatience of fanatics its leaders relied more and more on threats and coercion. Indeed, they were now encouraged to do this by the Party itself, and they were allowed to proceed in 1929 with a campaign of terror aimed at breaking the will of the fellow-travellers, forcing them to choose between total submission or elimination from the literary scene.

The method which RAPP employed to force a showdown with the organization of fellow-traveller writers established a precedent for the technique which became all too familiar in the Stalinist decades to follow. The technique was that of picking on certain scapegoats and starting a campaign of vilification with the object of terrorizing a whole group into submission. In this first case of its kind in the cultural field, the victims were the chairman of the All-Russian Union of Writers, Boris Pilnyak, and the head of the branch of the Union in Leningrad, Evgeni Zamyatin. There is a close parallel with the Zhdanov campaign in 1946 which started with the denunciation of Zoshchenko and Akhmatova. In both cases the victimization of the chosen scapegoats was the signal for a sharp change in literary policy and a general purge, instigated by the Central Committee of the Party —that is, in effect, by Stalin personally. The alleged offences of the victims were of relatively little importance in the minds of their denouncers compared with the terroristic effects for which they offered a suitable pretext. The only striking difference between the case of Pilnyak and Zamyatin and that of Zoshchenko and Akhmatova is that the former showed certain defects of orchestration which were perhaps not surprising in view of the relative inexperience of the instigators and the fact that the tragicomedy was enacted in a society which was not yet entirely broken and which still had to learn the futility of resistance.

By later standards the campaign was clumsily handled, and as an attempt to compromise Pilnyak and Zamyatin morally it was a failure. The original charge against them was that both had arranged for the publication abroad of works which had not been passed by the Soviet censorship. A few months previously a story by Pilnyak called *Mahagony* had been published in Berlin; and a few years before, in 1924, without any repercussions at the time, Zamyatin's anti-utopian novel *We* had been published in Prague in a Russian émigré journal. Both writers were able to demonstrate beyond any doubt (and it is characteristic of the ham-handedness of the campaign that they were allowed to do so in public) that they were quite blameless on the score of having deliberately published these works abroad. Zamyatin had, in fact, done his best to prevent the publication of *We* in Prague, and the manuscript of Pilnyak's *Mahagony* had been sent by his literary agent in Leningrad to a Russian publisher in Berlin in accordance with what was then a perfectly legal procedure whereby Soviet writers obtained protection under the international copyright laws. What happened in the case of Pilnyak's manuscript was that the Berlin firm, which performed this service for Soviet writers, published *Mahagony* prematurely without waiting for it to be passed for publication in Moscow.

When both authors were able to show that they were not guilty of evading Soviet censorship control, the RAPP instigators of the affair changed their tack and concentrated, quite irrelevantly as far as the original charges were concerned, on the alleged *anti-Soviet* nature of the works in question. They were said to be symptomatic of the work of many fellow-travellers who were now bluntly told that they must make manifest their 'solidarity with the proletariat' or forfeit the right to call themselves *Soviet* writers. The word *Soviet* in this context was henceforth to be interpreted not as a mere territorial designation but as a definition of the writer's political allegiance. After a series of rigged meetings in the various writers' organizations, resolutions were adopted in accordance with which Pilnyak and Zamyatin were removed, together with the whole of the old leadership of the All-Russian Union of Writers. At the same time the rank and file membership was 're-registered', and as many as one half were purged. This was separating the bourgeois goats from the proletarian sheep with a vengeance. To mark the radical change in the literary situation, the All-Russian Union of Writers was now renamed the All-Russian Union of *Soviet* Writers. Pilnyak set a sinister precedent for years to come by making a grovelling recantation, whereas Zamyatin wrote a defiant letter to Stalin asking permission to emigrate—which extraordinarily enough was granted.

Despite one or two muted protests, this blatant frame-up

marked the end of creative freedom in Russia for fellow-travellers and Proletarians alike. The following two decades saw the increasing terrorization of intellectuals into abject conformity, and the debasement of literary and artistic taste in accordance with what are now freely admitted to have been Stalin's personal whims.

For two years, until 1932, RAPP was allowed almost complete control over the literary scene, and its leaders as well as most observers naturally imagined that its policy was that of the Central Committee of the Party and that it had come to stay. In 1932, however, it was quite suddenly and without any warning disbanded. In a brief and offhand decree, the Central Committee announced that in view of the great progress in Socialist construction and the consequent immeasurable strengthening of proletarian cadres, there was now no need for different literary organizations (most of the other organizations apart from RAPP still existed in theory at this time), and that henceforth there would be one unitary organization to be called the Union of Soviet Writers, membership in which would be essential for anyone who wished to practise professionally. The decree stated significantly that the Union must have a communist fraction in it. At the same time similar unitary organizations were set up for musicians and artists.

Odd as it appeared at the time, this sudden liquidation of RAPP is completely explicable in terms of Stalin's temperament. RAPP consisted for the most part of genuine fanatics who really believed that they were the chosen spokesmen of the proletariat. It was characteristic of Stalin during the Thirties that he mistrusted and suspected true believers in anything but his own infallibility. Particularly he distrusted those for whom Marxism, in however primitive a form, was a sincerely held credo. It is not surprising, therefore, that having used RAPP as an instrument to bludgeon non-Party intellectuals into conformity, he now abruptly got rid of them. A number of them, including their leader Averbakh, were, needless to say, subsequently accused of Trotskyism, like so many other communist intellectuals of the Twenties, and shot.

During the Thirties, Stalin showed a clear preference for broken and compliant intellectuals with a bourgeois and fellow-travelling past who could be relied upon to make any compromise without reference to political principles or ideals, in the face of Stalin's increasingly outrageous deviations from Marxism. The most noteworthy examples were in the field of historical studies. After the denunciation of the old Marxist historian Pokrovsky, the bourgeois historians Tarle and Vipper were rehabilitated and recalled in order to glorify Russian despots of the past.

Having herded the writers into a single organization, firmly controlled by a communist fraction subservient to Stalin, the logical next step was to give them a unitary doctrine. Socialist realism, on which membership of the Union of Writers was made conditional, was promulgated at the first congress of the Union in 1934. This was done by Zhdanov, who first emerged on this occasion as Stalin's lieutenant in cultural matters. Since it was now intended to exploit literature for a purpose quite alien to it and in a way which contradicted almost everything ever said on the subject by Marx and Engels, who had never advocated outside interference in the creative process, Zhdanov justified the new situation by invoking the authority of a hitherto little-known article by Lenin entitled *Party Organization and Party Literature*. This has been written by Lenin in 1905, and it had never before occurred to anyone that it was particularly relevant to the problem of literature in the sense of *belles-lettres*. In using this document as the main authority for the Party's new policy of enforcing total control on the writers and dictating to them in matters of content and form, Zhdanov was certainly resorting to conscious fraud. As the notes which Lenin made for this article show, he was writing of literature in the most general sense, and primarily had in mind not creative writers but, as he said in one of his notes, such '*littérateurs* as Akselrod, Martov, Parvus, Trotsky, Potresov and Plekhanov'. Lenin was writing after the 1905 Revolution, when a number of parties existed legally, and he was simply insisting that anybody who wrote for Social Democrat journals must stick to the Party line. He was worried about the lack of Party discipline displayed by what he called 'intellectual supermen', and he demanded that they become 'screws and cogs' in the Social Democrat mechanism. Zhdanov pointedly ignored another passage in Lenin's article which said: 'Everybody is free to write and say what he pleases, without the slightest restrictions, but every free association (and a party too) is also free to expel such members who use the party's platform to preach anti-party views. Freedom of speech and freedom of the press must be absolute. But the freedom of association must also be absolute.' By 1934, as Zhdanov well knew, there was no longer freedom of association in the Soviet Union.

Nevertheless, this article of Lenin's was used as the source of the central concept of socialist realism, namely *partiynost* (Party-mindedness): the idea that the Party may use literature for whatever purpose it may think fit at a given moment, and that it is the duty of any true Soviet writer to accept Party guidance without question. As an aesthetic theory socialist realism is muddled, self-contradictory and eclectic, owing far more to nineteenth-century pre-Marxist publicists, such as Belinsky and Chernyshevski, than to the Marxist classics. It appears to have been devised by Gorky in consultation with Stalin. For Gorky the principal intention was no doubt to keep Soviet literature in the mainstream of the classical realist tradition, of which he himself was the last great representative, but for Stalin, as well as being in keeping with his own pedestrian tastes, it must have seemed an attractive way of subordinating literature and the arts to his own extra-literary purposes.

The greatest difficulty for the writers about socialist realism was that they were expected to employ the realist style of the nineteenth-century classics in a spirit which was quite alien to its creators. The new doctrine drew a sharp distinction between 'socialist' realism and the 'critical' realism of the classics. The latter, it was said, had used the realist method to *negate* the society in which they lived, whereas the Soviet writer was required by the same method to *affirm* the new Socialist order which was *ex-hypothesi* the most benevolent and the most nearly perfect ever establishd on earth. It was the writer's duty, therefore, not only to describe it 'realistically in its revolutionary development' (Zhdanov's phrase), but also to assist the Party in its task of completing the social transformation now in progress, of consolidating the gains already made, and of educating the people in the ways of virtue. Since, in Marxist theory, consciousness always lags behind social and economic change, there were still admittedly many wayward citizens who were slow to recognize the benefits of the new order, their minds being infected by 'survivals of capitalism'. One of the writer's principal duties was now to expose and hold up to scorn these 'survivals', and thus hasten the day when all would model themselves on the New Man. Stalin summed it all up by saying that the writers should be engineers of human souls. His only other known contribution to literary theory was his advice on how to be a good socialist realist: 'Write the truth.'

The second half of the Thirties, until the war, is notable for the steady deterioration of literary standards and the gradual disappearance from the scene of most writers of any standing. Many fell silent, and many were shot or imprisoned during the terror of 1937.

Paradoxically, the outbreak of war brought a sense of relief, even of liberation to Soviet intellectuals. This feeling has been well described by Pasternak in *Dr Zhivago* in the famous passage where one of the characters speaks about how the outbreak of war 'broke the spell of the dead letter'. In retrospect it is of course quite understandable. There was now a genuine atmosphere of national unanimity in the face of a real and truly terrible external enemy, instead of the bogus unanimity artificially created by Stalin in the face of a largely imaginary internal enemy. A true wartime feeling of comradeship, often forged and tested in front-line conditions, replaced the hideous mutual suspicion created and deliberately fostered by the terror of 1936–38.

For literature the war was entirely beneficial. Most Soviet writers were at the front as war correspondents, and were able to write reportage of lasting value, which on the whole faithfully reflected the everyday tragedy of war. For a time at least, they were released from the obligation to distort reality and parody human nature. But the most surprising development in literature during the war was that some journals, particularly in Leningrad, published verse and prose unconnected with the theme of the war, which was quite out of keeping with socialist realism. The most extraordinary example is Zoshchenko's *Before Sunrise*. This is a highly pessimistic autobiographical sketch in which the author seeks the cause of his own unhappiness by a kind of Freudian self-analysis. Admittedly this work was stopped after two instalments, but the fact that it could have appeared at all is indicative of the comparative relaxation of the Party's grip on writers and their publishers during the war.

This interlude, which went on for a short time after the war, was brutally brought to an end by the famous decree of the Central Committee on the journals *Zvezda* and *Leningrad* in 1946. This was the first of the notorious so-called Zhdanov decrees, which also affected philosophy, music, cinematography, and indeed every sphere of intellectual activity. The effect and purpose of these decrees was to restore the situation as it existed on the eve of the war. Many reasons have been advanced for this most brutal intervention in Soviet cultural life, which seemed to show complete contempt for public opinion and the prestige of the Soviet Union abroad. The main factor was certainly Stalin's desire to destroy the solidarity among intellectuals which had sprung up during the war. He regarded mutual trust among people as tantamount to a conspiracy against himself. He had to restore as quickly as possible the atmosphere of mutual distrust on which his absolute rule depended. The orgy of mutual denunciations, the hounding of scapegoats such as Zoshchenko, Akhmatova and Pasternak, which followed the first Zhdanov decree had a devastating effect, and the period between 1946 and 1953 was utterly sterile in terms of literary production. Furthermore, in this period socialist realism was enforced to such a point of absurdity that literature ceased to fulfil the crude didactic functions assigned to it by the Party; the almost total divorce from reality, the projection of the communist millennium into the present, the unbearably false optimism, and the increasing standardization of style and plots made it difficult to distinguish one play, novel, or poem from another, and the reading public, far from being educated in the spirit of service to socialism, was bored and exasperated almost beyond endurance. This was even admitted in the year or so before Stalin's death. The emptiness of the theatres during the performance of new Soviet plays made the lack of public interest in Soviet literature all too conspicuous. Needless to say, the blame for this was put not on the Party's literary policy or the manifest absurdities of the doctrine, but on the writers themselves for somehow failing to apply it correctly. The fact is that the writers had been so intimidated by the denunciation of Zoshchenko and Akhmatova and many subsequent campaigns that they had taken refuge in what appeared to be the safest of stereotyped formulae. They no longer even dared to expose 'survivals of the past', for fear of being accused of slandering Soviet reality. As a critic wrote after Stalin's death, the lives of Soviet people in literature were supposed to 'take place under a sugary sky to the cheerful laughter of "militant" men and women'. Nobody dared mention the seamy side at all, and satire, even of the most innocuous kind, disappeared. Formerly, at least there had been the so-called struggle between the 'good' and the 'bad' to enliven the plot of a Soviet novel or play. Now, in sheer self-defence, the writers played safe by depicting only the conflict between the 'good' and the 'better'. The emasculation of literature had become so evident by 1952 that the writers were accused of having evolved the 'rotten theory of lack of conflict', and they were suddenly urged in a *Pravda* editorial to produce satire like Gogol and Shchedrin, but no new Gogols or Shchedrins stepped forward. Everybody remembered too vividly what had happened to Zoshchenko in 1946.

Not only the satirists but the writers in general wisely bided their time until after Stalin's death in March 1953. In my contribution to this symposium I have tried to relate the varying fortunes of Soviet literature in the post-Stalin period until the summer of 1962. It only remains for me to comment briefly on the most recent turn in Party policy occasioned by Khrushchev's remarks during a visit to an art exhibition in Moscow on 1 December 1962.

This was the signal for a brusque reversal of the trend towards 'liberalization'. By November 1962 it seemed as though the Party leadership and Khrushchev personally had come to accept and tolerate the existence of a 'right' and 'left' wing among the writers, which expressed itself increasingly in the classical form of a split between generations, the 'fathers' and 'sons'. More than this, there were visible signs that the Party might even be prepared to give active support to the 'left wing'. Among the conspicuous tokens of this support were the appointment of such young writers as Evtushenko and Voznesensky to responsible posts in the writers' organizations and on editorial boards, and the appearance of ever 'bolder' prose and verse, such as Solzhenitsyn's *One Day in the Life of Ivan Denisovich*, which was published by specific permission of the Party Central Committee. Many people not unnaturally thought that its publication was preparatory to impending trials of Stalinists and the expulsion of certain particularly notorious members of the Union of Writers.

The right wing was quick to exploit Khrushchev's indignation at the specimens of abstract art he saw at the exhibition, and at a moment when their cause seemed to be lost, they tried to bring about a total reversal of the liberal trends of the last few years. At the end of December 1962 and again at the beginning of March 1963 the intellectuals of Moscow and Leningrad were berated by Ilyichev, the head of the Ideological Commission of the Party Central Committee, and by Khrushchev himself, for having entered the dangerous path of 'ideological co-existence' with the bourgeois West. This was now pronounced to be impermissible, and was sternly condemned by Khrushchev and Ilyichev in Zhdanovist language. With appropriate quotations from Lenin they tried to show that the Party has always drawn, and is obliged to draw, a clear distinction between art which serves the bourgeoisie and art which serves the 'toiling masses', and that only 'Party guidance' and the acceptance of the supposedly Leninist principle of *partiinost* can prevent the line between them getting blurred. They reiterated the familiar point that art and literature, as part of the 'superstructure', are an instrument in the hands of the class which controls the 'base', and that hence an abstract painter or a formalist poet objectively, if not subjectively, puts himself at the service of the bourgeoisie and thus helps the bourgeoisie in its insidious design of weakening the resolve of the Soviet people in the construction of communism. The lesson is, therefore, that there can be no question of ideological co-existence between varying trends at home or between the Soviet Union and the outside world.

Some time in the second half of 1962 it was evidently borne in on Khrushchev that the more tolerant policy which he himself had inaugurated by his speech to the writers in 1959 could easily lead to an irreparable loss of Party authority over the Soviet intelligentsia. It was clear from much recent literature, particularly the poetry of Voznesensky and Evtushenko, that the younger generation, with the encouragement of certain older patrons like Ehrenburg, were groping towards ideological positions which had more in common with the uncommitted and, for the most part, un-Marxist standpoint of their Western coevals than with the rigid and discredited dogmatism of their 'fathers' at home. After a period of hesitation, during which Khrushchev may have thought that by giving the left wing its head he might somehow gain its support and lure it on to the path of compromise, he was evidently moved by the sight of the canvases painted by 'donkeys' tails' at the art exhibition to intervene decisively in the controversy between the 'conservatives' and the 'progressives' and thus fulfil his duty as guardian of the Party's authority in all ideological matters.

In abruptly upsetting the balance between the two 'camps' in literature, Khrushchev has achieved nothing except the alienation of the liberal intelligentsia, and has certainly turned many who were content to be loyal oppositionists into implacable opponents. It is no use employing Stalinist methods of intimidation at a time when most people, particularly the younger generation, have lost the conditioned reflexes induced by Stalinist terror.

MAX HAYWARD

St Antony's College
Oxford
July 1963

1

THE TRANSITION FROM RUSSIAN
TO SOVIET LITERATURE

Gleb Struve

1. *Literature and the October Revolution*

In approaching the subject of Soviet literature one is faced at the outset with the double problem of terminology and chronology: What is Soviet literature? When did it come into existence? To begin with, I should like to point out that, for the sake of exactness, one should really distinguish between *Soviet* literature and *Soviet Russian* literature. When I first published, in 1935, my English book on Soviet literature, which was the first comprehensive survey in any language of post-revolutionary literary developments in Russia, I deliberately called it *Soviet Russian Literature*. This term was retained in the subsequent revised and enlarged editions, published in England in 1944 and in the U.S.A. in 1951 (I am not responsible for the omission of the word 'Russian' in the French and German versions of those editions). In making this distinction I am in agreement with Soviet historians of Soviet literature: the two recently published Soviet histories of Russian literature since 1917, which are the first such works in Russian to deserve the names of 'histories'—the three-volume one published under the auspices of the Soviet Academy of Sciences and the two-volume one published by the University of Moscow—are both entitled *History of Soviet Russian Literature*. The designation 'Soviet literature' is reserved by Soviet scholars for the totality of the literary output inside the Soviet Union: in other words, it includes the literatures of all the nationalities inhabiting it. Nevertheless, Soviet historians of Soviet Russian literature often speak of it loosely as 'Soviet' literature, and this is even more true of the Sovietologists outside the communist world. In this paper, too, I am going henceforth to use the words 'Soviet literature' in this looser sense, when I really mean Russian-language literature, to which my remarks will be confined.

What is, then, Soviet literature, and when did it come into existence? The author of the introduction to the three-volume *History of Soviet Russian Literature*, Professor L. Timofeyev, begins with the words: 'The history of Soviet literature begins with the establishment of the Soviet system in our country.' He then goes on, however, to qualify somewhat his statement, and at the same time to underline the ideological implications of the term 'Soviet literature', by saying: 'The sources of Soviet literature can be traced back to the beginning of the third period of the liberation movement in Russia, to the nineties of the nineteenth century' (this refers, of course, to Lenin's famous periodization of Russian history).[1]

Is it possible, however, to regard the October Revolution of 1917 as the demarcation line between the pre-Soviet and the Soviet periods in Russian literature? Leaving aside the fact, usually completely ignored by Soviet literary historians, that after the Bolshevik Revolution Russian literature came to be divided into two streams—literature inside Russia and literature in exile—and that to this day these two streams still run parallel to each other, is it possible to regard all literature produced in Russia since 1917 as coming within the concept of 'Soviet' literature?

Notwithstanding Timofeyev's rather sweeping chronological assertion, he himself as well as some other joint authors of this composite *History* in the course of their survey never tire of referring to 'un-Soviet' and even 'anti-Soviet' writers and works within the general framework of postrevolutionary Russian literature inside Russia. I recall that when my English book on Soviet literature was first reviewed by a Soviet literary scholar (Professor Anikst) one of the main reproaches he levelled against me was the inclusion in my survey of such 'anti-Soviet' writers as Zamyatin and Zoshchenko.

Anikst wrote:

Why does he need to introduce Zamyatin who did not create any

1. *Istoria russkoi sovetskoi literatury v trekh tomakh. Tom I; 1917–1929 gg.* Moscow 1958, p. 7.

single work of significance? This adept at mimicry and falsification, whose whole conception of life was culled from literary reminiscences and bore no relation whatsoever to reality, left no trace in literature and has been completely forgotten by the present generation of Soviet readers. The secret is easy enough to guess: Zamyatin once wrote a malicious satire on socialism entitled *We*, and our 'objective' Mr. Struve ... devotes eight pages to a detailed rehash of the contents of this lampoon which is noteworthy neither for its wit nor its talent; and he smacks his lips audibly as he churns out this anti-Soviet propaganda.[2]

(The sentence, in the above passage, about Zamyatin and the present generation of Soviet readers is truly priceless: how could those readers remember *We* when they were never given a chance to read it?)

A little earlier, none other than Professor Timofeyev, in a letter to the editor of *Kultura i Zhizn*, had also taxed me with including in my survey various 'émigrés and renegades'. He named Zoshchenko, but did not name Zamyatin, although the reference to 'émigrés' obviously meant him.[3] This distinction, within the framework of Soviet literature, between 'genuine' Soviet writers and those who were regarded as foreign bodies within the organism of Soviet literature and branded as 'un-Soviet' or 'anti-Soviet', was of course based on ideological and political criteria. It was quite natural and understandable at the height of the Zhdanov era when both Timofeyev's letter and Anikst's review appeared in print. (In those days Zamyatin's name was even unmentionable in a Russian-language Soviet publication—Anikst's review was written for the benefit of a foreign audience.) But this approach has not been abandoned to-day and is illustrated again and again in the three-volume *History* published between 1958 and 1961. The number of Soviet writers who would have been dismissed as 'un-Soviet' between 1946 and 1956 was very great. It has been greatly reduced since. But the fact remains that while Alexander Blok and Andrey Bely are, for Timofeyev and other Soviet scholars and critics, part and parcel of Soviet literature, Zamyatin, Klyuev and Klychkov are not: they are 'un-Soviet'

2. Alexander Anikst, 'Slander in the Guise of Scholarship', *Soviet Literature*, 1947, No. 10, p. 62.
3. *Kultura i Zhizn*, 9 March 1947.

or 'anti-Soviet', they are outcasts. (Zoshchenko no longer is, but
his works still require expurgating.)

It is, however, possible, in my opinion, without adopting Timofeyev's purely ideological criteria (one suspects, though, a certain
admixture of expediency in this ideological approach), to distinguish in the earliest period of Soviet literature between those who,
no matter what their political attitude was, continued the prerevolutionary tradition and belonged to the main stream of Russian literature, and those who were part of the new, Soviet, period
of it.

Let me refer here to the rather extreme view expressed by the
well-known prerevolutionary literary scholar and critic R. Ivanov-
Razumnik, a friend of Blok, Bely, Klyuev and Esenin, and the
main ideologist, in the early days of the Revolution, of the so-
called 'Scythianism'. Like Blok and the other above-mentioned
poets, Ivanov-Razumnik 'accepted' the October Revolution. A
Populist of vague socialist-revolutionary sympathies, he joined in
1917 the Socialist-Revolutionaries of the left, the only Russian
political party which concluded an alliance with the victorious
Bolsheviks and for a short time accepted posts in the new Soviet
government (the break between the allies came after the Brest-
Litovsk Treaty). As a literary figure he was very active and
prominent until about 1923. In 1918 he was the literary editor of
the newspaper *Znamya Truda* and the magazine *Nash Put* in
which Blok published his poems *The Twelve* and *The Scythians*.
He also edited several almanacs. Arrested in 1919, together with
Blok, Zamyatin, Remizov and some others, he was kept under
arrest longer than the others, but nevertheless was soon released.
Later, he fell out with the new regime, and between 1933 and
1941 spent many years either in prison or in exile. An end was
put to his original literary work, although he continued to do
some editing for Soviet publishing houses even while in exile. His
main contribution to literature in those years was the editing of
six volumes of Saltykov-Shchedrin's works. He was also entrusted
in 1930 with the editing of Blok's complete works, but his comments to the first seven volumes of that edition were cut out,
though much of the material collected by him was used by the
new editor, Vladimir Orlov. In 1941, when the war was already
on, he was released for the last time and allowed to rejoin his
family in Tsarskoye Selo. There he fell into the hands of the

Germans and became eventually a wartime émigré: the Germans removed him to a camp in Germany but later he was released. He died in Munich in 1945. Before his death he wrote an interesting account of his experiences in prisons and exile. He also wrote a short booklet entitled *Pisatelskie sudby* ('Writers' Destinies') which was published posthumously in New York and deserves to be better known that it actually is.[4] It contains some valuable information about such writers as Sologub, Zamyatin, Klyuev, Mikhail Bulgakov and Zabolotsky. Although not free from some inaccuracies (Ivanov-Razumnik had to write from memory in 1942–43), it was the first intimation of the fate of some Soviet writers purged under Stalin, who were later to be rehabilitated (among them, Pilnyak, Kirshon, Kikhail Koltsov). Even though Ivanov held a rather dim view of Soviet literature, he did not dismiss it summarily. His final conclusion was, however, that nearly all that was of real and lasting value in it, especially in poetry, had been produced by writers of the older generation who were mature men when the Revolution swept over Russia. He named such works as Khlebnikov's *The Night Search*, Bely's *The First Meeting*, Vladimir Gippius's *The Countenance of Man*, and the poetry of Klyuev, Esenin, Pasternak and Voloshin. The name of Mandelshtam was strangely absent from this list. Of Akhmatova, it was said that she had fallen silent after 1923. There was no mention of Blok, but it was clear that Ivanov-Razumnik, who had been directly responsible for the first publication of *The Twelve*, did not regard it as part of *Soviet* literature. Speaking of prose fiction, he was ready to admit that about a dozen postrevolutionary prose writers might find a place in the future history of *Russian* literature (he named Babel, Neverov, Bulgakov, Zoshchenko, Ilf and Petrov, Leonov, Olesha, Pilnyak, Fadeyev, Sholokhov and Ehrenburg— none of whom he seemed to rate very highly; he spoke rather slightingly of Zoshchenko and somewhat condescendingly of Babel as a writer who had exhausted his potential with *Red Cavalry*). What is more important is that after discussing these prose writers he once more arrived at the conclusion that in prose, too, the most valuable achievements belonged to prerevolutionary writers. He mentioned Andrey Bely's *Moscow* and *The Masks*

4. R. Ivanov-Razumnik, *Pisatelskie sudby*. 'Literaturny Fond', New York, 1951.

and Prishvin's *Kashchei's Chain* as the works which, to him, were the high points not only in Russian but also in European literature; he also named Alexei Tolstoy's *Peter the First* (about the dramatized version of it he related a rather amusing anecdote), the novels of Sergeyev-Tsensky and, somewhat surprisingly, Novikov-Priboi's *Tsushima*.

I am not concerned here with Ivanov-Razumnik's individual estimates of Soviet and pre-Soviet writers and I do not necessarily share them. In the long run, he may be quite right in his contention that there is really no such thing as 'Soviet' literature, that there are only works of literature produced in the Soviet period, and that very few of them will retain their place in *Russian* literature when viewed in the proper perspective in time. The point I wish to make here is that, in the earliest period of literature with which I am dealing, there was little that was specifically Soviet, that much of this literature—and, in fact, much of the best in it—belongs to 'un-Soviet' writings (to use Timofeyev's terminology). This is certainly true of some of the best poetry published between 1918 and 1923—for example, of the last volumes of Gumilyov (*Kostyor, Shatyor, Ognenny stolp*), of Akhmatova's poetry (*Podorozhnik, Anno Domini*, after which her voice was silenced for many years), of Sologub's, Kuzmin's, Voloshin's, Tsvetayeva's, or Mandelshtam's *Tristia*, of the books of verse by Georgi Ivanov, Adamovich, and many others, published in the early 1920's, or of Andrei Bely's *The First Meeting*. This is even true, in my opinion, of such works as Blok's *The Twelve* and the postrevolutionary poetry of Esenin. In a different way it is true, of course, of such works as Zamyatin's *We*, the first émigré book by a non-émigré writer—a description that fits also Boris Pasternak's *Doctor Zhivago*, Abram Tertz's *The Trial Begins* and *Fantastic Tales*, and various other works that have been smuggled out of Russia in the last few years.

If we take Blok's *The Twelve* (written in 1918) and Zamyatin's *We* (written in 1920), we have, on the face of it, two very different cases. Blok's poem has often been acclaimed as the first major work of Soviet literature, as its starting point. It was hailed by those who sympathized with the Bolsheviks as a glorification of the Revolution, and denounced by those who were irreconcilably opposed to them as Blok's betrayal of his ideals. Zamyatin's *We*, read by him at writers' gatherings and announced for publication in number eight of *Zapiski Mechtatelei* (this interesting journal, edited by Andrey Bely, was, however, discontinued after the sixth issue), is the first work known to have been banned by Glavlit (there may have been others); it first became known in translations, and its full Russian version appeared only in 1952. The author himself, although he continued to write and publish in the 1920's, came to be treated as an 'inside' émigré. By 1929, he was hounded out of Soviet literature. Reduced to silence, he decided to leave Russia. His case is quite unique in the annals of Soviet literature: as a result of a personal letter addressed to Stalin himself and backed by the intercession of Gorky, Zamyatin was allowed to leave Russia with his wife and ended his life as an émigré *tout court*. And yet, to my mind, there is more justification for regarding Zamyatin's post-revolutionary work as belonging to Soviet literature than to include in it *The Twelve*. Soviet students of Blok are, of course, fully aware of the fact that this poem is not a glorification of the Bolshevik Revolution. They all agree that Blok did not and could not 'grasp' the true meaning of 'October'; but to-day they are trying very hard to put the best possible interpretation on the poem, which would enable them to claim it as part of Soviet literature. This applies especially to the ambiguous conclusion, which has aroused so much dispute, and which Blok himself could neither explain nor fully understand. But this has not always been so, and in one of the earliest Soviet studies of Blok, by Pavel Medvedev (who later became one of the victims of Stalin's purges), we read by way of a comment on the final vision of the poem:

In its [the Revolution's] rumble Blok heard the tender footsteps of Christ. The poet recalled [Him] once more—'the only one, the bright, a little sad'. Blok did not betray himself, he tied up the end with the beginning. He concluded his revolutionary symphony with a Te Deum full of tender emotion; in its music he heard the trumpets of the archangels.[5]

There is no doubt, of course, about Blok's sincere and, at least to begin with, wholehearted 'acceptance' of the October Revolution. This acceptance, which antagonized so many of his literary

5. P. Medvedev, 'Tvorcheski put Aleksandra Bloka', in *Pamyati Bloka*, 2nd enlarged edn., Petersburg, 1923, p. 203.

and personal friends, is sufficiently well documented in his diaries, notebooks and letters, and in the memoirs of his contemporaries. It is very much stressed in all recent Soviet writings about him, including the three-volume *History*. That it found its reflection in *The Twelve* is evident enough. There is, however, equally little doubt about his subsequent disillusionment, which grew apace as time went on. For his disillusionment there is much less direct documentation available, perhaps because some of it has been suppressed or is being withheld: not all of Blok's diaries and note-books of the last two years have been published. In the memoirs of Blok's contemporaries there are more than enough hints at this growing disillusionment with the Revolution which Blok had hailed in a spirit of moral maximalism and to which he addressed Brand's demand of 'All or nothing!' Such a hint is to be found, for instance, in the account of a meeting with Blok in Korneli Zelinsky's recent volume of literary memoirs (*Na rubezhe dvukh epokh*—'At the Borderline of Two Epochs', Moscow, 1959). But the most telling evidence of Blok's mood of deep dis-illusionment, if not despair, is his famous speech at a meeting commemorating the anniversary of Pushkin's death in February 1921, six months before his own death. This speech, 'On the Mission of the Poet', is duly printed in Soviet editions of Blok's works, but the comments on it are usually very perfunctory and unilluminating. Soviet students of Blok and historians of litera-ture prefer to dwell at some length on such essays of Blok's as *The Intelligentsia and the Revolution* and *The Downfall of Humanism*, without attempting to unravel the true meaning of the Pushkin speech. The full story of Blok's changed attitude toward what was going on in Russia—and perhaps to his own poem about the Revolution (despite his often quoted statement to the contrary)—still remains to be written. It will be possible to give the true and full story only when independent scholars are given access to all the relevant documents. In this connexion one little-known, or forgotten, and somewhat enigmatic episode should be mentioned. It concerns the publication of two verse fragments of Blok's which amounted to a recantation of *The Twelve*—a recantation dictated by something like religious re-pentance. One of these fragments was alleged to have been part of a letter written by Blok, not long before his death, to a friend in Finland. It was published by the addressee in a serious Russian émigré newspaper—the Berlin *Rul*—soon after Blok's death. The article containing this extract from Blok's letter and a second one a little later, with another verse fragment of Blok's allegedly received from someone in Moscow, bore a signature that looked like a pseudonym—'Leo Ly' (in Latin characters).[6] Although quite sensational, *if* authentic, this publication seemed to arouse little interest and response among the Russian émigrés (though in some émigré writings on Blok its authenticity was taken for granted). Nor did it provoke, to my knowledge, any refutation from the Soviet side. What is more, it was never followed up and no one, it appears, took the trouble of examining seriously its claims to authenticity. I have my doubts on this point (the poem does not have the true Blok ring, although one must bear in mind that it is written as an informal letter in verse). Nevertheless, it is something that would deserve investigation; and until its authenticity is convincingly disproved, it should be added to the 'dossier' of *The Twelve*. Not many students of Blok abroad seem to be familiar with it.

In claiming *The Twelve* as part of Soviet literature, Soviet scholars like to stress its negative reception by anti-Soviet Russians. In support of this they usually quote the pronouncements of Zinaida Gippius and Ivan Bunin. In doing so, they ignore all the utterances by the Russian émigrés in which the artistic value of the poem was very highly appraised. Of particular interest in this respect is my father's review of *The Twelve* in *Russkaya Mysl*, and the fact that Blok himself thought it necessary to copy it *in extenso*—without any comments—in his Diary.[7]

2. *Silent Musae Inter Arma: 1918–20*

The initial period in Soviet literature can be roughly subdivided into two main periods: the first more or less coincides with the Civil War and so-called War Communism; the second begins with the inauguration of the New Economic Policy in February 1921. The Latin saying at the head of this section of my paper must not be taken too literally: the Muses were not silenced completely or at once. Such works as *The Twelve* and

6. Leo Ly, ' "Dvenadtsat" (Sobstvenny kommentarii A. A. Bloka)', *Rul*, No. 237, 28 August 1921, and 'A. Blok—v poslednie dni', *ibid.*, No. 266, 1 October 1921.

7. *Dnevnik Al. Bloka: 1917–1921.* Ed. by P. N. Medvedev. Leningrad, 1921, pp. 236–39.

The Scythians by Blok, Gumilyov's *The Pyre* and new editions
of his early books of poetry, Gippius's volume of political verse,
Mayakovsky's *Mystery-Bouffe* and some of Esenin's work, all appeared in 1918. But, on the whole, the saying does hold good, and
this is especially true after the summer of 1918.

What were the principal factors which determined literary
developments in the earliest period in Soviet literature? The most
important of them, the crucial one, was the almost overwhelmingly hostile attitude of the Russian intelligentsia, including the
writers, to the new regime. Very few writers welcomed, or even
'accepted', the new order of things, and just as few believed in its
durability. Even Maxim Gorky's attitude to the October *coup
d'état* and to the policies of the new government was unequi-
vocally hostile, and Soviet historians of literature cannot
completely ignore his series of articles entitled 'Untimely
Thoughts' in his newspaper *Novaya Zhizn*.[8] Two examples can
illustrate this predominantly hostile attitude of the literary
community to collaboration with the new regime and to
those who were willing to place themselves in its service. In
November 1917 the newly elected Executive Committee of the
Soviets issued a call for cooperation to the literary and artistic
intelligentsia in Petersburg, and invited its representatives to
Smolny, the headquarters of the new government. Not more than
half a dozen people responded to this call, and the only writer of
prominence among them was Vladimir Mayakovsky. About a
month later, a regular meeting of the literary society called
'Sreda' took place in Moscow. This society was, for the most part,
composed of writers who were realists in their literary method
and progressives or even radicals in their political outlook. The
meeting was presided over by Ivan Bunin's brother Julius. Ivan
Bunin himself, Chirikov, and several other well-known writers
were present. One of the members rose to make a statement to the
effect that one of their fellow members, Alexander Serafimovich
(who was also present at the meeting), had just accepted the post

8. In 1917 and 1918, Gorky regularly published in *Novaya Zhizn* articles on
topical subjects under the general title 'Nesvoevremennye mysli' ('Untimely
Thoughts'). Most of them have not been included in the thirty-volume edition
of his *Complete Works*. Among the regular contributors to Gorky's paper
in those days were, however, many men later prominent in Soviet literature and
journalism, such as Lunacharsky, Steklov, Desnitsky (Stroev), Vyacheslav
Polonsky (Gusin), and others.

of literary editor of the Moscow *Izvestia*, the official organ of the Moscow Soviet of Workers' and Soldiers' Deputies. 'Thereby he has joined the present usurpers of power,' said the speaker according to the report of this incident in *Pravda* and *Izvestia*, 'and there should be no place for him among us.' Evgeny Chirikov, an old friend and colleague of Serafimovich's in Gorky's *Znanie*, supported the speaker, adding that, despite his old friendship with Serafimovich, he would now refuse to shake the latter's hand. Serafimovich then asked for the floor and said : 'Yes, gentlemen, a gulf, a deep gulf has been dug between you and the people— workers, peasants and soldiers. And the writers who used to write so touchingly, so beautifully about the poor peasant, have found themselves on one side of this gulf while the peasant is standing on the other. It is not since yesterday that I have been writing. My writing manner is known, it has not changed. Needless to say, if at least one protesting voice were to be raised, I would not remain. But it is important for me to know whether all those present share the view that has been voiced here.' Complete silence was the answer to Serafimovich's words, and he left the meeting.[9] There was no formal vote for expulsion, but this is what it amounted to : the negative reaction was unanimous. Collaborating with the 'usurpers of power' was regarded as a disgrace, as a sell-out, as a betrayal of the traditional principles and values of the radical Russian intelligentsia.

The majority of the writers persisted in their hostile, or at best neutrally aloof, attitude for quite a long time. The situation was to change somewhat in 1919, when the closing down of practically all non-political periodicals and the hardships caused by Civil War and the Allied blockade, reduced the old intelligentsia to a point of near-starvation. Then it was Gorky who came to their rescue: pursuing the double aim of relieving the material plight of the intelligentsia and of forcing it to at least a partial capitulation, he provided employment for it in such enterprises as 'World Literature', a vast and ambitious pet idea of his, a publishing concern which was to provide the Russian public with new editions, often in new translations, of all that was best in world literature, from the Babylonian epos to the French Symbolists. Such institutions as the House of Writers and the House of Arts were also

9. An account of this meeting was published in *Izvestia Moskovskogo Soveta Rabochikh i Soldatskikh Deputatov* on 5 December 1917.

set up with Gorky's aid and under his sponsorship, and in them many writers, scholars, and artists received accommodation, while various lectures and study circles organized in connexion with these institutions enabled them to carry on their professional activities. Another outlet for these activities was provided by the numerous 'workshops' of the Proletkult which in those days was run independently of the Soviet government.

There were, of course, some exceptions to the general rule from the very first. A number of *avant-garde* writers, in the first place the Futurists led by Mayakovsky, rallied to the new regime as soon as the old government was overthrown. As revolutionaries in art, they tended to identify themselves with the Bolshevik Revolution and even staked out their claim to be its principal spokesmen in arts and letters. They were encouraged in this by the Soviet Commissar for Education, Anatoly Lunacharsky, and many of them were given leading posts in his Commissariat. The new government was also supported by many 'proletarian' writers who were associated with the Proletkult which had come into existence earlier in 1917, still under the Provisional Government, and was headed by the oldtime Bolshevik Bogdanov. Several of the older, established writers also rallied to the new regime; they included, apart from the already mentioned Serafimovich, such well-known poets as Valery Bryusov, who even joined the Communist Party, Alexander Blok and, to a lesser degree, his friend Andrei Bely whose poem *Christ Is Risen!* was a pendant to Blok's *The Twelve*. Maxim Gorky began to support the new regime after the unsuccessful attempt on Lenin's life in the summer of 1918.

Until that summer the so-called 'bourgeois' press continued to exist: various newspapers connected with the non-Bolshevik progressive parties, such as the Mensheviks, the Socialist-Revolutionaries and the Cadets, openly voiced their anti-Soviet views. Many prominent writers—Remizov, Prishvin, Sologub, Shmelyov, Mandelshtam, Ehrenburg and others—were among their regular contributors. In one of them Ehrenburg published his famous poem entitled *Prayer for Russia*: it was an outspoken indictment of Bolshevik rule and a lament for Russia's fate. Some of these newspapers were from time to time closed down for violating the new Soviet decree about the press, promulgated in January 1918, which had greatly curtailed freedom of the press.

As a rule, they would reappear, sometimes the very next day, under a new name. This situation changed radically in the summer of 1918 when, in connexion with the attempt on Lenin's life, on the one hand, and the flare-up of the Civil War, on the other, all independent, non-Bolshevik periodical publications were summarily suppressed. By this time many well-known writers had found their way out of Soviet Russia and settled in the territories governed, in the south and in the east, by anti-Soviet forces. With Russia torn and divided by the Civil War, literature was also divided into two camps. In Soviet Russia, military and political emergencies, combined with such factors as shortage of newsprint, led to drastic curtailment of literary activities. This curtailment became particularly pronounced in 1919 when these activities were practically confined to such *avant-garde* groups as the Futurists and the Imagists, and to various groups of proletarian writers. By the summer of 1919, even these groups, owing to the exigencies of the war, were deprived of their media of expression when the Soviet government decided to close down all but the most essential periodical publications: the only literary magazine to survive this drastic measure was *Proletarian Culture*. Of all the forms of literature, poetry fared best: it could dispense with the printed word; poems could be recited at public gatherings and in poets' cafés, and this period came to be spoken of as the period of oral, or café literature. It was at this time that Mayakovsky devoted his main attention to propaganda poetry, inaugurating his ROSTA posters—satirical drawings and cartoons with sharp, terse verse captions—serving the need of combating the enemies of the New Order, the 'Whites'. Another form of literary art that flourished during the Civil War, for it also could dispense with paper, was the mass propaganda theatre. Few books were published in 1918 and 1919, but it is significant that such an outspokenly anti-Soviet work as Zinaida Gippius's volume of political poems could still appear in 1918.

The defeat of General Denikin in 1919, followed by the Red Army's occupation of much of the Black Sea coast (with the exception of the Crimea), led to the first substantial exodus of the intelligentsia from Russia. Many writers, including Ivan Bunin, became political émigrés in 1919. Their ranks were further swelled in 1920, after the collapse of Admiral Kolchak's government in Siberia and the final débâcle of General Wrangel's armed forces in the Crimea, whereupon his supporters were evacuated *en masse* abroad. From the end of 1920, one can date the division of Russian literature into two branches: Soviet literature and émigré literature.

By the end of 1920 civil war in Russia was, to all intents and purposes, over. This, and the New Economic Policy proclaimed by Lenin a couple of months later, which signified a partial return to a bourgeois economy, created conditions in which a literary revival became possible. This literary revival, aided by the setting up of private publishing enterprises and by renewed contacts with the outside world, extended well beyond the period under review here. But the early part of this period, the years 1921–23, had several unique features that mark it off from what was to follow.

3. *The Double Face of Literature: 1921–23*

The Soviet literary scene between 1920 and 1923 offers a picture of great diversity and richness. To analyse it in terms of individual writers and works would require much more space than I have at my disposal. I shall dwell therefore on what seem to me to be its salient general characteristics.

Poetry had occupied a position of near monopoly in Russian literature from 1918 until 1920. The new period, which began in 1921, saw an expansion of prose writing and the appearance of a number of new prose writers, several of whom came to hold later a prominent place in Soviet literature. But even in this period poetry predominated over prose fiction. Much of it, and certainly some of the best, was written by prerevolutionary writers and can hardly be said to belong to *Soviet* literature.

In 1922, Valery Bryusov, the old *maître d'école* of Russian Symbolism, whose whole-hearted adherence to the new regime, to the point of joining the Communist Party, had astounded many people, published in *Pechat i Revolutsiia* (1922, No. 7, pp. 38–68) a survey of Russian poetry for the period 1917–22, which was highly symptomatic. It was entitled *Vchera, segodnya i zavtra russkoy poezii*, 'The Yesterday, the To-day, and the Tomorrow of Russian Poetry'. For Bryusov the communist of 1922, the Symbolists and their offspring the Acmeists were the 'Yesterday' of Russian poetry; the Futurists, of whom he had been rather critical before the Revolution, its revolutionary 'To-day' (he singled out as its most remarkable representatives Pasternak and Mayakovsky, but gave also credit to Khlebnikov for his experimenting with words); and the proletarian poets, among whom he selected a few talented or promising ones (Sadofyev, Gastev, Kirillov, Gerasimov and Kazin), its true 'Tomorrow'. Bryusov treated his former fellow Symbolists very cavalierly. 'The whole quinquennial period of 1911–22', he wrote, 'was not marked by a single outstanding work signed by a poet coming from the ranks of the Symbolists.' With such a sweeping statement Bryusov seemed to be dismissing not only Balmont, Bely and Sologub (and he went on to make clear that they no longer existed for him as poets), but also Blok's *The Twelve*. When, later in the article, he came to discuss Blok specifically, he said that Blok's postrevolutionary work boiled down to a rehash of old themes and motifs (strangely enough, Bryusov, who as a critic and literary scholar had always attached importance to meticulous accuracy, included among Blok's 'new' works his lyrical drama *The Song of Fate*, reprinted after the Revolution). Of *The Twelve* Bryusov had the following to say: 'Blok's most powerful revolutionary work of the revolutionary period remains the poem *The Twelve* which *is, of course, antirevolutionary in spirit* [the italics are mine—G.S.], but in which the poet did all the same establish a contact [*soprikosnulsya*] with the element of the Revolution.' This somewhat ambiguously worded appraisal ('revolutionary', but 'antirevolutionary in spirit') is remarkable for its reserve: Bryusov obviously did not regard *The Twelve* as a revolutionary eye-opener.

Several other Symbolist poets (Vyacheslav Ivanov and Maximilian Voloshin, as well as such younger *epigonoi* as Vladislav Khodasevich and Marina Tsvetayeva) were condescendingly patted on the back by Bryusov. He also bestowed some lukewarm posthumous praise on Nikolay Gumilyov for his unquestionable mastery of poetic craft. For him, Gumilyov in his last volumes of verse (here again we note a strange lapse on Bryusov's part: among those volumes he mentions a volume of Gumilyov's early prose—*The Shadow from the Palm-Tree*) remained 'a master of plastic description', equalling at times Leconte de Lisle and Baudelaire (a strange juxtaposition!), but essentially a relic of the past, exemplifying 'refined aestheticism', full of exoticism and archaeology—in other words, 'a skilful imitation of some old classical model'. Of the other Acmeists (Gumilyov, however, was

for Bryusov not an Acmeist but a latter-day Symbolist), Mandelshtam and Akhmatova fared even worse at Bryusov's hands. The
former was dismissed in one sentence as a priest of 'pure art' while
the latter's postrevolutionary poetry was described as something
of which a pupil at any good poetry workshop would be ashamed.

In retrospect these judgements of Bryusov's strike us as singu-
larly shortsighted and inept. Akhmatova's *Anno Domini*, which
Bryusov specifically mentioned, is now almost unanimously recognized as the book that greatly enhanced her stature as a poet:
it contains some of her best mature poetry. Gumilyov's *The Pyre*
and *The Pillar of Fire* opened up new vistas before his poetry and
held out a great promise, cut short by his premature tragic death
before the firing squad. His influence was long felt in Soviet
poetry. Although for over thirty years his name had been kept
behind a curtain of silence, recently a prominent Soviet critic,
Victor Pertsov, spoke of the 'keen interest' which young Soviet
poets evinced in Gumilyov's work, while another and even better
known critic, Kornely Zelinsky, described Gumilyov as an excellent poet and likened his fate to that of André Chénier who had
also paid with his life for siding with the counterrevolution.[10]
There has been some evidence of Gumilyov's poetry, not reissued
in Russia since 1922, circulating in manuscripts, and quite recently there was a complaint about the high prices which Gumilyov's volumes fetch in secondhand bookshops: as a remedy for
that situation the desirability of publishing a volume of his
selected poems was suggested.

Mandelshtam's *Tristia* and *Second Book*, published respectively in 1922 and 1923, and partly overlapping, revealed him as a
poet of great originality and power, and of growing stature, developing in a new direction. How Bryusov could have overlooked
this is difficult to understand. Mandelshtam's status among all
lovers and connoisseurs of poetry has never been so high as it is
to-day, and the great interest shown in him by the younger Soviet
poets is also attested by Soviet critics. The same is true of Marina
Tsvetayeva, a volume of whose selected poetry was published last
year.

10. See V. Pertsov, 'Poiski novogo i velikie traditsii', *Literaturnaya Gazeta*,
26 February 1962, and K. Zelinsky, 'Russian Poetry Today', *Survey*, No. 40
(January 1962), pp. 49–67. Zelinski's essay is introduced in a note signed 'G. K.'
Cp. also G. Struve, 'Dnevnik chitatelya. O poluzapretnoy literature', *Russkaya
Mysl* (Paris), No. 1819, 31 March 1962.

Bryusov was also quite off the mark in regarding Sologub and Vyacheslav Ivanov as 'spent forces', as relics of the past, just as in underrating Khodasevich and in ignoring completely Mikhail Kuzmin whose postrevolutionary poetry has to this day received insufficient attention and is in part still unknown. Certainly all these poets produced some of their best work after the Revolution. Some of them (Sologub, Voloshin, Kuzmin and Mandelshtam) remained in Russia (and the two last-named went on writing and publishing for quite a long time); others, such as Vyacheslav Ivanov, Khodasevich and Tsvetayeva became émigrés (Tsvetayeva, however, went back in 1939—only to end tragically by taking her own life two years later). Not one of them, however, can in my opinion be regarded as part of Soviet literature.

On the other hand, the proletarian poets whom Bryusov saw as masters of the poetic tomorrow, were to be completely forgotten a few years later—and some of them even banned from Soviet literature along with counterrevolutionary Symbolists and Acmeists. They have been rehabilitated (posthumously—with the exception of Kazin who is still alive), but one can hardly view them as a great force and vital influence in Soviet literature.

To complete this picture of Bryusov's lack of foresight, one should say that Pasternak attained greatness by developing away from Futurism and by keeping aloof from the *sovremennost* in which Bryusov saw a pledge of the poetic future. Even Mayakovsky's poetic destiny would probably have surprised Bryusov had he lived to see its unfolding. And Futurism as such was for Bryusov the poetic 'To-day' only in terms of 1917–22: he did not visualize its great impact on Russian poetry throughout the 1920's.

When I say that poets like Sologub, Gumilyov, Akhmatova, Kuzmin and Mandelshtam, who produced some of their best work after 1917, are outside the pale of Soviet literature, I find myself in full agreement with most of the Soviet historians of literature to-day. Not one of those poets was as much as mentioned in the two-volume *Outline History of Soviet Literature* published soon after Stalin's death (1954–55). Granted that this *Outline History* has since been superseded and that in the new three-volume *History* we find many names that were absent from the earlier survey. But even though the names of the above-mentioned poets (and the same applies to a number of others) are to be found, if not in the body of the work, then in the appended 'Chronicle' of literary events (and even Gumilyov's name, though not in the index, is actually mentioned a few times), their work is not examined or discussed. Sometimes it is not even mentioned, the names themselves being brought up casually, often in a polemical context, as representatives of counterrevolutionary trends or of harmful influences on certain Soviet writers. They are not treated as part of Soviet literature.

Let us look more closely at the individual subsequent destinies of some of these writers. A volume of Sologub's verse was published in the late Thirties in the 'Little Series' of *'Biblioteka Poeta'*. It included some very good poems of the Soviet period, and the introduction by Orest Tsekhnovitser quoted from some of his 'anti-Soviet' poems and made it clear that in Sologub's archive there was a great deal of unpublished poetry (some very interesting information on Sologub's archive will be found in the earlier mentioned pamphlet by Ivanov-Razumnik).[11] A little earlier, Sologub's famous prerevolutionary novel *The Petty Demon* had been reissued in Soviet Russia. But nothing more was heard of Sologub until 1958, when one of the provincial Soviet publishing houses (in Kemerovo, of all places!) brought out, most inconspicuously, a new edition of *The Petty Demon* with an appropriate very brief introduction to the effect that the novel was a masterful picture of the decay of Russian bourgeois-gentry society. This may be followed by a volume of Sologub's selected poetry, but to claim Sologub as part and parcel of Soviet literature would require a very wild imagination. The same is true of Kuzmin, of whose literary resurrection there is as yet no hint. There are, on the other hand, enough hints of a possible, at least partial, rehabilitation of Gumilyov and Mandelshtam. But if Gumilyov, shot for his participation in a counterrevolutionary organization, is rehabilitated, it will hardly be as a *Soviet* poet. It would also require ideological sleight-of-hand to restore Mandelshtam to *Soviet* literature. His physical fate need not have been what it was, but his expulsion from Soviet literature was not an accident or a whim of Stalin's. After all, even the readmission of Akhmatova, first in 1940, after a long period of voluntary or enforced silence, and then again in the 1950's after the sentence of ostracism imposed by Zhdanov, is only a recognition of the place

11. See 'Pisatelskie sudby', pp. 13–19.

due to her in *Russian* literature. The three-volume *History of Soviet Literature* has nothing to say about her poetry, except for a few casual adverse remarks. This readmission differs from that of Bunin only in that in Bunin's case it was, and could only be, posthumous, while in Akhmatova's case it happened during her lifetime. What is significant is not that Akhmatova had been re-admitted into Soviet literature, but that the latest collection of her poetry, covering the period from 1909 to 1960, has been compiled with a definite bias and represents a carefully sifted selection. The same is true of Bunin. In the introduction to the latest edition of his late prose (1961) Konstantin Paustovsky proclaims *The Life of Arsenyev*, not only *the* masterpiece of Bunin (this is in complete agreement with the opinion voiced a long time ago by many émigré critics), but also one of the most remarkable works in world literature, noting with pride that this work belongs to Russian literature. In reading this one cannot help recalling the indignation which, in the Soviet Union, greeted the award of the Nobel Prize to Bunin, based primarily on that work. More significant, however, is the fact that this very work in this very same edition is published in what is euphemistically described as 'somewhat abridged form'. 'One of the most remarkable works in world literature', of which the Russians can be justly proud, is thought to need ideological pruning before being made available to Soviet readers.[12]

One of the features, then, of this early, transitional period in postrevolutionary literature is the place occupied in it by non-Soviet, or 'un-Soviet', writers and works. This feature is related to another important characteristic of this period—the relative freedom of discussion as exemplified in particular in many short-lived periodicals which sprang up during this period and ventured to express independent and unorthodox opinions. Alongside the first periodicals launched between 1920 and 1923 [13] (all of which were to play an important part in Soviet literary life in the years to come, though most of them faded out long before World War II), there mushroomed in those days slim and ephemeral

12. K. Paustovsky, 'Glavy iz vtoroy knigi "Zolotaya roza"', in *Tarusskie stranitsy*, Kaluga, 1961, pp. 28–34. Cp. also Paustovsky's Introduction to Ivan Bunin, *Rasskazy-povesti-vospominania*, Moscow, 1961.

13. *Kniga i Revolyutsia* in 1920, *Pechat i Revolyutsia* and *Krasnaya Nov* in 1921, *Sibirskie Ogni* and *Molodaya Gvardia* in 1922, *Na Postu* and *LEF* in 1923.

publications which represented those whom the three-volume
History characterizes as the forces of anti-Soviet opposition. *Dom
Iskusstv, Literaturnye Zapiski* (published by the House of
Writers), *Vestnik Literatury; Knizhny Ugol* (which had been appearing earlier and was now resumed, and which is sometimes described to-day as the principal nest of counterrevolution), *Zapiski
Mechtatelei* (of which one number, containing pieces by Blok,
Bely, Sologub, Vyacheslav Ivanov and Remizov had appeared—
by a fluke it would seem—in 1919, and four more issues, one of
them double, were published in 1921–22), *Rossia, Novaya Rossia,* and a few others. As a rule, they were closed down after two
or three issues. There was one case when a similar independent
journal (*Novaya Evropa*), to be edited by E. Zamyatin and K.
Chukovsky, was announced but apparently never came out. All
these journals represented foreign bodies in Soviet literature and
are branded as such in the three-volume *History* and various
other Soviet sources.

It was in *Literaturnye Zapiski* that Lev Luntz published his
famous article which came to be regarded as the literary manifesto of the Serapion Brothers, and in which, in the name of the
latter, he proclaimed that art should be independent of politics,
that it need not reflect the epoch, and that they, the Serapions,
were not interested in Bunin's or Blok's political views.[14] These
and other such heresies immediately came under fire from the
big guns of orthodox Marxist criticism. In the same journal the
Serapions published their facetious autobiographies (Zoshchenko's was particularly irreverent, and this was recalled by
Zhdanov in 1946). There, too, the well-known former critic of
the Populist *Russkoye Bogatstvo*, Arkadi Gornfeld, had the
courage (or the cheek) to say of the Russian émigrés that their
contact with the European cultural milieu might prove to be
beneficial for literature, adding: 'We do not have enough data for
any forecasts, and we must remember that critics had often
treated Chateaubriand and Senancour, Nodier and Benjamin
Constant as "émigré literature", and that *Les Contemplations* and
Les Miserables, My Past and My Thoughts and *Small Town
Okurov* were all written in exile.'[15]

14. See 'Serapionovy bratya o sebe', in *Literaturnye Zapiski* (Petersburg),
No. 3, 1 July 1922, pp. 25–31.
15. See the review of the almanac *Severnoye Utro*, signed transparently
'A. G-d', *ibid.*, No. 2, 23 June 1922, p. 13.

In *Dom Iskusstv* Zamyatin published his article '*Ya boyus*' ('I Fear') in which he wrote that true literature could exist only where it was produced not by efficient officials, but by madmen, hermits, heretics, dreamers, rebels and sceptics, and voiced his fear that Russian literature had 'but one future—its past'. Although Zamyatin was to continue working in Soviet literature, he came to be looked upon as an 'inside émigré' and is now treated as such in retrospect. There is as yet no sign of his being rehabilitated, but his great influence on the budding Soviet writers of the Twenties is grudgingly admitted. It was Zamyatin who became (together with Gorky, who was then living abroad in a kind of self-exile) the *spiritus movens* of the last truly independent literary journal to be published in Soviet Russia—*Russky Sovremennik* ('The Russian Contemporary'), of which four issues, replete with valuable literary material, appeared in 1924.

It is curious to note that some of the 'anti-Soviet' tendencies and moods of the early Twenties, of which the Soviet press spoke at the time and which, if anything, are rather overstressed to-day, came to be officially associated with the movement known as 'Change-of-Landmarks' (*Smena vekh*). This movement originated abroad, among the émigrés. Its principal ideologists were Professor N. Ustryalov in Harbin and Professor Yu. Klyuchnikov in Paris (both of them, as well as several of their supporters, returned later to Russia—to disappear eventually in the limbo). In 1921 they published in Prague a volume entitled *Change of Landmarks*, and early in 1922 they launched in Berlin, then the main literary centre of the Russian émigrés, a daily newspaper called *Nakanune* ('On the Eve'). Their central idea boiled down to the belief that the New Economic Policy was more than a tactical move, that it signified the first step toward the restoration, not only of a bourgeois economy, but in general of the pre-Bolshevik order of things. Allied with this was the conviction that the Bolsheviks were willy-nilly serving the national interests of Russia and should therefore be supported by all patriotic and state-minded Russians. The attitude came to be known as National-Bolshevism. For a time, it found quite a sympathetic response among certain émigré circles, especially since the exponents of this movement fell back, in their ideology, upon the ideas expounded in 1909 by the authors of *Vekhi* ('Landmarks'). Thus the name they chose had, in a way, a double significance.

There can be no doubt about the sincerity and genuineness of Professor Ustryalov's convictions. But there can be little doubt either that he and some of his convinced followers had been joined by all sorts of unscrupulous timeservers, and that there was also an element of 'Zubatovism' in this movement. The movement was primarily an émigré movement, and one of its practical prime objects was to call upon the émigrés to return to Russia and place themselves, in the interests of the country and its long-range goals, in the service of the new regime. This meant playing upon the émigrés' patriotic feelings. The movement had some repercussions both in Russia and among the émigrés. In Russia, a number of writers and journalists voiced their sympathy with the ideas of Ustryalov and Klyuchnikov; this sympathy found its expression in some of the 'anti-Soviet' periodicals mentioned above, in particular in *Rossia* and *Novaya Rossia*, in the writings of Professor Adrianov, of the well-known prerevolutionary Populist journalist V. G. Tan-Bogoraz, of Peter Guber and others. Several poets and fiction writers contributed to these journals, although the latter were speedily denounced as organs of 'Change-of-Landmarkism'. Outside Russia, a number of writers and journalists began contributing to *Nakanune*. The most prominent among them was Alexei N. Tolstoy, but there were also some younger ones (Alexander Drozdov, Gleb Alekseyev, Roman Gul and others). Later, Tolstoy drew the necessary conclusions from his own 'change of landmarks' and returned to Russia, to win eventually for himself a prominent position in Soviet literature. His act of repentance was preceded by an open letter (published in *Izvestia*) to the venerable leader of the left-wing émigrés, the ex-revolutionary Nikolai Chaikovsky.[16] In this letter Tolstoy tried to justify his step by patriotic and idealistic considerations. He wrote: 'My conscience calls upon me, not to climb down into the basement [he had compared émigré life to life in a basement], but to proceed to Russia and knock at least a small nail of my own into the storm-battered ship of Russia. Following the example of Peter [the Great].' In commenting in *Izvestia* upon Tolstoy's letter, the well-known Marxist literary scholar, Peter Kogan, waxed enthusiastic and hailed it as a sign of a serious split among the émigrés. He also went to the length

16. Tolstoy's letter to Chaikovsky was published in *Izvestia* on 25 April 1922; it was reprinted from the Berlin *Nakanune*, No. 17, 14 April 1922.

of comparing it, for its historic significance, to Chaadayev's first 'Philosophical Letter' and Belinsky's famous letter to Gogol.[17]

Tolstoy's example, however, was followed only by a few little-known younger contributors to *Nakanune* (Alexander Drozdov, Gleb Alekseyev, Georgi Venus). Not one of them made a name for himself in Soviet literature and, with the exception of Drozdov, none seems to have survived the great purges of the Thirties. The only other prominent writers to return to Russia from their exile—and this more than fifteen years later—were Alexander Kuprin (in 1937) and Marina Tsvetayeva (in 1939). In both these cases personal reasons played the primary role. It is true that three other prominent figures in the field of arts folowed the earlier example of Tolstoy at different times: the composer Sergey Prokofyev and the well-known painters Ivan Bilibin and Vasili Shukhayev. Of them, Prokofyev alone gained a prominent place in Soviet culture.

On the other hand, at about the same time as Tolstoy's break with the émigrés (later in 1922), the ranks of the émigrés were greatly reinforced, both numerically and qualitatively, by the expulsion from Soviet Russia of more than 160 prominent scholars, writers and journalists, as 'internal enemies'. The émigrés owed much, indeed, of the spiritual richness and variety of their subsequent activities to this unique action of the Soviet government, for the group included many outstanding philosophers who were regarded as undesirable because of their religious outlook. It is interesting and significant to note also that it included all but one of the surviving authors of *Vekhi* ('Landmarks') who had still been living in Russia, viz. Nikolai Berdyaev, Father Sergius Bulgakov, Semyon Frank and Alexander Izgoyev; the only other of the 'seven humble ones', as Merezhkovsky had called them, still alive, Peter Struve, had become an émigré much earlier. The only one to remain in Russia (where he died in 1925) was Mikhail Gershenzon.

This brings me to another characteristic and unique feature of the Russian literary scene in 1921–23: the close contact between the two branches of Russian literature, the blurring of the borderline between them.

Their meeting-place was in Berlin. The inflation-ridden Germany of Post World War I years had not only attracted many

17. See *Izvestia*, 25 April 1922.

homeless Russians by a prospect of cheap living and easy money, but also provided conditions which were propitious to the setting-up of publishing houses, newspapers and magazines. At the same time, Germany was in those years the only country in Western Europe with which Soviet Russia had established diplomatic and commercial relations. The newly founded private publishing firms in Russia found it advantageous to set up branches in Berlin and often to do their printing there. One of the most flourishing publishing businesses, whose books appeared with the double imprint 'Petrograd-Berlin' or 'Berlin-Moscow', was that of Zinovi Grzhebin, a personal friend and benefactor of many a writer then still living in Russia. There was also 'Petropolis' which published Gumilyov, Akhmatova, Kuzmin, and other prerevolutionary poets.

Germany was also the only foreign country to which Soviet citizens could get visas without too much difficulty. After the lean years of the Revolution many of them felt the attraction of the relative amenities of the German capital. Between the end of 1921 and the beginning of 1923 many well-known Russian writers found themselves in or near Berlin: Gorky (who later went on to Italy), Andrei Bely, Remizov, Shklovsky, Khodasevich and many others. Some came ostensibly for health reasons, others received assignments from 'World Literature' or some other literary organization or publishing enterprise. Many never went back: such well-known recruits to the ranks of the émigrés as Alexei Remizov, Ivan Shmelyov, Boris Zaitsev, Vladislav Khodasevich, Marina Tsvetayeva, Georgi Ivanov, Georgi Adamovich and Nikolai Otsup, not counting the already mentioned deportees, all passed through Berlin in those years. Andrei Bely very nearly stayed behind, but at the last moment changed his mind and returned to Moscow. There was no clear demarcation line between émigré and Soviet writers, and at one time there was a large group of those who sat between two stools, as it were: Soviet writers who had not quite made up their minds whether to go back or stay in the West, and émigré writers who were planning to return to Russia. There were even some of whom one could not say at any given moment whether they were Soviet or émigré: this was true of the veteran poet and philosopher Minsky, and also of Ilya Ehrenburg.

There were quite a number of publishing houses which published indiscriminately the work of émigré and Soviet writers. There were also journals and magazines in which the two groups rubbed shoulders. This may not have been true of *Nakanune* where self-respecting émigrés who were not contemplating a 'change of landmarks' would not have dreamed of appearing: most of its contributors were drawn from the ranks of Soviet writers, including some well-known ones (Mikhail Bulgakov, Ovadi Savich, Osip Mandelshtam), and those of the émigré adherents of Ustryalov and Klyuchnikov. But the situation was different in *Russkaya Kniga* (later renamed *Novaya Russkaya Kniga*), edited by Alexander Yashchenko, a professor of International Law, who later disappeared somewhat mysteriously and was said to have been a paid Soviet agent. His journal specialized in literary criticism, literary news and bibliography, and its contributors included émigrés, Soviet writers and halfway-house people like Ehrenburg and Roman Gul, now one of the joint editors of the New York *Novy Zhurnal*, who at that time had 'changed landmarks', but without taking the final step of returning to Russia. Both Ehrenburg and Gul contributed to Yashchenko's journal some of the major book reviews. Ehrenburg also wrote for it an article, characteristically entitled 'Au dessus de la mêlée'—this was the line Yashchenko's journal was trying to maintain. Next to articles by such a staunch anti-communist as Julius Eichenwald (one of Trotsky's deportees), *Novaya Russkaya Kniga* printed pieces by Boris Pilnyak and other Soviet writers.

Another magazine on the pages of which Soviet and émigré writers met was *Spolokhi*, edited by Alexander Drozdov, who was later to follow Alexei Tolstoy as a repatriate. In *Spolokhi* the true émigrés predominated, but there was also a sprinkling of Soviet contributors.

Of much higher quality were *Epopeia* and *Beseda* ('Colloquy'). The former was edited by Andrei Bely and published material of high literary quality, incuding the continuation of Bely's own memoirs of Blok, begun in *Zapiski Mechtatelei*. *Beseda* had a rather unusual character. It was started by Gorky who edited it in close collaboration with Andrei Bely, Vladislav Khodasevich and Professor F. Braun, a Russian-German scholar who, after the war, became a professor of the University of Leipzig. Gorky had meant his literary-scientific and non-political review for distribution in Russia, but when the first number was published he was surprised to discover that it would not be admitted across the frontier.[18] Five or six issues of *Beseda* were published containing some interesting articles by Khodasevich, Bely and others, but its circulation was officially limited to the émigré public. One of *Beseda*'s highlights was Lev Luntz's provocative article 'To the West!'

Mention should also be made of *Veshch* ('Thing'), a magazine designed to propagate modern art, of which Ilya Ehrenburg was one of the editors. This was, of course, the time when all *avant-garde* trends in art were welcome in Soviet Russia, but it is significant that Ehrenburg chose to publish his magazine abroad: he was himself then a semi-émigré, though a Soviet citizen.

In other centres of Russian emigration there was no such literary coexistence. Only for a short time the Change-of-Land-marks movement issued its magazine *Smena Vekh* in Prague which was the centre of the émigré younger generation.

There was also in Berlin a sort of literary club, called—like the one in Petrograd—'Dom Iskusstv', which met in a café on Nollen-dorf-Platz and became the personal meeting place of writers from the two worlds. For a time it was presided over by Nikolai Minsky. Its membership was open to writers and artists without distinction of political allegiance or views. It established contacts with the House of Arts and the House of Writers in Petrograd. Many well-known émigré writers were its members, or at least attended its meetings at which poetry was recited and stories read. Newcomers from Soviet Russia, whether they intended to 'choose freedom', or entertained no such idea, were regular visitors, and at the meetings of Dom Iskusstv in Berlin one could hear in those days Andrei Bely, Khodasevich, Tsvetayeva, Otsup, Boris Paster-nak and Vladimir Mayakovsky recite their work. Literary co-existence was also maintained on a purely personal level: some examples of it are related in Ehrenburg's Memoirs.

This situation persisted through 1923. It came to an end by 1924, partly because, with the revaluation of the German mark, Berlin lost most of its commercial and other attractions for the Russian émigrés; Russian publishing houses and periodical pub-lications began to close down, and the bulk of the writers them-

18. See 'Pisma Maksima Gorkogo k V. F. Khodasevichu', in *Novy Zhurnal* (New York), Nos. 29, 30 and 31 (1952), especially, No. 30, pp. 194–95, and No. 31, p. 200.

selves moved on to Paris; and partly because in Soviet Russia the internal conflict in literature—between the proletarian writers and the fellow-travellers—became more accentuated, and hobnobbing with the émigrés could no longer be tolerated.

In literature inside Russia there was, in those years, a marked change-over from poetry to prose. The appearance of the Serapion Brothers in 1921 was quite symptomatic. The overwhelming majority of them were prose writers. Most of them had sat at the feet of Zamyatin and Shklovsky. They were not a literary school and were heading in different directions. Zamyatin was one of the first to see this. Some, like Vsevolod Ivanov and Nikolai Nikitin, were strongly influenced by Pilnyak who, himself very much influenced by Andrei Bely and Remizov, was rapidly becoming one of the leading and most influential figures in Soviet literature. Besides Pilnyak and the Serapions, the years 1922–23 saw also the appearance of such major prose writers as Isaac Babel and Leonid Leonov. They should, however, be seen within the framework of the next period.

If I were asked to characterize in a terse formula the general spirit prevailing in literature in those early years, especially in the truly Soviet sector of Russian literature—for I insist that Russian literature in those days was still divided into two sectors (just like Russian trade under NEP)—I would choose the formula of Revolutionary Romanticism. On this point I have no quarrel with the authors of the three-volume *History of Soviet Russian Literature*. Or should I rather put it this way: on this point they agree with me.

In conclusion, it should be mentioned that a number of valuable critical and literary-historical studies, free from any ideological preconception, were produced in Soviet Russia in the first NEP years. This was a field in which less and less valuable work came to be published as time went on—especially after the end of the 1920's.

2

LITERATURE IN THE NEP PERIOD

Helen Muchnic

The NEP period began in 1921 with Lenin's proclamation of a policy that ordained a measure of individual freedom and ended in 1928 with the inauguration of the first Five-year Plan which revoked this freedom. It began with the end of the Civil War and the victory of communism; it ended on the eve of fascism. It was the most outspoken, the most varied and experimental period in Soviet literature, the Russian phase of that exuberant literary revival which characterized the Twenties in the West. Here were the same excitement, the same interest in new ventures, the same boldness of thought. Relations with the West were freer at this time than they were ever to be again. But despite all this, the literary achievement of these years is not comparable to that of the West. Why this was so, it is of course impossible to say with absolute certainty. But there are reasons which suggest themselves, and some of these I shall bring forward in the course of this survey.

In the field of criticism, this was the period in which the Formalist school reached its heights, in Eichenbaum's, Zhirmunsky's, Tynyanov's, Shklovsky's, Tomashevsky's, Vinogradov's, and Jakobson's studies of Tolstoy, Gogol, Dostoevsky, of Bely and Anna Akhmatova, and in their works on the theory of language and style. It was in this period also that a group of freedom-loving writers formed the Serapion Brotherhood and received an unexpected official accolade, first from Leo Trotsky, who called them 'fellow-travellers' in his *Literature and Revolution,* and then from the Central Committee of the Communist Party, which two years later, in 1925, gave them its endorsement. On the other hand, this was also the period of the 'On Guard' attacks and of the uncomfortable gyrations, under pressure of semi-official demands, of Mayakovsky's LEF. The controversies about the nature, the function, and the place of art were heated, and whatever one may think of their fairness or intrinsic merits, one cannot deny that they generated intellectual excitement.

In the realm of poetry and fiction, this was the period which marked the rise of remarkable artists, some of whom were to attain an assured status in the history of Russian letters, while others did not fulfil the promise of their early work. Sholokov's *Tales of the Don* came out in 1925, *The Quiet Don* was started the next year and its first volume was published in 1928, Babel's *Red Cavalry* appeared in 1926, Zoshchenko's *Of What the Nightingale Sings* and Olesha's *Envy* in 1927. There were also the experimental novels of Vsevolod Ivanov, Pilnyak, Neverov, Fedin and Leonov—*Armoured Train* and *The Naked Year* in 1922, *Tashkent, City of Plenty* in 1923, *Cities and Years* and *The Badgers* in 1924, *The Thief* in 1927.

It was now, too, that older writers published some of their finest things. Mandelshtam's *Tristia* and Anna Akhmatova's *Anno Domini* came out in 1922, Pasternak's *The Lofty Illness* in 1923, his short stories in 1925, *The Year 1905* in 1926, and *Lieutenant Schmidt* in 1927. Mayakovsky's *About What? About This* was done in 1923, his *Vladimir Ilych Lenin* in 1924, and *To Sergei Esenin* in 1926, which Esenin himself worked on his *Pugachev*, and wrote many a poignant lyric and his autobiographic *Anna Snegina*. Andrey Bely, in Berlin, brought out his journal, *Epopeia*, in 1922 and published in it his fine memoirs of Alexander Blok; and in 1921 Zamyatin's *We*, which was written the previous year, was exported out of Russia to begin its extraordinarily influential career abroad. In the official literary camp, we have Furmanov's *Chapayev* in 1923, Gladkov's *Cement* in 1925, Fadeyev's *The Rout* in 1927. In 1928 Ilf and Petrov presented the world with their lighthearted *Diamonds to Sit On*. In short, these years were rich in the extent and variety of their literary output.

Nevertheless, with all their differences, the productions of the NEP period were not so varied as, on the face of it, they may appear to be. They had much in common, for they were held together in the grip of a concealed but effective injunction, a felt, imperative demand which lay at the root of all expression. Their variety was due to the measure of freedom granted by the age, but the age was not free in essence, and they were circumscribed and united by its limitations. Perhaps, indeed, there was now so much talk of freedom precisely because freedom was by no means assured. A dogmatic spirit, arising from uncertainty, exerted an overwhelming sway even over those who revolted against it. And to my mind, one poet alone was able, without shutting himself away from his age, to withstand its insidious, constricting power. This poet was Pasternak, but because his genius was always unemphatic, because his very depth precluded showiness, the extraordinary strength of his independence was not fully appreciated in the loud, assertive Twenties, nor indeed was it wholly realized in his own work until much later.

In their special tragic way, the Russian Twenties were, in large part, like the American, brilliant and flashy. Although their flamboyance had a different origin, a different outcome, and somewhat different manifestations, it was equally pervasive. The Formalists, for one, their high seriousness and scholarship notwithstanding, were part of it. Their insights were brilliant, their theories extreme, their pronouncements dogmatic. And brilliance, extremism and dogma were characteristic of the age, engendered perhaps by the despair of those who, having something to say, know that they will not be heard unless they shout. At any rate, whatever the reason, everyone, beginning with Gorky and the Futurists, shouted in Russia. Of writers who succeeded in making themselves heard, Chekhov's was perhaps the last quiet voice before Pasternak's. There is a world of difference between the calmly given opinions of these two artists, even between the not so quiet ones of Tolstoy and Blok, and the theories of Formalists, the manifestos of Futurists, the proclamations of the Serapion Brothers, 'On Guardists' and other literary groups, a difference, I mean, not in the views themselves—which are sufficiently divergent—but in purpose, tone and method. It is the difference between statements made by individuals, on the one hand, which, however dictatorial or rhetorical, are expressions and explanations of the work and the personalities of their exponents, and on the other, pronouncements of schools and groups; on the one hand, for example, Tolstoy's moralistic arguments in *What Is Art?*, or Blok's lyricism in *The Spirit of Music*, or Chekhov's fragmentary remarks about his writing—all of them formulations of their thoughts and practices, having the same root as their impulse to creation; on the other hand, programmes for action, impositions of belief, plans of attack—battle cries of warring factions, and as such tied to the theories of the enemy. Would even the Formalists, the most learned and scholarly of all these groups, have developed their radical theories and carried their minute researches to extremes had they not been impelled to do so by a general disregard of formal values, a scorn of technique, and an over-emphasis on psychology and morality in art? Were not their favourite terms: 'playing with reality', 'the verbal gesture', 'making things strange', a sharp retort to the hazy insistence on such equivocal concepts as 'truth' and 'goodness', which plagued the theories they were combating? Certainly the Serapion Brothers, at one with the Formalists in their love of precision and their belief in the sovereignty of art, issued their famous manifesto of 1922 in open protest against the demands that were being made on artists. They had come together, they declared, 'at a time of widespread regimentation, registration, and barrack-room regulations'; all they had in common was a belief in artistic autonomy; they were 'no school ... no band of imitators'; they demanded 'but one thing: that a work of art be original and real, and that it live its own peculiar life'. It is surely a measure of Russia's tragedy that not only was there need for such elementary declarations of artistic independence as this, but that they could have been made only during this brief NEP period of relative freedom.

The document, important in itself, marked also the launching of a series of works which were remarkable for their novelty—either of form, or feeling, or outlook. The importance of innovation was constantly emphasized by the Formalists. It was implicit in Shklovsky's celebrated analysis of Tolstoy's style as the method of *ostranenie*, defined as a freshness of approach, through which everything was seen as for the first time, unobscured by the routine concepts formed by habit—the opposite of the cliché in speech, of commonplaceness in viewpoint, of dogma in thought. Such novelty and independence were, according to the Formalists and the Serapion Brothers, the *sine qua non* of artistic excellence. But Tolstoy's penetration is not given to every man. And with some writers novelty was sought for its own sake. If one had little to say, one could at least find new ways of saying it. And so, there was much experimentation with narrative structure. It was in keeping with Eichenbaum's theory of literary composition as a 'playing with reality', and it was encouraged by Shklovsky, whose infatuation with *Tristram Shandy* pointed the way to peculiar constructions, and by Lev Luntz, who attempted to arouse interest in plot as an important, and hitherto neglected, device in Russian literature.

But the reality that writers were trying to 'play with' was a very sombre reality indeed. Most of them, understandably, were impelled to write about the immediate past, the 'terrible years' they had just lived through. Their theme was war, famine, revolution; their task was to explain and to make memorable the horrors they had known. But these events were too close, the issues involved too complicated for unprejudiced assessment, and explanations too difficult, except for those who could swallow the ready solutions of propaganda. Because of this, the best war books of the period were those which, without attempting to present events in the perspective of history or philosophy, confined themselves to the recreation of scattered episodes. Such were a few of Sholokhov's early tales, Babel's *Red Army*, Ivanov's *Armoured Train*. They gained in intensity whatever they may have lost in breadth, while more ambitious works like Pilnyak's complicated *The Naked Year* or Fedin's *Cities and Years* were artistic failures. To my mind, at any rate, the highly mannered structure of these two books was not so much an appropriate design for intricate ideas as a substitute for understanding; and, in the last analysis, what they exhibit is the complexity of confusion rather than any insight into complexity.

Pilnyak, the first to deal with the Revolution in fiction, took his cue from Alexander Blok. He chose as epigraph the famous lines:

> People born in barren years
> Do not remember the path they've trod.
> We, the children of Russia's terrible years
> Are unable to forget anything at all.

and he evidently modelled the whole novel on *The Twelve*, filling in Blok's outline with circumstantial details, transforming Blok's concentrated image of Russian society into an elaborate mosaic, which included all classes and interests of both ancient and modern Russia, from the aristocracy to the peasantry and the proletariat, and from commerce, the professions, theology and art to various forms of dilettantism, debauchery and eccentricity. In style, too, the book is a composite, a patchwork of history, journalism, poetry. And it is full of literary echoes: in addition to those of Blok, also of Bely, Gogol, Dostoevsky, Tolstoy, Remizov and the ancient *byliny*. These were no doubt intentional, contrived as a counterpart to the mosaic of style and content and thus designed to represent the whole history of Russia, literary as well as social. The book contains unforgettable passages, such as the nightmare scene of Mara Junction, where masses of human beings, in a desperate attempt to escape starvation, fight for a foothold on an already overloaded train, packed inside and out with miserably pathetic refugees. As a whole, however, the work is not so much history as an exalted, romantic, bewildered parable of the Revolution. Pilnyak admitted as much in a preface to a collected edition of his writings in 1923. 'The hero of these books', he wrote, was he himself,

I, my life, my thoughts and my actions. And if after thirty or forty years, a new generation will read these books and will think about them, they will see and feel in them the living human blood of a living man in the years of Russia's magnificent storms and floods, and will smile at my ravings and will justify my romanticism, the romanticism of a 'village idiot', visiting the world in its 'fateful moments'—then my work will have been justified.

Well, forty years later the reader is moved to weep rather than smile at the 'ravings' of this 'living man', and not only because he knows what happened to him subsequently, but because in retrospect his enthusiasm seems to have been sadly misplaced and his parable piteously inadequate, because the reader can now see that he was attempting to play with a monstrous reality which was far beyond his grasp, that the popular concept of the Revolution as a storm was insufficient, and that the rhetorical passage with which Pilnyak closed his book by way of poetic summary was ingenuous rather than profound:

The forest stands austere, like cleated spars, and like carrion-birds the storm flings itself upon it. Night. Was it not of the storm that the true *bylina* was composed about the death of the *bogatyri*? Again and again the stormy birds of prey fling themselves upon the forest spars; they howl, they scream, they cry, they whine in spitefulness like peasant women, they fall dead, and after them come other carrion-birds; they do not diminish, they still arrive,—like serpent heads, two for every one that is cut off, but the forest remains standing, like Ilya Muromets.

Today such grandiloquence and such structural contrivances seem more pitiful than moving.

Fedin's *Cities and Years,* cooler, more rational than Pilnyak's novel, is equally ambitious and intricate. Its action embraces six years, from 1914 to 1922; its scenes shift between Germany and Russia; its plot is arranged in unchronological order, the conclusion being given in the prologue and the beginning in Part II, and only then, with several gaps in the time sequence, does the narrative proceed consecutively. It is, furthermore, divided into chapters in such a way as to form an elaborate symmetrical pattern: there are nine parts, of which the first and the last, a kind of prologue and epilogue, have three chapters each; the second and eighth parts, containing the decisive action of the story, are each composed of five chapters; and each of the remaining five parts, leading up to and explaining the decisive action, is divided into four chapters. It is a scheme that reminds one of Remizov's *The Clock,* without serving, however, so far as I can see, the symbolic purpose of Remizov's design, which was intended, through the circular motion suggested by both title and form, to exemplify an underlying metaphysical idea: that static and episodic human events occur within the inescapable circle of time. Fedin's intention seems to have been, quite simply, to be interesting in a novel way, to treat history in terms of adventure, and thus to create suspense and avoid the tedium of ordinary chronicles. Through its construction, the novel does achieve the atmosphere of a detective thriller, and differs from other war books in being chiefly concerned not with fighting but with ethics and the psychology of a complicated character. But to be merely ingenious about such matters as these strikes one as inadequate, not to say flippant.

Leonov's first novel, *The Badgers,* which, like *Cities and Years,* was published in 1924, exhibits the same interest in structural eccentricity. It is full of crudely inserted episodes, flashbacks, disappearances and sudden re-emergences of important characters. Here, too, history is treated as an exciting adventure. And Leonov's later novels are even more elaborate exercises in the obliquities of narrative method.

Such is the tendency of some of the most conscious artists of the period, who set themselves the task of modifying traditional literary procedures. They are distinguished, on the one hand, from artists like Babel and Vsevolod Ivanov, whose work is novel because their perceptions are original; and, on the other, from those who, like Fadeyev and Furmanov, following in Gorky's footsteps, see themselves as bearers of a vital message and are not interested, therefore, in formal innovations, but simply in express-ing what they conceive to be new in a way that is most familiar and most readily understandable. About the importance of Ivanov's and Babel's achievement there can be no doubt; their powerful, laconic sketches of war are little masterpieces of tragic understatement. Concerning Furmanov and Fadeyev, however, opinions differ. Furmanov's *Chapayev*, in fact, is usually dis-missed by Western critics as a mere piece of ordinary reporting. I think that it may be rather more than this and that it deserves, perhaps, somewhat more serious critical attention than it has received. A piece of reporting it undeniably is, a piece of propa-ganda also; and yet, this reporting and this propaganda are so wholehearted, the book is done with such devoted, such naive enthusiasm, that all unconsciously an engaging self-portrait emerges from it. It is an honest book—more honest than many of Gorky's, I would say. Its propaganda comes not of duty but convictions, as the expression of an uncomplicated and com-pletely absorbing experience. For these reasons it seems to me to possess greater artistic merit than it is usually accorded, where-as Fadeyev's much more sophisticated book is derivative and inferior. But however this may be, *Chapayev* and *The Rout* (along with other novels of the same kind but of lesser consequence) throw into sharp relief, by contrast to those of the Babel-Ivanov and the Pilnyak-Fedin categories, one of the major issues of Soviet literature: the relative importance for art of novelty and tradi-tion, the whole question, raised by the Formalists, of the relation of technique to content, of the primacy of technique over content.

The pervasive topic of war was part of a larger and even more compelling theme which imposed itself on everybody—the theme of the present, in whatever aspect it might be seen. The immediate moment was of prime significance. One might view it in comparison with the past or as a step toward the future, or one might examine it in itself, so fateful did the age appear—and not only to Communists—that every one was bound to scruti-nize it, to try to understand what it stood for, what it portended. I wonder whether there was anywhere, at any time, a period so self-conscious as this one, so filled with a sense of its historic import. In the first issue of his *Epopeia*, Andrey Bely explained its title in a preface choking with the excitement of his prophetic announcement that mankind was about to attain the pinnacle of culture in the advent of the Proletarian State—an event that, in the course of human history, only the birth of Christ could equal. Thence, said Bely, the epic quality of the era, thence the title of his journal. Bely's was but a turgid proclamation of something that seems to have been almost universally believed. It was a period of heightened emotionalism, a romantic period. The years of fighting were seen in an exalted light, and now that the fight- ing was over and the country was to be rebuilt, 'heroes of industry' were replacing heroes of battle. In a poem of 1923, Mayakovsky addressed the miners of Kursk, praising their unostentatious heroism. Their monument, he said, would be raised in the in- dustry of the future; the pattern of their names would be woven in the sky by the smoke of the million chimneys which their labour was helping to build. Serafimovich's *The Iron Torrent* came out in 1924, Gladkov's *Cement* in 1925.

Mayakovsky was one of those ardent revolutionists who were at first shocked and disillusioned by the NEP. There is a caustic denunciation of it in *About What? About this*: Where

> the scourging, the judging October had thundered,
> you have disposed yourselves,
> have set out your dishes
> under its flame-feathered wing.
>   . . .
> Chicken love!
>   Love of brood hens!

But by the following year Mayakovsky had come to terms with it, and in his epic elegy, *Vladimir Ilyich Lenin*, presented it as an example of the Great Leader's wisdom. NEP was a temporary measure, a necessary piece of strategy, a sudden changing of the ship's course to rescue 'the colossus of Soviet Republics' and bring it safely 'into construction docks'. Far from betraying the ideals of the Revolution, it was a step toward realizing them.

The prevailing temper of the times, in short, was to justify the losses and sufferings of the preceding years and to defend the privations still demanded in building the emergent Utopia, in

which everyone was constrained to believe. Hopefulness was in
the air, as well as a continued faith in the ideals for which the
Revolution and the Civil War had been fought. A reverence for
novelty was implicit in these views: a new civilization was
evolving, and with it a new morality and a new art. One must
look ahead; if one looked back, it was only to see how the past
could serve the present. And one must find new modes of expression appropriate to its greatness and splendid expectations. But
although no writer could escape this compelling theme, not every
one could be happy in it. And so, although much was written
that was genuinely enthusiastic, in which the artist's inspiration,
that is, was not in conflict with generally accepted attitudes, there
was also a good deal that was forced, contrived, and meretricious.
'With good intentions hell is paved,' wrote Pasternak in 1923,

> And the opinion is now held,
> That if with them one paves one's verses too,
> All one's sins will be forgiven.

Pasternak himself was moved by something other than 'good intentions'. But it was, surely, the insistence of the age on the immeasurable importance of social and historic themes that brought
him at this time out of his room, where he had been 'smoking
with Byron and drinking with Edgar Allan Poe', out into the
contemporary world to write, between 1923 and 1927, *The Lofty
Illness*, *The Year 1905*, and *Lieutenant Schmidt*. He treated history in his own way, but the fact remains that the age made its
irresistible demands even on him, made it imperative for him
to deal with history.

There were also authors who felt the tragedy, or the pathos,
of these insistent demands, to whom it seemed that whatever the
significance of the historic moment, it was not consistently, at all
times, to all men, uniformly uplifting, heroic and benign. In
Zoshchenko's early stories, the glorious present appears drab and
petty, and the men who are caught in it are defenceless, absurd,
and insignificant as Gogol's pathetic Akaki Akakiyevich Bash-
machkin. In the guise of the supposed narrator of his *Sentimental
Tales*, the 'fellow traveller I. V. Kolenkorov', Zoshchenko explains what he is doing. 'This book', says Kolenkorov in a preface
of 1927,

was written at the very height of NEP and the Revolution. The reader, of course, has the right to demand from the author real, revolutionary content, big with those planetary programmes and heroic pathos—in a word, full of high ideology. Unwilling to involve the unwealthy purchaser in unnecessary expense, the author hastens to announce, in profound pain of spirit, that in this sentimental book there will be little that is heroic.

His book is written, he says, about man in all his 'unalluring beauty'. And unheroic man appears in Zoshchenko's world in a rather sardonic, though pitying, light. 'Of what does the nightingale sing?' asks Lizanka in a tender moment. And Bylinkin, whom she is about to marry, replies: 'He wants to eat [*zhrat' khochet*], that's why he sings.' Their sweet romance is presently broken up because of a chest of drawers. Bylinkin cannot live without it. He has been 'steeled in battle', he says, he 'knows what life is, and not by a single step will he depart from his ideals'. But his future mother-in-law, fond though she is both of him and of her daughter, will not be parted from her chest of drawers. A quarrel ensues, he leaves, and finds himself another wife. Other characters in Kolenkorov's tales are more pathetic than Bylinkin. And all of them are anti-heroes, quiet little men, unregarded, hurt by life, cast off by a society in which they are superfluous. What Zoshchenko likes to point out is that though these men are not popular heroes, by any stretch of the imagination, they do exist nevertheless, are real, and have their lives to lead. His stories, melancholy and very touching for all their humour, are a condemnation of a society that cares too little about the private fortunes of ordinary men. 'The author doesn't know', Kolenkorov is made to say,

'what is most important, what is, so to speak, most splendid in our life, that for which, generally speaking, life is worth living on this earth.

Maybe it is service to one's country, maybe it is service to one's people—and all that kind of tempestuous ideology. Maybe that's so. Most probably it's so. But then in private life, in the day-to-day design, there exist also, in addition to these lofty ideas, other small little notions, which are principally those that make our life interesting and attractive.'

There is, for example, the notion of love. Doesn't it seem to the reader that 'the precious feeling of love' is 'the most precious, the most attractive in our life?' The author 'does not affirm this. He positively does not affirm. He hopes that there is in life something even better and more beautiful. Only sometimes it seems to the author that there is nothing higher than love.' The stories are mostly about how hard it is to come by 'this most precious feeling', how elusive it is, how easily missed or how easily lost. 'The author confesses that in our stormy years it is positively shameful, positively embarrassing even, to come out with such trivial ideas, with such commonplace talk about individual man.'

On the more tragic level, the same protest, the same excuses are made by Esenin and Mayakovsky. From the beginning of the Revolution, Mayakovsky had devoted himself to propagandist work. But as soon as conditions permitted, he turned to poetry about himself. In 1921 he wrote his autobiographic *I Love* and in 1923, *About What? About This*, that extraordinary analysis and dramatization of love, 'the small, private' theme, as he called it, which was unmentionable but inescapable. Mayakovsky's whole life was a self-willed, defiant submission to what he conceived to be his public role. He sacrificed his private life and his private voice, 'stepped on the throat of his own song', 'made himself all will', to be what he thought the country required of him. But he made his martyrdom well known in a kind of anguished bravado, which was at once both praise and reproof of the age to which he immolated himself. Esenin's laments are equally poignant, but not so dramatic. His defiance took the form of rowdiness; he was not, in his own eyes, a tragic martyr, but a lost soul, a drunken tramp who had wasted his life, although— as he wrote in verses that are unintentionally more pathetic than his outspoken complaints—he was determined to grasp the glory of the Soviet State and to change his feeling and his language in appreciation of it:

> Great and glorious publisher! In this book
> I give myself up to feelings new,
> I learn to comprehend in every moment
> Russia raised up by the Commune.
>
> It may be that my pencil whispered
> to the paper clumsily about many things,

> my soul, not yet awake, sang hoarsely,
> not understanding our festive days.

In 1926, when Esenin killed himself, Mayakovsky felt in duty bound to pass judgement on him. *To Sergei Esenin* is a bitter reproach: a poet, says Mayakovsky, has no right to take his own life, when there is still much for him to do in his country—a reproach that only four years later was to reverberate ironically in the minds of those who remembered it, when Mayakovsky himself chose the way out which he here condemned.

These two poets rise up out of the controversies of the period, like symbols of what is most tragic in it, towering above fictional heroes and giving the lie to their inhuman fortitude. They are, on a grander scale, the discarded men of Zoshchenko's stories, while Yuri Olesha and Evgeni Zamyatin draw a satiric picture of the conditions that destroyed them. With all their differences, *Envy* and *We* are both laments for the loss of human values in a mechanized world, powerful and unequivocal indictments of a society in which individual lives count for nothing except insofar as they can be of use. And although it may be unfair to lay Esenin's and Mayakovsky's destruction at the door of their society, it is surely not unfair to see its callousness as a potent contributing factor.

It was, however, Pasternak whose work, even in this period, gave the subtlest and deepest analysis of what was taking place. His stories in prose, *Il Tratto di Appelle*, *Letters from Tula*, *Aerial Ways* and *The Childhood of Luvers*, which were published as a volume in 1925, were all built, as Stefan Schimanski pointed out astutely in his introduction to the English edition, on 'one single leitmotif ... the problem of replacing something that has been lost so as to restore the equilibrium that has been upset'. This is not the moment to discuss Pasternak's treatment of this theme, nor of the way it throws light on the intricate philosophy he was at this time evolving. But I would like to suggest that the theme itself may have been given him, in these years of shifting values, by the ever present experience of loss, both physical and spiritual, actual and threatened, the loss of everything that men hold precious—life and love, a sense of purpose, of meaning, of identity. This suggestion may be disputed, but what does seem to me unquestionable is that in this respect, as also in others, Pasternak retained a position of independence, not through indifference or evasion, but, on the contrary, through genuine involvement in the lives and thoughts of his contemporaries. He was involved in his world, but not lost in it; and he could view it in the dispassionate light of his historic and philosophic knowledge, of his supreme integrity as artist and thinker. The same is true of his historic poems, *The Year 1905* and *Lieutenant Schmidt*. Like other works of the time, they too were an attempt to reconstruct and interpret the revolutionary events of twentieth-century Russia, to portray the hero of modern times; and the staccato, nervous brevity of their language was, like Babel's and Mayakovsky's, the speech of a restless, anxious period. But they stand apart in the originality of their appraisals, in their profoundly appreciative, sympathetic and non-partisan judgement of men. Pasternak is a superb example of the cliché that a great artist is both of his age and ahead of it. Mayakovsky, Babel, Zoshchenko, Sholokhov belonged wholly to their age—Esenin, partly to the past. There was no artist at this time, in my opinion, of a stature comparable to Pasternak, who alone belonged to both the present and the future.

It will not do to belittle this brightest period in Soviet Russian literature, to minimize the contributions of the Formalists, of Akhmatova and Mandelshtam, of Mayakovsky and Pasternak, of Babel and Zoshchenko, of Zamyatin and Ilf and Petrov. The literature of the NEP period stands on its own merits, and not only in relation to the darkness in which it was soon to be engulfed, though to the eye of hindsight it seems doubly brilliant in this contrast. And yet one must acknowledge that even this bright epoch is not comparable to the analogous period in the West. Why? Two easy answers suggest themselves. First, it is impossible to legislate about genius or account for it; and apart from Blok, who died in 1921, and Pasternak, who did not come fully into his own until somewhat later, there happened to be no Proust, or Joyce, or Yeats, or Thomas Mann in the Russia of the Twenties; and, secondly, the gifted artist who was starting out at this time was not given a chance to develop: his talent was presently snuffed out. Perhaps these are the right answers: either that, despite much promise, the writers of the time did not have the stuff of greatness in them, or that, given more leeway, a Leonov or a Pilnyak might, in time, have produced work of universal

significance. Perhaps. But another answer, and in my opinion a
more valid one, may be given. This is that the spirit of the age
itself—its apparent freedom notwithstanding—was a stifling one.
Debates were possible, experiments were welcome. But the very
stridency of the former and the artificiality of the latter were in
themselves a sign of anxiety and constraint. It was an age of
fighters. And the fighter is not free, his hand is forced by the
enemy. It is a rare individual, maybe only a genius, who, driven
into and fixed in the posture of defence, can still maintain the
freedom of his mind and heart. Mayakovsky was rebellious, not
free; and the same can be said of Esenin. Zamyatin and Zoshchenko were isolated, rather than free. Akhmatova and
Mandelshtam retained their freedom, but only within the limits
of strictly inward experience. Pasternak alone was able to take in
his world and still remain himself. And although his accomplishment appears all the greater for the hostile atmosphere in which
it unfolded, there is no way of estimating how much was lost to
art in this epoch that seemed propitious, because it granted a
modicum of outward freedom, but which caught hold of the
minds and spirits of its artists and tacitly, but imperiously, made
its demands on them.

In sum, the NEP period was a time of unprecedently varied
artistic productivity, some of it of lasting importance. It was also
a stirring time of intellectual excitement, but this excitement had
its dangers: the urgency of the debates created an atmosphere
of partisanship, of narrow, passionate commitments that made
independence difficult. The freest minds were fettered by the self-
consciousness of an age which took itself with wonderful seriousness, believing that the destiny of mankind lay in its hands and
that upon the articulate members of the population devolved the
duty of formulating and directing the ideals of all men. The
artist's view of himself as a spokesman for humanity became inescapable, and often led to bombast, to the showy, exaggerated
and artificial rather than the original—characteristics which
were true, to a degree, even of the Formalists and the fellow-
travellers, whose excessiveness was the emphatic answer, given by
men who valued independence and respected the mind, to a
threatening philistinism, which was soon to find embodiment in
the official doctrine of Socialist Realism. In the case of those for
whom the public role was unnatural and difficult, this imposed

self-consciousness operated not as liberation but constraint. No one escaped completely. And that is why this period dramatizes, perhaps more poignantly than any other, the essential aesthetic and moral debate of modern times: the debate on the possibility of the mind's freedom, when freedom itself is conceived as an offshoot of commitment. Thence, the banding together of even the most ardent advocates of independence in schools and groups; thence, the expression of even personal experience in terms of *pro* and *contra*; thence, also, the individual tragedies of suicide and exile. It is, in short, a period which can most justly be characterized as tragic, because it exhibits all the factors of struggle, idealism, the clash of wills, the defeats and the possibilities which are implicit in the concept of tragedy. Through our knowledge of what happened later, it appears as a period of immeasurable loss; but it is also so full of spiritual strength, of such splendid potentialities for the life of the mind and artistic creation, that one is inclined to see it in the symbol of Pasternak's stories, the symbol of wonderful restitutions, in which loss itself figures as the instrument of redress, transforming bereavement into an unprecedented, unexpected, illuminating understanding of man's fate.

3

THE YEAR OF ACQUIESCENCE

Edward J. Brown

1. *Introduction*

The year 1930 was a crucial and a tragic one in the history of Soviet literature. The year 1956, which marked a stage in the emergence of literature from the rigours of dogmatism, has been called a 'year of protest'; 1930, another year of critical change—but in the direction of Stalinism—might be called a 'year of acquiescence'. Acquiescence took many forms, from the suicide of Mayakovsky to Pilnyak's transmogrification of *Mahagony* into a Five-year Plan novel. Soviet literature in 1930 was poised between the old and the new. The relative freedom and variety of the Twenties had not yet been completely eroded, and at the beginning of that year the many groups that had come into being under the liberal policies announced in 1925 still existed and still carried on their occasionally lethal polemic in the public press. But the political climate was becoming cold to difference and dispute, and during 1930 the number of independent groups was sharply reduced. Consolidation of literary forces for the attainment of political and economic ends was the official policy during that year, and 'consolidation' meant organizational unity as well as ideological conformity. The final organizational 'reform' which would bring all writers into one big union was still two years ahead, but 1930 saw the absorption by RAPP, the Russian Association of Proletarian Writers, of many formerly independent groups and individuals. The followers of Pereverzev joined RAPP; the 'Smithy' and the Constructivists asked for admission; members of the defunct LEF group joined during the year, notably Mayakovsky, and the writers of *Pereval* came under heavy pressure to conform. Stalin himself directly intervened on at least two occasions—an omen of future development.

2. Reform of the Union

Some of the important developments of the 'year of acquiescence' were initiated late in 1929. Two events in particular were indicative of future trends. The first of these concerned the so-called fellow-traveller wing of literature, and the second the proletarian, or party-oriented, writers.

In August 1929 the two leading figures in the Union of Writers, which was the organization of the fellow-travellers, were Pilnyak, chairman of the Moscow section, and Zamyatin, chairman of the Leningrad section. The Union was at that time a body concerned less with the ideology of its members than with their interests as writers. The prestige and influence in that Union of Pilnyak and Zamyatin is evidence that its dominant group was not in tune with the official Soviet mind, nor ready to accept a political role for literature. Indeed the Union was often attacked as a focus of heterodoxy and free thought, and as early as August 1929 Efim Zozulya caused a mild flurry when he resigned from it on the grounds that it 'did not possess an ideological platform in touch with the times' and that it included 'a variety of elements ranging from communists to mystics'. And that was no doubt true, since its membership was open to all writers.[1]

The Russian Association of Proletarian Writers (RAPP), with heavy backing from the Party, was at that time engaged in a campaign against 'neo-bourgeois' elements in Soviet literature. The 'struggle against neo-bourgeois literature' was, in 1929 and 1930, a euphemism for the campaign to reform the Union of Writers and make it into an obedient instrument of Party policy. Vilification of the Union's leaders, Pilnyak and Zamyatin, who had published abroad novels that could not be published in the Soviet Union, was the method used. Though many Soviet writers had contracts with foreign publishers, the action of Pilnyak and Zamyatin was hysterically attacked in the press as 'treason', and 'traffic with the enemy'. Statements condemning their 'traitorous' behaviour were obtained from many writers, including Mayakovsky, who said that Pilnyak's deed was like 'betrayal in battle'. Such statements were featured in successive issues of the *Literary Gazette*, and were used to cover and confuse the efforts of Pilnyak

1. See Max Hayward, 'Pilnyak and Zamyatin: Two Tragedies of the Twenties', *Survey*, No. 36, April–June 1961.

and Zamyatin to defend themselves. These two were forced under pressure to resign from their posts in the Union and the whole executive board was replaced. The novelist Leonid Leonov was elected chairman of a new executive board, the name of the organization was changed to the Union of *Soviet* Writers and a new statement of principles declared among other things that 'literature is not only a reflection of life but a mighty weapon of social action. . . . Soviet literature has a single great aim: while reflecting and explaining the world to remake it'. The new Union, having rid itself of those relics of the bourgeois past, Pilnyak and Zamyatin, presented Soviet writers with a purpose and a programme.

3. *Consolidation of Proletarian Forces*

The second event which served as a prelude to the year of acquiescence was the Party demand for 'consolidation of forces' within the proletarian or communist wing of literature. In December 1929 an editorial in *Pravda* asserted that RAPP was carrying out a line in literature 'closest to the line of the Party', and from this drew the conclusion that all proletarian literary forces should close ranks around RAPP. The article expressed suspicion of the fact that Marxists were broken up into 'competing groups', and that these not only disagreed but fought one another violently. The events which followed publication of this article offer clear proof that the ideas expressed in it represented a considered and authoritative Party view. Controversy was suddenly damped down. The journal *Pechat i revolyutsia*, which had been at odds with the leadership of RAPP and their journal *Na literaturnom postu* on many points of literary criticism and theory, published a statement regretting the acrimonious nature of the controversy, and acknowledged RAPP, using the exact words of the *Pravda* editorial, as an organization carrying out a line in literature 'closest to the line of the Party'. The 'consolidation of forces' meant in practice that many proletarian writers and critics from groups which had been hostile to RAPP now joined RAPP, ostensibly of their own accord. The members of the 'Smithy', for instance, asked the executive board of RAPP to admit them as a body, but were told that each member must apply individually for admission. The effect of this, of course, would have been to liquidate the 'Smithy' as a group. After lengthy negotiations the

Smithy was admitted to RAPP, but certain members were denied admission.

4. *Defeat of Pereverzev*

Soon after the publication of the *Pravda* article calling for consolidation, a group of literary figures connected with the Communist Academy and the Institute of Red Professors, who had been followers of Professor Pereverzev, published a declaration of their intention to join RAPP as the 'basic proletarian literary organization'. Their collective application for membership made one condition, that they be allowed to continue to defend their own views on questions of literary theory, even if those views differed from the views of the RAPP leadership. But the RAPP leaders demanded, as a minimum concession, repudiation of Pereverzev and his ideas. Libedinsky's comment on this event points up the authority and importance which had been conferred on RAPP by the Party:

> After the defeat of Pereverzev, the entire body of his followers entered our organization . . . The comrades understood that outside our organization it was impossible to work, that one must work inside it.

The 'defeat' of Pereverzev was one of the significant events of the year of acquiescence. Pereverzev was a Marxist literary theoretican of high standing and wide influence. Textbooks on literature used in the schools were full of his doctrines. His theory was an attempt to apply Marxism scientifically to the investigation of literary phenomena. He maintained that 'the image' is the basic ingredient in a work of literature, and that a given writer's system of images is determined by the position he occupies in the productive process. Each writer's system of images, moreover, he held to be subconsciously determined, and not capable of being altered by conscious thought or reformed in response to directives. Understandably, his theory came into conflict with the campaign to 're-educate' various bourgeois writers in the spirit of the proletariat. And his dictum that 'a bourgeois writer cannot produce a proletarian character, nor a proletarian writer a bourgeois character' found no favour with 'proletarian writers' who were almost without exception bourgeois in education and origin. Obviously such ideas as these were unwelcome in 1930, when the demand was that all writers, proletarian and bourgeois, carry out literary directives given them by the Party and the government.[2]

5. The Taming of Mayakovsky

The best-known incident in the 'consolidation of proletarian forces' was the entry of Mayakovsky into RAPP in February 1930, just two months before his suicide. He had abandoned the 'Left Front of Art' (LEF) in 1928, and in October 1928 a new organization called REF had been formed under his leadership, the purpose of which, he said, was to combat 'apolitical and aesthetic tendencies in LEF, and to place political action and social purpose in the forefront of the artist's attention. While insisting on a certain freedom in the selection of means—that is, in the development of literary method and form—Mayakovsky proposed to give special emphasis to *purpose* in his poetry.

But in February 1930 he abandoned his comrades of REF and joined RAPP. The reasons for his action are not known in detail, but it was certainly in part a reaction to the *Pravda* editorial of December 1929. His announcement of adherence to RAPP, read at a meeting of the Moscow branch of the organization on 6 February 1930, was written earlier, and is actually dated 3 January 1930.[3] Libedinsky in his volume of reminiscences, *Sovremenniki*, claims that Mayakovsky had decided to enter RAPP late in 1929. Sutyrin, who was secretary of RAPP at the time, said, according to Volume XIII of Mayakovsky's *Collected Works*, that Mayakovsky first announced his intention of joining early in January but that nothing could be done about it then because a number of key officials of RAPP were absent from Moscow. The announcement of his intention to join RAPP reveals in its language that this action was an answer to the call for 'consolidation of forces':

> In order to realize in practice the slogan for the consolidation of all the forces of proletarian literature, I request that I be accepted as a member of RAPP.
>
> (1) I have not, and have never had any disagreements as to the literary-political line of the Party, which is being carried out by RAPP.

2. The best statement of Pereverzev's viewpoint at the time under discussion is V. F. Pereverzev, 'Problemy marksistskogo literaturovedenia', *Literatura i marksizm*, No. 2, 1929.

3. V. V. Mayakovsky, *Polnoe sobranie sochinenii*, Vol. XIII, p. 350.

(2) Stylistic and methodological differences can be resolved with benefit for proletarian literature within the Association.

I believe that all active members of REF should draw the same conclusion that I have drawn, a conclusion dictated by all our previous history.

V. Mayakovsky [4]

The date of this document, 3 January 1930, presents an interesting problem. Why was there a delay of more than a month in accepting Mayakovsky into RAPP? Why should there have been any delay in acknowledging the capitulation of a powerful adversary? Sutyrin's explanation does not cover the case. There is evidence that the bureaucrats in control of RAPP were afraid of the poet and did not very much want him in their organization. There is evidence, further, that Mayakovsky himself forced their hand. The evidence in question is Libedinsky's account of how Mayakovsky became a member of RAPP on 6 February 1930:

In February, 1930, I arrived at a conference of RAPP, and at the door Sutyrin, a member of the secretariat, met me.... He looked a little bit upset. 'I have to consult you on one question,' he said. 'You know, Mayakovsky is here and he says he's going to speak now and announce he's joining RAPP. I said I'd have to consult with some of my colleagues, with Fadeyev or Libedinsky....'

'What is there to consult about?' I asked, though I was myself somewhat upset. I rejoiced at the entrance of Mayakovsky into RAPP, but for me, too, it was somewhat unexpected....

The leaders of RAPP looked upon Mayakovsky's adherence with a kind of worry. It was as though we were concerned lest our weak vessel be hurt by the weight of such an elephant....[5]

Libedinsky admits that Mayakovsky was not warmly welcomed into RAPP, and that in this mass organization he felt isolated and alone. His comrades of REF did not join him and he had no new friends in RAPP. 'I know,' said Libedinsky, 'that from February until April, 1930, the secretariat of RAPP constantly hauled Mayakovsky over the coals—and in a trivial and didactic fashion. Mayakovsky's plays, indeed, could not be fitted into the framework of RAPP dogmas.'

The account in the *Literary Gazette* of 10 February 1930 of the meeting at which Mayakovsky joined RAPP bears out Libedin-

4. *ibid.*, p. 134.
5. Yu. Libedinsky, *Sovremenniki*, Moscow, 1958, p. 173.

sky's memory of the cold reception accorded the poet. The secretary, Sutyrin, pointed out that many people joined RAPP because
of the advantage membership conferred on them, and that some
others who came in had an exaggerated notion of their own importance. Among the latter he included Mayakovsky.

The capitulation to RAPP which was exacted from Mayakovsky was probably the one event which made his suicide inevitable. In his suicide note he included a special paragraph for his
comrades of RAPP: 'Comrade RAPPists, don't think me a
coward. Really, it couldn't be helped.' And the suicide note contains a reference, too, to the fact that the attacks upon him had
not ended with his capitulation.

The pressures upon Mayakovsky to join RAPP had been many
and various. The manuscript of his play *The Bath-house* had been
held up for two months in *Glavrepertkom*, the Chief Committee
on the repertory of Soviet theatres. Difficulties had arisen because
of the sharply satirical attacks in it on contemporary personalities
and tendencies and on the bureaucratic nature as exhibited by
recognizable commissar types from Lunacharsky to Yermilov.
The third act of the play contains an undisguised mockery of the
literary slogans advocated by RAPP itself: 'For the living man',
and 'Learn from the classics'. Some of these barbs were softened
at the behest of *Glavrepertkom*, and permission to produce the
play was finally granted on 9 February, just three days after Mayakovsky joined RAPP. There may well have been a connexion
between the two events.

6. *Pereval*

Pressure to conform was also brought upon the writers of the
organization *Pereval* in 1930, and a public discussion of their
work was held in April. The occasion for the discussion was the
appearance of the collection of their stories and poems, *Rovesniki*,
containing Ivan Katayev's story *Milk*. This story was immediately singled out for censure, and was even found worthy of an
article in *Pravda*. In Katayev's story a 'committee of the poor and
middle peasants' eliminates a *kulak* from control of a dairying
collective, but the narration is so contrived that the *kulak* emerges
as an interesting, attractive and sympathetic character. In the
welter of charges against the *Pereval* group, which included impu-
tations of deviation and disloyalty, the most persistant was that a

'humanistic viewpoint' prevented them from seeing life in terms of the class struggle. They defended themselves vigorously at the public debate held in Moscow, but were obliged to publish a new 'Declaration of Principles' which, like the statement of the re-organized Writers' Union, retained certain basic literary prin-ciples while attempting to adjust to the new demands. Their analysis of the contemporary literary situation, included in that document, is one of the most informed and perceptive state-ments produced in the Marxist milieu.[6]

7. The Litfront Affair

In the process of mass adherence to RAPP by groups that had formerly held aloof from that organization, each group insisted on the right to differ with the leadership on matters of form and style while accepting its overall political programme. The im-mediate effect was a factional struggle within RAPP that involved in the end much more than matters of style or literary method. The faction that took issue with the leadership called itself the *Litfront*. Its most important members were Semyon Rodov, a poet of the 'Smithy' and a leader of the early 'On Guard' move-ment; the playwright Vsevolod Vishnevsky, author of agitational dramas such as *The First Cavalry Army* and *Unforgettable 1919*; T. Kostrov, editor of the *Komsomol* newspaper, that stern young man with no sympathy for tender feelings to whom Maya-kovsky directed his poem from Paris about love; V. Zonin, a critic associated with the 'Smithy'; Boris Kushner and some others formerly of the 'Left Front of Art'; Bespalov and Gelfand, who had been on the editorial board of the magazine *Pechat i revolyutsia* and were followers of Pereverzev; and one of the lead-ing figures in the early proletarian literary movement, the agi-tator-poet Alexander Bezymensky. Bezymensky was the most active and articulate member of the *Litfront*, and its spokesman, as we shall see, on important occasions.

At the Sixteenth Congress of the Communist Party in June 1930 the factional struggle in RAPP was dramatized by the pre-sentation of two speeches on literary problems, one delivered by the playwright Vladimir Kirshon speaking for the leaders of RAPP, and a second by Bezymensky, who held up to ridicule the dominant literary programme and the principal writers of the

6. 'Pereval i iskusstvo nashikh dnei', *Literaturnaya gazeta*, 14 April 1930.

proletarian movement, to the applause and amusement of the
assembled delegates. These two speeches provide a key to the
issues which at that moment divided proletarian literature. Kirshon's talk was a dull statement, in an ill-natured political idiom,
of the official line in literature. In it he attacked a number of
prime targets: Pilnyak, liberal professors, officials of Glavlit who
allow the publication of works containing 'shades' of bourgeois
philosophy, the *Pereval* writers for their generalized 'love of all
humanity', intellectuals who 'accept' the revolution but treat proletarians with condescension, the 'menshevik' literary theorist
Pereverzev and all his crew, and an 'unprincipled bloc' calling
itself the *Litfront* which, he said, attacks 'our whole programme
and all our literary slogans'.

Bezmensky's answer was a poem in the pseudo-Mayakovsky
style which he had made his own and could use with amusement
and verve. The subject of his poem was the 'break' on the front of
literary production, the causes of which he found in the work of
the principal leaders of RAPP. He spoke of the industrial transformation of the country, using with poetic emphasis words such
as rails, tractors, blast-furnaces, dumpcars, excavators, kolk-
hozes and the like, contrasting this progress with the backwardness of Soviet literature in reflecting it. Punning on the title of
Fadeyev's famous novel, he asserted that in literature we 'have
suffered a rout'. He complained of the lack of socialist planning
in the production of literature. 'Fadeyev is still, after five years,
trying on his Tolstoyan jacket, *The Last of the Udegs*. Chum-
andrin chews over the sex problems of Soviet bureaucrats in
Fabrika Rable. And in a country replete with heroes of the blast
furnace, the mine and the kolkhoz, Libedinsky in *The Birth of a
Hero* salivates over the problem of ladies' hair.' Libedinsky's
notion that every communist must know himself and his own
motives thoroughly through 'active self-analysis' Bezymensky
slanderously caricatured, quoting him out of context to the effect
that 'nothing can take the place of self-analysis, not even devotion
to the revolution'. And he linked Libedinsky with Voronsky's
theory of art, accusing him of having borrowed from that discredited source his notions about 'immediate impressions' in
literature. Bezymensky demanded a correct 'class' orientation
instead of 'humanism' and called upon literary men to take active

part in the struggles of the moment. 'We do not need', he said, 'Tolstoys in Marxist clothing.'

The literary discussion of 1930 revolved around issues that are still alive in Soviet literature, and the confrontation before a Party Congress of Kirshon and Bezymensky has some points of similarity to the later confrontation of Surkov and Sholokhov in 1956, and of Tvardovsky and Kochetov in 1961. The main point at issue in 1930, as in 1961, was the place in literature of individual lives and private experience. The RAPP leaders produced novels about particular human beings, whom they presented in private as well as in civic situations. The *Litfront* called for de-emphasis of psychology and the 'inner man' in favour of stylized images of revolutionary heroism which would inspire the masses.

The *Litfront* deplored the length of proletarian novels and begrudged the time required to produce a *Quiet Don*, or a *Last of the Udegs*. The novel form itself they regarded as outmoded, and they called for a 'revolution in literary genres' that would bring to the fore political poetry, stories and dramas of production, sketches and pamphlets. The *Litfront*'s most powerful argument for support from the Party was that its method would 'liquidate the backwardness' of Soviet literature, and convert it into a mighty weapon of Party propaganda, free from psychologizing and 'self-analysis'.

The *Litfront* had support within the Party, and for several months during 1930 it had access to the public press. The *Literary Gazette* under the editorship of Olkhovy was distinctly favourable to the *Litfront* in its editorial tone, and in the weight of articles it published. *Pechat i revolyutsia*, until it became *Literatura i iskusstvo* in September 1930, supported the *Litfront* programme. In this respect, too, the literary situation bore some resemblance to the present day, when opposing factions in literature are identified with certain periodicals, the liberals with *Novy Mir*, and the conservatives with *Neva* and *Oktyabr*.

As in later periods, certain books and authors served as emblems of the opposing parties. The controversy between the *Litfront* and the leadership of RAPP was to a large extent carried on in terms of the relative merits of *The Birth of a Hero* and two plays produced during the year 1930, Bezymensky's *The Shot* and Vishnevsky's *The First Cavalry Army*.

The leaders of RAPP had tied themselves firmly to Libedinsky's *The Birth of a Hero,* a novel that attempts to explore in depth the consciousness of an earnest and intelligent Bolshevik, Shorokhov, and to reveal in his inner monologue the dialectic of history. The novel is an ambitious project, and it is not wholly without merit. The hero is shown in 'dialectical' opposition to the static forces of bureaucratism in the Party and bourgeois stability in family life. His most important opponent is his young assistant Eidnunen, for whom all life has fallen into static patterns, and thought is simply a process of labelling. His second enemy is his young wife Lyuba, whose programme for family life is narrow and selfish, aimed only at propriety, comfort and reproductive activity. But Shorokhov's radical nature negates these negations of revolutionary movement, and he at last frees himself from their influence:

And suddenly he felt himself a new and youthful creature by comparison with her . . . And in the desolation . . . of this large room he sensed the barely visible elements of Lyuba's family world: vari-coloured embroidery on the window sill; a quiet new meat grinder glistening in the corner, and her comfortable worn slippers under the bed. And he looked upon all this, which had before been so sweet to him, as a new manifestation of the old enemy, as the elemental repetition of immemorial and hateful forms of life. He had fought with them all his life, all his life he had exposed them, tearing the hypocritical masks from them; and now he had even found them inside himself: his own inner Eidnunen had been covering them up. And never before had he been so deeply . . . armed against them as now, and he looked sharply and coldly at Lyuba—as one looks at an enemy.

The Shot and *The First Cavalry Army*, the examples of the *Litfront* method, are alike in that they reject realism of character, setting and plot, in favour of episodic action, agitational statement and exciting dramatic propaganda. *The Shot* deals with shock workers and bureaucrats, and in skilfully constructed verse dialogue modelled on the Griboyedov iambics of *Gore ot uma* exposes the hindrances to production in the Party apparatus and reveals the heroic remedies needed to remove them. There is hardly a trace of individual psychology in the play; indeed there are properly speaking no individual characters. Vishnevsky's *The First Cavalry Army* is in a sense a dramatic answer to Babel's

Konarmia, and was published in 1930 with an approving preface by General Budyonny. Its first scenes provide a quick, graphic treatment of the Czarist army and the first world war. There follows a series of scenes on the formation and the campaigns of the Cavalry Army. Each scene is a complete unit, a characteristic episode in which the dramatist reveals in a single tableau the heroic enthusiasm and monumental proportions of the Red Cavalry. The work is a frank and conscious effort at myth-making. The dramatist himself is present in the *Vedushchi*, a kind of chorus which appears at intervals on the stage to explain in poetic prose the historical sense of the drama. Vishnevsky, like Bezymensky in *The Shot*, avoids individual psychologism and private lives; he features no individual heroes.

8. *Stalin's Intervention.*

Though the factional fight came to an end when its principal figures, including Bezymensky, abandoned the *Litfront* and condemned factionalism in the name of the consolidation of proletarian forces, yet the victory of the RAPP leaders was only apparent. The *Litfront* controversy of 1930 was the occasion for the direct intervention of Stalin in literary affairs, and though he seems to have deplored the factional fight, he did intervene on the side of the *Litfront*. On 19 March, the day on which Bezymensky's play *The Shot* was to be discussed under the auspices of the *Komsomol* newspaper, Stalin dispatched a personal letter to the author, in which he said:

I have read *The Shot* and *A Day of Our Life*. There is nothing petit-bourgeois or anti-Party in them. Both works, and especially *The Shot*, should be considered as models of revolutionary proletarian art for the present day.[7]

The existence of this letter undoubtedly influenced the course of the discussion, and it is one of the earliest documented cases of direct intervention by Stalin in literary affairs. The nature of his intervention gave clear warning that the days of Averbakh and the 'On Guard' leaders of RAPP might be numbered, and demonstrated his preference for the purposeful propagandist element in literary works.

7. J. V. Stalin, *Sochinenia*, Vol. XII (1949), p. 200.

Another case of intervention by Stalin occurred later in the year, and though not directly connected with the *Litfront* controversy, again helped to tip the scales against the 'On Guard' leaders of RAPP. This case involved Demyan Bedny, a favourite of theirs, out of whose name they had fashioned a wonderful new slogan: 'For the Demyanization of poetry'. Bedny published in *Pravda* on 7 September 1930 a poem entitled *'Slezai s pechi'* ('Get off the Stove'). The poem is a bitter commentary on both the Soviet management and the workers in the Donbas area, where there had been great difficulty in maintaining an adequate labour force because of a heavy turnover among the workers. The poem is a reaction to newspaper articles describing the large-scale desertion of the factory back to the village by peasant workers recruited for the Donbas enterprises. It is a sharply pointed indictment of both the Soviet bureaucracy and the peasant labour force, which exhibited in the Don area immemorial Russian characteristics: laziness and indifference on one side and supreme ignorance on the other. The poem is clear in placing the blame on the Russian people for their traditionally slavish mentality. Libedinsky, who was especially sensitive to the ignorance and backwardness of the peasant mass, praised the poem in the highest terms. Its publication in *Pravda* and subsequent reprinting in a mass edition indicate that many highly placed people found it acceptable reading. But there was a sudden and complete reversal. The Central Committee of the Party intervened to have the poem condemned as a slanderous, unpatriotic attack on the Russian nation, and Bedny rejected his own poem as a mistake. That Stalin had himself intervened in this affair became clear when in 1951 the thirteenth volume of his collected works appeared, containing a letter he wrote to Bedny concerning this and other things:

What have you done? Instead of understanding the meaning of the greatest revolutionary process in history and rising to the heights of a singer of the advanced proletariat, you've gone off somewhere into the valleys . . . You announce to the whole world that Russia in the past was a vessel of filth and indifference, and that present day Russia is no better, that laziness and the desire to 'sit on the stove' are to all intents and purposes national characteristics of the Russian people—and that means, of Russian workers—who, after accomplishing the October revolution did not cease to be Russians. And you call that Bolshevik criticism! No, my honoured Comrade

Demyan, that is not Bolshevik criticism but a slander on our people. It is the degradation of the USSR, the degradation of the proletariat of the USSR, the degradation of the Russian proletariat. And after that you expect the Central Committee to be silent! Just who do you take us for? [8]

The year 1930, then, marked the personal intrusion upon the literary scene of Stalin, whose flatly dogmatic epistolary statements were injected into the literary disputes of that year; and it is significant that the weight of Stalin's intervention was exercised against the leaders of RAPP, and in favour of patriotic, agitational literature. Stalin's letter to Bedny reveals, moreover, a paranoid streak in the mounting anger he allows himself to feel, not at Bedny's poem, but at his own description of it.

Perhaps it is important to realize that Stalin's intervention was not spontaneous, but was in a sense solicited by the writers themselves. The letters to Bedny and to Bezymensky were both answers to requests from those writers for statements about the works in question. Writers embroiled in controversy sought to use Stalin against their adversaries and were therefore themselves to some extent responsible for establishing the pattern of authoritarian control. By 1930 the power structure within the Party was such that the Central Committee could enunciate doctrine as to the content and style of literature, and Stalin could speak in the name of the Central Committee.

9. *Real Proletarians*

Another major event of 1930, the 'draft of shock-workers into literature', demonstrated the mystical power possessed by the notion of a purely proletarian literature to be produced by actual workers. The so-called 'draft' was an effort to recruit into literature and enrol in RAPP 'worker-writers' from the plough and the factory, and thus to create a literature saturated with working-class character and attitudes, something that had so far never come into being. The typical proletarian writer of the Twenties was not of the working class at all, but was simply an intellectual who had mastered communist ideology but was still a stranger to the actual manner of life of proletarians and above all to the work that they do. The proletarian novels of Libedinsky, Mitrofanov, and Semyonov do not portray proletarian characters or the work-

8. *Op. cit.*, Vol. XIII (1951), pp. 23–27.

ing-class milieu but rather the mores of the communists themselves. The mass recruitment of 'worker-writers' should, it was
believed, correct this anomaly and provide a literature of
genuinely proletarian provenance. Proletarian organizations
carried out the 'draft' at a feverish tempo, with the high hysterical
note of a military campaign. Literary circles formed in the
factories, RAPP expanded its 'working-class nucleus' and workers
were promoted to be Honoured Writers. The 'worker-writer' became in official Soviet jargon the central figure in literature;
fellow-travellers and proletarian writers of intellectual background
were obliged to yield their place to him. There were complaints
from the fellow-travellers that the unfair competition of pure-
blooded proletarians was making it difficult for them to publish.
The damage done to literature is shown graphically in the issues
of *Knizhnaya letopis* for 1931, where, under the general heading
belles-lettres there are a number of sub-divisions: agitational
belles-lettres, production *belles-lettres*, belletristic sketches and
the like.

10. *Themes of Reconstruction*

For the fellow-travellers the most important result of the
changed atmosphere was the pressure upon them 'to come into
close contact with Soviet reality', or, in plain words, to offer literary support to the labours of the Five-year Plan. Trips around
the country to visit various industrial enterprises were organized
for them by the State Publishing House and the newspapers
Pravda and *Izvestia*, the purpose of which was to break down the
'isolation' of writers within their own little world. Most of the
leading fellow-travellers took part in these expeditions. Leonov,
Pilnyak, Ivanov and Zozulya, for instance, travelled to Turk-
menistan in May 1930. Pantaleimon Romanov was taken along on
trips to factories and collective farms. Valentin Katayev was an
interested observer of the construction at Magnitogorsk. Gronski,
the editor of *Izvestia*, who was a relatively liberal man, included
in these expeditions writers like Pilnyak and Romanov whose
reputations had been damaged by vilification, thus offering them
an opportunity to rehabilitate themselves by writing propagandist stories and sketches.

During 1930 two novels by fellow-travellers appeared which
signalized the adoption by their authors of reconstruction

themes: Marietta Shaginyan's *Hydrocentral* and Leonid Leonov's *Sot*. And Sholokhov, on a visit to Moscow in 1930—according to some authorities as a result of talks with Stalin—decided to postpone completion of *The Quiet Don* in order to write a novel on a topical theme: the collectivization programme in the Don region.[9] In order to survive as a writer it was becoming in-increasingly necessary to deal with themes of the immediate present, and very few writers escaped the pressures generated by the Party.

11. *Conclusion*

To sum up, the year 1930 marked a critical turning point in Soviet literature. The main features of emergent Stalinism were apparent in the outcome of the disputes and discussions that took place. The primacy of politics in literature was evident in the purge of the Union of Writers. The drive for organizational uniformity was apparent in the consolidation of communist forces in RAPP. The organic hostility to independent and outsize genius showed itself in the treatment of Mayakovsky. The angrily dogmatic rejection of Pereverzev was evidence that Marxist literary science must admit in theory the possibility of organization, encouragement and direction of literary production by the Party. The condemnation of the *Pereval* writers meant that no considerations of human pity or tolerance would be allowed to confuse writers and take their minds off the main task. And the struggle within RAPP between the leadership and the *Litfront* was a clear indication that psychological realism—the examination of individual experience—would eventually give way to revolutionary romanticism and the cult of the positive hero. The main ingredients of literary Stalinism, including the direct intervention of Stalin himself, are clearly present in 1930, but they are not yet unmixed, and debate and discussion are still possible, within ever more restricted limits.

And today in Soviet literature there is evidence of the resurgence of literary attitudes which in 1930 were about to disappear. Today there are parties in the literary field, and the literary magazines are divided between the parties. Two points of view—at least—are allowed to exist and even to be expressed at important gatherings such as Party congresses. The 'humanism'

9. I. Lezhnev, *Put Sholokhova*, Moscow, 1958, p. 246.

and 'sincerity' of the *Pereval* writers and their search for immediate, unspoiled impressions of reality seems to have come to
life again in the works of many young writers: Voinovich,
Nekrasov, Tendryakov and Kazakov. The revival ever since
the death of Stalin of an interest in personal life and private
emotion is evidence that political perspectives and positive heroes
may not indefinitely dominate Soviet literature.

But what of the apparatus of political power, the Party and
its current spokesman, Khrushchev? We have seen that in 1930
Stalin's authority was invoked and exercised to settle disputes as
to literary form and content, and in 1957 Khrushchev's authority
was similarly invoked to condemn certain works. This evidence
that the authoritarian system still persists leads to the question
whether any basic change has taken place so far as literature is
concerned. A careful examination of Khrushchev's actions and
of his statements on literature suggests that there have indeed
been basic changes. For example, the writers accused of deviation
in 1957 were slow to recant, sat silent at meetings called for the
express purpose of attacking their position, and as late as May
of that year Khrushchev complained that Dudintsev and Aliger
had not, up to that time, reacted properly to criticism. The fact
that those writers remained free and unharmed is perhaps the
best evidence of the real changes that had occurred since the days
of Stalin.

Khrushchev's speech in 1959 at the Third Congress of Soviet
Writers did contain crudely phrased ideological demands of a
general nature, but as a statement from the highest authority in
the Party it was a novel performance. The novelty is apparent,
not so much in the content of Khrushchev's speech as in its
style. He announced in off-hand phrases that affairs in the literary
world had reached a satisfactory state. He now defended some
writers whom he had attacked in 1957, among them Dudintsev,
but he did so casually, without any solemnity. Dudintsev has seen
the error of his ways, he said, and 'you don't kick a man when
he's down'. The speech was unprepared, off-hand, rambling,
studded with 'sayings' and proverbial wisdom, and what is most
important, frankly and cheerfully ignorant of literature. It was
radically different from Stalin's flat pronouncements, it was a
complete contrast to the patterned and paragraphed dogmatism
of an Averbakh or a Zhdanov, and it offered prescriptions for

literature only in broad general terms. Khrushchev's performance at the Third Congress of Soviet Writers suggests that in the literary domain the Party now permits a tentative search for answers to questions of form and content in place of the dogmatic assumption that answers can be supplied when asked for by the Central Committee or by its spokesman. As Max Hayward has pointed out, the spread of this new liberalism into other areas might very well pose a threat to the Party's control of all aspects of Soviet life.

4

THE FIRST WRITERS' CONGRESS:
A SECOND LOOK

Rufus Mathewson

The radical and the artist argue in Flaubert's *L'éducation sentimentale:*

... Sénécal protesta. L'art devait exclusivement viser à la moralisation des masses! Il ne fallait reproduire que des sujets poussant aux actions vertueuses; les autres étaient nuisibles.

— Mais ça dépend de l'exécution! cria Pellerin. Je peux faire des chefs-d'oeuvre!

— Tant pis pour vous, alors! on n'a pas le droit ...

— Comment?

— Non! monsieur, vous n'avez pas le droit de m'intéresser à des choses que je réprouve! Qu'avons-nous besoin de laborieuses bagatelles, dont il est impossible de tirer aucun profit, de ces Vénus, par exemple, avec tous vos paysages? Je ne vois pas là d'enseignement pour le peuple! Montrez-nous ses misères, plutôt! enthousiasmez-nous par les sacrifices! Eh! bon Dieu, les sujets ne manquent pas: la ferme, l'atelier....

Pellerin en balbutiait d'indignation, et, croyant avoir trouvé un argument:

— Molière, l'acceptez-vous?

— Soit! dit Sénécal. Je l'admire comme précurseur de la Revolution française.

— Ah! la Révolution! Quel art! Jamais il n'y a eu d'époque plus pitoyable!

— Pas de plus grande, monsieur!

What remains to be said about socialist realism? Flaubert's scorn for a 'virtuous' art, restated by successive generations, guided the best part of Western and Russian literature past the swamp of political uplift. In the past thirty years in the USSR socialist realism has produced little the world cares about. We know all we need to know about this theory—its inner contradictions, its political function, its artistic 'criteria', its fabricated tradition. Indeed, what can we say about it? Nothing, perhaps, except that it may be coming to an end in the turmoil that followed Stalin's death. It is still *named* as the doctrine that must guide Soviet writers, but so much has occurred since 1953 that one is tempted to proclaim the end of some kind of era, the end, in any case, of Stalin's socialist realism. Men in all branches of literature seem to be trying to return to the genuine Russian tradition as it was before it was interrupted by socialist realism, by RAPP, or in some cases by the October Revolution. Whatever is coming to an end now, the sense of an era passed invites reflection on how it all began. What did men expect the new era to accomplish, what kind of hopes and expectations were invested in it? How were men persuaded to commit themselves with such enthusiasm to an undefined and untested doctrine?

It is time, perhaps, to look back with all the advantages of hindsight at that great literary circus which inaugurated the era of socialist realism in August 1934, the First All-Union Congress of Soviet Writers. It is the central event of the period, and offers a cross-section view of the state of the Soviet literary sensibility after the First Five-year Plan and before World War II.

It is worth recalling the facts and figures of the Congress. Five hundred and ninety Soviet delegates attended twenty-six sessions over a period of two weeks and listened to more than two hundred speeches and reports. Sixty per cent of the Soviet delegates were affiliated with the Party. Forty foreign guests—among them the Germans Oskar-Maria Graf, Klaus Mann, Theodor Plievier, Ernst Toller; the Frenchmen André Malraux, Jean Richard Bloch and Louis Aragon. ('Fraternal greetings' were sent to Romain Rolland, André Gide, Henri Barbusse, George Bernard Shaw, Theodore Dreiser, Upton Sinclair and Heinrich Mann.) The literary business was interrupted repeatedly to hear greetings delivered personally by workers, Red Army men, *kolkhozniki*, students, etc. Zhdanov gave a short orientation lecture (hindsight tells us it was the most decisive utterance made at the Congress); Gorky spoke at length on the evolution of world literature and the Soviet place in it; Bukharin gave an old-fashioned Bolshevik address on poetry and poetics; Radek gave another on world literature and 'the tasks of proletarian art'. Lesser figures presented reports on the national literatures, drama and children's literature.

An overwhelming sense of irony accompanies a reading of the stenographic report of the Congress.[1] It is enough to list the names of the participants—Bukharin, Babel, Yashvili, Radek, Malraux—or to record the bright expectations of the doomed. It is tempting but ultimately fruitless, I think, to record in detail the shambles history was to make of this strange gathering. The unfortunate Fadeyev's remark about the Politburo—'they are bound together by the manly, principled, iron, gay friendship of epic heroes—suggests all that now strikes us as fatuous and terrible about the Congress. No doubt Fadeyev meant what he said and he was no more mistaken than Babel, who thought he would go on writing, or Bukharin, who though he would go on governing, or Feffer who spoke with confidence of the future of Jewish literature, or the dozens of unknowns who sought to imagine the happy tomorrows that lay ahead.

There is no doubt that the hopes for a genuinely new and great literature were widespread. 'Where are the new Shakespeares?' was a question urgently asked (first by Malraux) and repeatedly discussed. Grandiose perspectives were invoked: Aeschylus, Phidias, Dante, Shakespeare, da Vinci were named as the real precursors of the great Soviet art about to emerge, an art that was to be the heir to all the best that had ever been done. The new era seemed to promise release from RAPP's harshness, and the expressions of optimism coincided with the political rhetoric which assured the delegates that the rotten art of a dying capitalism would soon be eclipsed by the new culture some called 'proletarian' and others called 'socialist'.

The monotonous repetition of *idées reçues* was interrupted at intervals by flashes of intelligence, wit and culture and by moments of genuine concern for the fate of Russian literature. Important questions were asked about the uses of the past and of other literatures, and about form and style, and properties of genres and the crucial matter of technical 'innovation'. These are problems which have reappeared with the Thaw. The increasing isolationism of the Stalin era assumed complete cultural self-sufficiency: the foreword to the new *Large Soviet Encyclo-*

1. *Pervy vsesoyuzny s'ezd sovetskikh pisatelei*—1934, Moscow, 1934. All subsequent quotations are taken from this text.

pedia announced in 1949 that the Soviet Union had become 'the centre of world civilization', but in 1934 these questions could still be posed. In these moments of enlightenment, we learn something of the actual state of the Russian tradition, of the real problems of language, style, structure and themes, and most important, of the state of mind of the genuine writers.

Maxim Gorky said in his opening address that of the fifteen hundred writers in the Writers' Union, it would be wise to expect no more than five geniuses and perhaps forty-five 'very talented' writers. His estimate is too generous perhaps, but the sense of his remark is certainly just. The drama of this tiny handful is the central story of the Congress and tells more of the actual state of literature than all the resolutions, reports and statistics.

Yuri Olesha made one of the most moving speeches of the Congress, embarrassingly frank, even abject, in its presentation of his personal and artistic problems. He spoke of 'my sense of beauty, of elegance, of nobility, of my entire vision of the world— from my view of a dandelion, of a hand, of banisters, of a leap— to the most complex psychological conceptions . . .' He spoke of the origins of his special 'vision' in his childhood and of his agonizing difficulties in bringing it into focus in socialist reality. In his sense of the privacy and uniqueness of his vocation, he brought to light an essential issue of the Congress: what room was there to be for the artist's special view of men and the world that is art's substance? Here was a small but very real talent, with its own fresh way of seeing and its own moral vision of man, struggling to put its resources at the service of a doctrine. Every writer, he said, finds in himself the moral qualities of his characters, the good and the bad, the coward and the hero. There is no doubt, he said, that his disreputable conspirator against the new machine-made society, Kavalerov, the hero of *Envy* (1927), was a part of himself, that the character saw the world through the author's own eyes. That is why the critics' attack on his hero's triviality and vulgarity was a personal attack as well. He described his despair and humiliation over these attacks, and then told of a discovery, a kind of personal vision, a patch of green grass seen through an archway in a crumbling wall, that had recently restored his own youth to him. Fleeting experiences of his childhood and youth are the sources of all that goes into his fiction, in effect of all he *knows* as an artist. (A book could be written, he said, called 'The Machinery of Transformation', exploring the complex way in which trivial childhood experiences become the images of the adult writer.) The rediscovery of his own youthfulness coincided miraculously with his discovery of the virtue and strength of the new Soviet youth. He found the way to connect the inner with the outer world in order to represent 'the moral order' of Communism and the genuine human relationships that characterized the new society.

This was a rare view of a literary sensibility at grips with the 'social command'. The 'personal vision' of experience was mentioned by few other writers, because it had never existed, or was kept secret, or had become identical with society's vision of itself. Vsevolod Ivanov's account of the path he had followed from the 'aesthetic' standards of the Serapion Brotherhood to the 'Bolshevik tendentiousness' called for by Zhdanov in his opening address, differed from Olesha's talk precisely because he had relinquished his personal vision for a mess of clichés. There was irony, too, in the final chapter of Olesha's drama. Soviet youth proved resistant to his creative designs on it. He began soon after to complain of premature old age. His speech to the Writers' Congress marked the end of his creative life.

Isaac Babel spoke more guardedly. His self-deprecation was intended to acknowledge criticism but to turn it aside. He kept his personal drama to himself. But his public frankness, his wry confession of failure (he had become a master, he said, of the 'genre of silence') suggests that he, like Olesha, felt he could rely on the good will of his listeners. He must have known that he was on exhibition (with Olesha and Pasternak) as proof of the tolerance of the new regime in literature but he must at the same time have felt the good faith behind the demonstration. A certain lightheartedness (his speech was punctuated with laughter) testified more persuasively to his convictions, perhaps, than the conventional sentiments he expressed. He spoke of the great unity of thought and purpose which binds together the writers—people who by their very craft are separated by ideas, tastes and methods of work—and the writer, in turn, with all the working people of the country. He used the phrase 'engineers of the human soul' twice without irony and recommended to the writers that they take lessons from Stalin in forging a spare, muscular prose. He was grateful for his country's patience with him for his long silences: 'in any self-respecting bourgeois country I would have starved to death long ago'. These remarks should not be read as bids for approval, strange as they sound today. They no doubt expressed his genuine acceptance of the Revolution and of the Soviet world. They were threaded through his speech as part of his view of the way art can be made honourably to serve the common cause.

If he and his fellow writers were to bring about the victory of 'Bolshevik taste'—and this would be a great political victory, he said—what must be the ingredients of the new 'style of our epoch'? He was concerned throughout with language. Words were essential in the struggle but they must be 'good words'. 'Artificial, vulgar, bureaucratic words play into the enemy's hands.'

He made his point with a brief anecdote, perhaps the germ of an unpublished story:

A worker neighbour beat up his wife. A crowd gathered. One says: he's no good, he beat up his wife. Another says: he is an epileptic. The third says: what the hell do you mean, an epileptic—he's a counter-revolutionary.

This incident, to Babel, indicated the spiritual understanding of the revolution among the people and guaranteed its victory. '*Poshlost* is the counter-revolution.' But our words do not keep step with our feelings. We must 'ennoble' the words.

The first scaffolding on the building of the revolution was being removed, he said. Its beauty is evident to all and we are seized with a kind of 'physical joy'. But the celebrators of this joy were often boring to the point of nausea. When this kind of person expresses himself in love he is so loud he threatens to burst our eardrums. If this continues we will all declare our love through megaphones like referees at soccer matches. Our new emotions must find expression, he said in effect, in a language worthy of them. 'The style of the Bolshevik epoch is in courage, in restraint. It is full of fire, passion, strength, fun.'

As Olesha defended his complex vision of life, Babel was celebrating an essential part of his own great gifts as a stylist. This style is the moral imagination at work. To define what he valued in art, he set it against the noisy, vulgar stereotype. He did it in a most engaging way but the conflict was a mortal one, as he may have realized, if only one standard was to prevail.

He spoke of one other quality in literature which is an essential part of his own best work. The reader demands art from us. We must give him the 'bread of art' but 'we must warn him, to avoid serious misunderstandings, that we will try to give him that bread. However, as regards the specifications for this bread it would be good to surprise him with the unexpectedness of art so that he will not say "a certified true copy" '. Babel's defence of the right to surprise implies the right to experiment and beyond that to respond freely to experience. On these grounds alone, Babel's terms for identifying his art with the Soviet cause were to prove unacceptable.

Pasternak's appearance, more than any other, testified to the 'amnesty' granted the non-conformist writer after RAPP's tyranny. He was a very important figure at the Congress: many speakers praised him; some patronized him. Bukharin called him 'one of the most remarkable masters of verse in our time', quoted him at length, and found the source of his strength and weakness in his dazzling originality.

Pasternak's own talk was brief, modest and deferential; it duplicated the patterns of the others in its efforts to present an aspect of his own view of art and to relate it to his terms for accepting the new Soviet world.

He was not 'a fighter', he said, before he began to read from his written text and he hoped others would undertake the polemics that might arise from his remarks. He was concerned above all with the language of poetry. In his definition he made a striking statement of his linking of art with politics. He had been sitting on the presidium for twelve days, he said, engaged in an extraordinary silent conversation, an exchange of glances, tears, signs and flowers, with the people who had spoken, above all with the members of the delegations—workers, farmers, soldiers, students—who visited the Congress. Pasternak's response to one of the workers illustrates exactly what he meant:

... when in uncontrolled impulse I wanted to lift the heavy coal-mining instrument, the name of which I don't know (laughter), off the shoulder of the girl worker from the Metro ... can the comrade on the presidium who laughed at my intelligentsia sensitivity understand that in that moment, in some instantaneous sense, she was a sister to me and I wanted to help her, as I would an old and dear friend.

The 'elevated poetic language' is born in conversation 'with our contemporary life', with the people who 'have broken loose from the anchors of private property' and are freely moving 'in the expanse of the conceivable'. This language has 'extended the boundaries of reality and has brought us into the area of what can be done, which, in the socialist world, is the area of what must be done'.

'What is poetry, if this is the way it is born . . . ?' His answer may have puzzled his listeners, but we now recognize in it a life-long conviction about his craft.

Poetry is prose, not prose in the sense of the totality of somebody's prose works, but prose itself, the voice of prose, prose in action, and not in the retelling. Poetry is the language of the organic fact, of the fact with living consequences.

Pasternak was saying, I think, what he has always said: the poet discovers the poem in the details, the facts, the prose of ordinary experience. Properly recorded, caught in its essence and in action, the mystery of life enters and makes the poem. I know of no other occasion when he brought this understanding of his work so close to Soviet reality. Though he had kind words to say for the 'many' good speeches made at the Congress, he found the authentic in the non-literary and the non-political, that is to say, in the human; in his sister, life.

He expressed concern at the end of his talk that writers were in danger of becoming 'literary dignitaries' partly because of the warmth with which the people and the state surrounded them. He invoked love for his native land and its great people as proof against the alienation caused by over-rewarding the writer, a fate that was never to threaten Pasternak.

Events like the First Congress are unlikely to get very close to the literary nerve. Babel had said that the problems of language that concerned him could never be settled by idle chatter or by resolutions and there was no shortage of either. But there are certain general questions that bear, indirectly at least, on the writer at work—the linked questions of form and of the attitude toward the past and toward other literatures. Much was said, but the results were confusing. One cannot even discern the outlines of a debate. Most agreed that for all the high hopes they entertained for the future, the shape of the new art was very elusive.

All agreed that capitalism was dying through economic breakdown or the spread of fascism, and that its rotting culture was dying with it. (Céline's *Le Voyage au bout de la nuit* was the primary exhibit on this point.) Many suggested, nevertheless, that style, technique, and structure could still be studied from Western models. Others disagreed, but little was said that was perceptive or exact or closely argued.

It is worth noting that certain dogmatic attitudes toward the past which we now associate with socialist realism had not yet taken shape. Belinsky, Chernyshevsky and Dobrolyubov had not yet been discovered as the fathers of socialist realism (Zhdanov did not mention them), nor had the Russian literary past been reworked to prove that it takes on its greatest value as a 'precursor', as an expression of the movement of political protest which came to its climax in October 1917. Nor had the anti-cosmopolitan, isolationist attitude come to dominate the view of the past. Tolstoy, Chekhov, Pushkin and, rarely, Dostoevsky, were referred to with admiration, but there was a general sense that, despite their excellence, they are not very useful as models. When the past was referred to it was more likely to be Shakespeare's name that was mentioned. (His ghost haunted the proceedings: Dinamov devoted his entire speech to showing that Soviet writers could learn all they needed to know by studying him.)

Gorky took his review of world literature all the way back to pre-history. His aim was clear: 'the role of the bourgeoisie in the process of creating culture has been greatly exaggerated'. Culture had been in decline since the Renaissance. Gorky maintained, in agreement with Tolstoy's *What is Art?*, and Soviet writers should look to the distant past, especially to folklore, to find models for a literature that celebrates the virtue of labour. Bukharin, on the other hand, in his learned address on Marxism and poetics, concluded that the new poet must emulate Pushkin, who stood on the very summit of world culture as its master. Radek's report on contemporary literature dealt largely with prose. The subtitle of his concluding section: 'James Joyce or Socialist Realism?' asks a question which answers itself. There is no doubt, he said, that we should learn from great writers like Proust his skill in representing the smallest movements of the human soul. The real question is this: 'Do we have our own main highway or will research abroad show us this main highway?' The answer was simple. Capitalism had 'shrivelled' intellectually: the triviality of the content was perfectly matched by the triviality of the form in world bourgeois literature. Proust and Joyce provided proof. The most refined techniques of analysis could find nothing in Proust's *salon* heroes because there was nothing there. Joyce's 'spiderweb of allegories and mythological reminiscences' were fantasies of the insane, and his immensely detailed 'picture' of his ordinary hero's life resembled 'a dung heap, swarming with worms, photographed by a movie camera through a microscope'.

Even if this 'method' faithfully recorded the trivial details of a trivial life, it was not able to respond to large events or ideas. The action of *Ulysses* took place in 1916 (sic!) and there was no mention of the Irish rising. The book, therefore, was simply 'untrue'.

Yet it would be 'foolish if our artists refused to learn from foreign artists ... The average French writer in the formal sense writes at the very least no worse than our very good writer.' Not form, not content—Radek told us that they are equally trivial in the best of bourgeois writers. What did he mean? He explained with the kind of industrial metaphor that confused the thinking of so many at the Congress.

A French or English worker handles his tools better than our new worker who has been at his bench only three or four years. Therefore, with respect to form we must learn much, not only from the classics of the old literature but also from the literature of a dying capitalism.

He spoke of 'form' but he clearly meant something neutral and disembodied, a skill analagous to an industrial technique. This has been a recurrent problem during centuries of Russian dependence on the West—to cleanse the borrowed foreign idea of all harmful ideological deposits.

We cannot conclude that anything resembling a decision was made at the Congress to break off contact with other literatures, or that the problem of form was either resolved, in the Congress's own terms, or set aside. Zhdanov himself had said blandly that socialist realism would be the heir to all the best in all literatures, and that mighty efforts were needed for the critical repossession of the literary heritage, with special emphasis on 'the genres, styles, forms and devices of literary creation'. And yet his speech contained all the ingredients of the narrowly politicized and formally stagnant literature which was to come in the years

ahead. The coexistence of these incompatible elements may be
noted throughout the Congress. The grounds for the subsequent
choice made between these contradictory attitudes can be found
in Zhdanov's exhortation to create 'works which respond to the
demands of the masses who are growing culturally'. If accessibility
were the only question, a Tolstoyan 'simplicity' might have been
the aim: *War and Peace,* for all the complexity of its composition, can be read by anybody. But the 'demands' of the masses,
as the Party interpreted them, called for clear 'pictures' of the
epoch, and, of course, for instruction.

The issue of a complex high art—as against the tastes of the
mass reader—underlay much of the confused discussion. André
Malraux made a number of politely critical remarks which chal-
lenged the vulgarians. 'The photograph of a great epoch is not
great literature,' he reminded the delegates. The task of culture
is to conquer the unconscious, to reduce experience to conscious
thought. Every great work of art is a 'conquest' in this sense, but
psychological depth and dimension are essential. 'Great poetic
discoveries', like Andrei Bolkonsky's victory over pain and vanity
at Austerlitz, enrich human existence because they teach men
how to live. Books liked by workers educated in literary study
groups, he said, would differ from those liked by their untaught
companions.

But you must know that only genuinely new works can support the
cultural prestige of the Soviet Union abroad—as Mayakovsky supported it and Pasternak supports it.

With respect to the mass reader Jean Richard Bloch was more
explicit: 'It is inevitable and necessary that there should be
writers for millions of readers, writers for a hundred thousand
readers and writers for five thousand readers.' The smallest group
will support those 'test pilots of literature', 'seekers after new
forms'. When a society has been seized with a dream as noble as
that of a classless socialist society, it is more than ever necessary
that 'literature should not be penetrated only by vulgar mass
conceptions'.

These warning words from Western Europe aroused interest
and some hostile comment but they did not shape the future. The
conquest of the unconscious did not occupy Soviet writers in the
following years, nor was a 'minority' literature ever encouraged.

The response to Leonov's *Road to the Ocean*, which contained a complicated time scheme based on patterns of reminiscence and other experimental techniques, was generally negative, precisely because it was too 'complex'.

Ilya Ehrenburg was the only Soviet writer who expressed similar views and he was at some pains to establish his right to say 'we' when he addressed his Soviet colleagues. He pointed out that a reader needed a high degree of culture to appreciate Mayakovsky and Pasternak. This remark was part of his generalized plea for tolerance, variety, privacy and sophistication, a plea which bears a remarkable resemblance to the position he has taken since Stalin's death. It was wrong to reproach Babel and Olesha for their silence: 'elephants are pregnant longer than rabbits'. The new forms could be achieved neither by blind rejection—or imitation—of the West, nor by a senseless eclecticism. Witness the atrocities of contemporary Soviet architecture. But new forms were indispensible: it was obviously reactionary to use the genres of 1900. Both Cézanne and the Dutch masters painted apples: the difference was in the way they did it. Art cannot be studied as a mere catalogue of themes. 'Group' writing was nonsensical: the making of art is an intimate experience that cannot be shared nor interfered with.

Apart from the invisible intentions of the Party and the shattering events of the next few years, the Congress was to find no clear definition of the *literary* problems envisaged. Its mandate on the central questions of form and tradition was contradictory, insubstantial, or—in Radek's case—unusable. The failure of the literary mind to defend itself in relatively open debate or to insist on the conditions for its own survival was very nearly complete. The minority of genuine writers announced the terms of their adjustment to the new doctrine, but were never able to put them into practice.

Flaubert's Sénécal was about to have his way with Pellerin.

5

THE ORGANIZATION WRITER
(1934–46)

Ernest J. Simmons

I

In the history of Soviet Russian literature the twelve years between 1934 and 1946 have sometimes been regarded in the West as a kind of pause that refreshes, a sort of lucid interval between two periods of extreme regimentation, that of RAPP and of Zhdanovism. And by a miracle of longevity in administrative tenure during the rigours of Stalin's rule, it fell to the lot of that Lord High Executioner of cultural freedom, Andrei Zhdanov, to herald the demise of the first period of regimentation in his speech at the First Congress of the Union of Soviet Writers in August 1934, and also to usher in the second period in his reports to the Leningrad Party *aktiv* in August 1946. Though these events are helpful in drawing up a schematic periodization of literature, their relevance to real change suggests the validity of the old saying that the more things change the more they remain the same. Revelations of the last few years, which have substantially increased our knowledge of the fearful happenings over the period 1934–41, enable us to evaluate and interpret more accurately the forces directing the course of literature at that time.

Indirect Party Controls during the reign of RAPP were simply transformed into direct controls covertly exercised by the Party fraction in the newly-formed single Union of Soviet Writers. And after the Central Committee decree of 14 August 1946 all subterfuge was dropped as the Party publicly and blatantly announced not only the subjects authors should avoid in their creative efforts, but also what thematic areas they must concentrate upon in novels, plays and poetry. In a very real sense Zhdanovism—the era of Party-organized literature and Party-organized writers—began with the First Congress of the Union of Soviet Writers in 1934. Whether this literary era has been replaced by another during the years since Stalin's death in 1953 is still dubious, despite the heartening struggle between 'liberals' and 'conservatives'—the Westernizers and Slavophiles, so to speak, of the new Soviet intelligentsia. That the Party will once again allow contending groups to exist at all and to voice their different creative approaches is a hopeful sign, recalling that wonderful first decade of artistic freedom and experimentation after October 1917, the only revolutionary period in Soviet literature.

However much mischief RAPP's aggressive supervision of literature caused, especially among fellow-travellers, the leadership of this Russian Association of Proletarian Writers advocated a theory of art not far removed from classical Russian traditions. Their slogans 'the living man' and 'tearing away the masks' were inspired by belief in the artist's right to tell the whole truth about both communists and class enemies in characterizations that must be as objective as they were human. If they accepted the Party's dictum that proletarian literature was an instrument for changing the world along socialist lines, they also insisted that its subject-matter must be treated independently, without simplification, and with respect for psychological truth. It is an artistic credo curiously resembling that of the 'angry young men' in Soviet literature today, with the difference that they are living in a society where the tragic struggle between the old and the new, so often the principal literary subject-matter of their predecessors, is of minor significance, and where the Party, full of confidence in ultimate victory, tends to exercise its artistic controls more benignly.

Not only regimented fellow-travellers welcomed the resolution of the Central Committee in 1932 which put an end to the existence of RAPP; Western students of the Soviet Union also hailed it as a long-delayed emancipation from the puerilities of the 'social command' in literature and from the wooden stereotypes of Five-year Plan novels and plays that had about as much variation as a row of telephone poles. This reaction, however, contained a large element of self-deception. No doubt the Party's cultural bosses—some said even Stalin—had also grown weary of the boring sameness of this literature, but they were aware that it had contributed its propaganda increment to the success of the

Five-year Plan. Yet the resolution was hardly prompted by the
Party's sudden realization that literature flourishes best when it
is uncontrolled. The fact is that the Party had become increasingly aware of the tendency of RAPP leadership to substitute its own administrative controls for the Party's and to urge
an approach to art that undermined the Party's conception of the
proper function of literature in a socialist state. The corner on
the road to 'socialism in one country' had been turned; proletarian literature and its contentious theorists had become obstacles to new tasks which would be required of all writers. In
the last analysis, however, the decision to dissolve RAPP and
replace it by a national Union of Soviet Writers was unquestion-
ably taken because Stalin, who according to Kaganovich was
associated directly in the decision, had consolidated his power
and felt strong enough to overcome any opposition to a design
to organize all literature to serve the propaganda and ideological
purposes of the Party. Then, on the level of administrative expediency, it was much easier for the Party to control one big
union of writers than RAPP and various other literary groupings.

Though writers still exercised a modicum of freedom at the
time of the dissolution of RAPP, no significant opposition developed. However, a few RAPP leaders, who had previously
deplored inept Party political interference in literary matters,
now bitterly attacked the resolution dissolving their organization,
and by implication they were also attacking the high Party officials responsible for it. And there is evidence that talented fellow-
travellers, the immediate beneficiaries of the dissolution of RAPP,
were not entirely happy over the future prospects of belonging
to 'a single Union of Soviet Writers with a Communist fraction
therein', which was designed 'to unite all writers upholding the
platform of Soviet power and striving to participate in Socialist
construction'. This formula plainly recalled RAPP's 'social command'. Their suspicions were further deepened by the dissolution of all other organized groupings of writers which had to
some extent guaranteed that plurality of views on art which the
fellow-travellers felt was necessary in order to develop a vital
and free literature. And the fact that the Organization Committee
required more than two years of effort to establish the proper
climate of 'unanimity' before the First Congress of Writers could

be held suggests that it had encountered considerable opposition to the launching of the Party's new literary programme.

II

Zhdanov's keynote speech at the Congress in August 1934 left no room for doubt in the participants' minds of the shape of things to come in Soviet literature. It must be tendentious, he declared, optimistic, heroic, serve the cause of socialist construction, and draw its heroes and heroines from the working men and women of the Soviet Union. Further, he asserted, writers must be guided by the method of socialist realism. He defined it as the depiction of real life in its revolutionary development, in which truthfulness and historical concreteness must be combined with the ideological remoulding and re-education of workers in the spirit of socialism. Though writers, he added, must shun conventional romanticism, revolutionary romanticism, which projects the heroic dimensions of Soviet characters as they will be in the future, was not only permissible but must be regarded as a definite aspect of socialist realism.

Here was a theory of literature potentially more confining than anything RAPP had ever proposed, a method that imposed upon the writer a tendentious and dogmatic artistic purpose. Yet the speeches and discussions, often by well-known authors, that followed Zhdanov's address failed to take serious exception to his design for a literature that categorically identified art with the political and propaganda position of the Party.

Now all qualified authors were expected to become members of the Union of Soviet Writers, which soon developed into a monolithic literary organization. With its administrative boards, its own publication facilities, and the various important services it provided for writers, the Union was able to exercise effective control over the whole national literary output. Finally, membership in the Union required acceptance of its statutes, which in effect compelled the writer's submission to the Party's political and social ideology, limited his choice of themes, and obliged him to treat them from the point of view of socialist realism. Gone was the relative freedom guaranteed the writer in the Central Committee's old 1925 resolution on literature. In some ten years after Lenin's death the totalitarianism of Stalin had wholly enveloped literature as it had everything else in the Soviet Union.

The full effect of the new order in literature was not felt for several years. The sense of emancipation after RAPP was heightened by freedom of literary contacts with the West, a by-product of the United Front movement accelerated by the growing menace of Hitlerism. Progressive foreign authors were cultivated, it was possible to discuss and write about the works of Proust, Joyce, Malraux, Dreiser, Hemingway, Dos Passos and Steinbeck without hopeless ideological gagging, and the novels, short stories and poems of many foreigners—over a hundred in the case of Americans—were published in translation during the Thirties.

Though the themes of literature were dictated by propaganda demands, after 1934 they were often treated with a degree of creative independence rarely observable during the years of RAPP. In large part this must be attributed to the fellow-travellers' return to the literary scene—they were now officially regarded as loyal participants in the nation's forward drive to communism—and also to able young writers, such as Vasily Ilyenkov and Yuri Krymov, who had not yet fully learned the lesson of conformity. For example, some of the starker realities of 'socialist emulation' or 'Stakhanovism' were apparent in the handling of industrial reconstruction and agricultural collectivization in such novels as Ilyenkov's much-discussed *Driving Axle* (1933) and *Sun City* (1935), and in Krymov's *Tanker Derbent* (1938), where the approved method of socialist realism was cleverly used to work out the purely human problems of a group of characters engaged in an exciting competition in shipping oil on the Caspian. *People from the Backwoods* (1938) by the older writer Alexander Malyshkin is also a construction novel which largely concerns an extensive building project in the Urals during the First Five-year Plan. In the sense that intense reconstruction was often the 'hero' of earlier Five-year Plan fiction, the same may be said of Pyotr Pavlenko's extremely popular novel *In the East* (1937) which concentrates on the feverish efforts of many ordinary men and women in building a new life in the Soviet Far East. But the shadow of military adventurism hangs over these peaceful activities—the threat of Japanese aggression. And in the last part of the novel Pavlenko prophetically describes a future war between Russia and Japan in the course of which he unwittingly gives the lie to official United Front propaganda by dwelling on the old dream of world revolution led by the Soviet Union.

Whether by design or accident the literary reforms of the Thirties coincided with and significantly influenced the intense nationalism which the Party promoted to consolidate the regime and arouse popular patriotism in the face of the growing threat of Nazism. Certainly it was no accident that in 1934 Pokrovsky's officially accepted Marxian interpretation of history, which had virtually eliminated formal instruction in Russian history in the schools, was denounced and replaced by conventional courses that espoused a patriotic veneration for the glories of Russia's past and for its great tsars and military leaders who had been instrumental in building the empire.

This resurgence of old-fashioned patriotic élan quickly found its reflection in historical novels and plays, genres that had been popularized in the previous decade by such writers as Aleksei Chapygin. A Marxian emphasis on the role of history had been cultivated at that time, but now, as though in anticipation of the need of national fortitude should the Germans invade, the stress was placed on great moments in the country's history when Russia had to fight for its life: the struggle against the Tatars in Sergei Borodin's *Dmitri Donskoi* (1937); the story of the destruction of the Russian fleet in the war with Japan in Aleksei Novikov-Priboi's *Tsushima* (1932–35); and Russia's heroic losing fight in the Crimean War in Sergei Sergeyev-Tsensky's *The Ordeal of Sebastopol* (1937–38).

Of the various novels and plays during this period devoted to historical figures, Aleksei Tolstoy's monumental *Peter I*, Part II of which appeared in 1933 and Part III in 1944, is by far the finest. One may quarrel with the author's interpretation of Peter's personality, but the total artistic accomplishment of the work is on a very high level. It has been claimed that Peter the Great became Stalin's favourite tsar and that one may perceive resemblances in the characters and activities of both rulers. Whether or not Aleksei Tolstoy had such an analogy in mind, his overidealized portrait of the tsar was entirely in the spirit of revived Soviet nationalism. Later, in his two historical plays on Ivan the Terrible (1942–43), there can be no doubt of Tolstoy's intentions; he set out to rehabilitate the tsar in keeping with the revised Party estimate of him as a true patriot and consummate statesman who, before Peter I, understood the necessity of Russia's expanding to the West.

Another group of novels in the Thirties, some of them by outstanding writers, was concerned with recent history, the Revolution and Civil War, subjects that had been extensively exploited in the Twenties. Only now the honest realism in the treatment of such themes by a Babel in *Red Cavalry* or a Fadeyev in *The Rout* was subjected often to d'istorting updating or rewriting of history, especially when it involved the activities of Stalin in the Revolution and Civil War. His role had to be exalted, for the process of mythologizing Stalin began in the Thirties and continued its dizzying tragi-comic course to the obscene deification accorded him on the occasion of his seventieth birthday. Its reflection in Soviet *belles-lettres* is an aspect of 'socialist realism' now belatedly rejected by the Party in the euphemism—'cult of the individual'. This kind of counterfeit glorification is shamelessly patent in Aleksei Tolstoy's novel about the Civil War, *Bread* (1937). In a work which in many respects supports his eminence as a historical novelist, Tolstoy does not hesitate to alter the facts of history in order to exaggerate Stalin's part and debase that of Trotsky in the defense of Tsaritsyn.

The blight of socialist realism is perhaps less obtrusive but certainly more fatal artistically in Aleksei Tolstoy's major novel, the trilogy *The Road to Calvary*. The first volume appeared in 1921 while he was still abroad as an émigré, but the second was published in 1926 after he had returned to Russia, and the third, written during the Thirties, came out in 1941. In the pages of this long work one may perceive clearly the ideological transformation that had come over the author between the publication of the first and the last two volumes. Basically the novel is concerned with the political, social, and moral changes experienced by a group of intellectuals during World War I, the Revolution, and the Civil War. The characters, including the secondary ones, are brilliantly realized, and the thrilling actions in which they are involved are described with captivating detail. But the independent judgement of events and objective analysis of intellectual and emotional experiences in the first half of the novel give way to a contrived and schematic treatment in the last half, where the leading characters are confronted with hard choices between their old loyalties or acceptance of the communist wave of the future.

And again, as in *Bread*, historical events and personalities of the Civil War are made to conform to the Party's official versions. Political opportunism is a fact of real life, but it must never be represented in art as political idealism. Of course, it may be argued that the political change of heart of the intellectuals is an honest reflection of the author's political transformation after his return to the Soviet Union, but it falsifies the logic of development in the personalities of these characters and renders the second half of the novel quite unconvincing. Aleksei Tolstoy, like so many devotees of socialist realism, failed to apprehend the truth of Chekhov's conviction that real art can never lie.

Another picture of the Civil War, in this case the peasant uprising in Central Russia in 1920, is to be found in *Solitude* (1936), the first novel of the young writer Nikolai Virta. It also was designed as a trilogy (the second volume, *Lawfulness*, appeared in 1937, but the third was never published). Although it lacks the vast scope and brilliance of Aleksei Tolstoy's trilogy, it is a skilful piece of fiction, and Virta seems to possess perhaps more objectivity than the older writer, for his two central characters, 'enemies of the people', are portrayed with a deep feeling for the personal tragedies of their lives. Valentin Katayev's tale of the early days of the Civil War in the Ukraine, *I, a Son of the Working People* (1937), rates much below his delightful novel of 1936, *Lone White Sail*, in which, against the exciting background of events of the 1905 Revolution in Odessa, he portrays the altogether charming relations of two nine-year-old boys.

In the revival of interest in Civil War themes during the Thirties, popular Red leaders in the struggle inspired biographical novels, such as Arkady Perventsev's *Kochubei* (1937) and Vsevolod Ivanov's *Parkhomenko* (1938). Though little effort was made to romanticize these heroes, a Party-line interpretation rather than historical truth guided the narrative of events in which they were involved.

Of course, the greatest novel of the Civil War, a revered Soviet classic, is Sholokhov's *Quiet Don*. The scope of its action—World War I, the Revolution, and Civil War—and the span of its writing and publication (1928–40), bear comparison with Aleksei Tolstoy's *The Road to Calvary*. Sholokhov's control over his basic material—the country life of peasants and Cossacks—is as masterful as that of Tolstoy in the case of the city life of intellectuals,

82   *Ernest J. Simmons*

but Sholokhov's treatment of the anguished moral and emotional problems involved in the terrible fratricidal struggle between Reds and Whites reveals a deeper sense of artistic integrity. In many tortured rationalizations Soviet critics have acclaimed the *Quiet Don* as the very quintessence of socialist realism, but any impartial observer would agree that the novel appears to have escaped the tyranny of strict ideological conformity and the literary flatulence that comes from imposed Party stereotypes of form and content. Gregor Melekhov, perhaps the greatest hero created by a communist author, and certainly one of the most human and appealing characters in the whole range of Soviet literature, is not the optimistic, iron-willed positive Soviet hero, the type continually called for by the Party, but an intensely tragic person, and in the end an enemy of the Soviet regime. He is an individualist. Perplexed in the extreme by the difficult choices erected by Revolution and Civil War, he reaches the conclusion that there is no final Red or White truth under whose wings all might shelter. Each man has his own truth, Gregor decides, and for him it was home, the farm, work, and most of all his eternal love for Aksinya. For these he fought the Red invaders of his Don region home as men had always fought 'for a piece of bread, for a strip of earth, for the right to live'.

The *Quiet Don* is not free of the tendentiousness of an author who accepts a communist political purpose in the historical forces which dominate the action of his story, but this purpose does not overtly obtrude, and with artistic honesty Sholokhov unhesitatingly reveals the cruelty, deception, ugliness, and occasionally the nobility of both sides in the Civil War. In the 1953 edition of the novel, however, Sholokhov appears to have submitted to the postwar demands made upon literature, history, and all intellectual endeavours, for he introduced substantial changes in order to bring the Communist Party and communist characters much more fully and favourably into the action, and, on the other had, to disparage the Whites still more and to emphasize their crimes. To be sure, one cannot be certain of the personal part Sholokhov played in this kind of editing, in which for example, a passage is added to credit the strategic successes of the Red Army in the south to Stalin's military genius, an alteration that will probably be expunged in later editions of the novel in deference to 'socialist realism', for since Stalin's death his military genius has been dismissed as 'unhistorical'.

Throughout most of his literary career Sholokhov has been a craggy, lonely figure whose artistic integrity has more than once brought him into conflict with the organization men in the Union of Soviet Writers and on one occasion, it seems, even with Stalin. Of late, however, he has been courted by Party leaders and appears to relish it. In speeches at the Second Congress of the Union of Soviet Writers in December 1954 and the Twentieth Party Congress in February 1956, he damns the 'cliques and factions' that control the Writers' Union which he tends to hold responsible for what he described as 'the dull stream of colourless, mediocre literature which in recent years has been pouring from the pages of our magazines and flooding the book market'. Khrushchev has recently honoured him with a visit to his home and invited Sholokhov to accompany him on his trip to the United States. Indeed, the artistic lapses and ideological conformity of the second volume of *Virgin Soil Upturned* (1960) suggest that Sholokhov himself may also be on his way to becoming one of the organization men of Soviet literature.

III

One of the insanely ironic facts of Soviet history is that while the purge and 'wrecker' trials were taking place between 1935 and 1938, and thousands were being shot or sent to labour camps in order to make Stalin's totalitarian rule unassailable, the official Party slogan designed to brighten the existence of a terrorized nation was: 'Life has become gayer, comrades!' If the exaggerated economic successes of the Five-year Plans lent some credence to the slogan, universal fear poisoned enjoyment of the gains. At no other time, unless it be from 1946 to 1953, was politics so crassly identified with culture. The theatres of Meyerhold and Tairov, brilliantly revolutionary and experimental, were denounced as 'formalistic' and soon the courageous Meyerhold, who dared to fight back, disappeared from the scene. Indeed, in the rush to conformity, 'formalism' became the pejorative term to stigmatize anything in the arts that deviated from the Party norm. Shostakovich's highly interesting opera *Lady Macbeth of Mtsensk* was tagged as 'putrid bourgeois formalism'; the work was banished from the stage and the composer fell silent. The same fate overtook Demyan Bedny's opera *Epic Heroes* in 1937, especially because it had treated satirically the tenth-century conversion of Russia to Christianity, an offence to the resurgent nationalism glorifying the nation's past.

Literature was even more destructively caught up in the political purges, which the memoirs of Ilya Ehrenburg now tragically affirm. Some of the old leaders of RAPP were accused of Trotskyism and though they vanished, their fates are not clear. Well-known authors such as Babel, Pilnyak and Kirshon were no doubt shot, and many others were either executed, imprisoned or ceased to write. Pressure was placed on authors to sign Party-publicized denunciations of their colleagues. (After Khrushchev's exposure of Stalin's terror, the ghosts of the 'rehabilitated' victims must have haunted these conscience-stricken proscribers.) A few older writers took refuge in silence—their mute condemnation of the whole macabre process.

In the failure to differentiate between appearance and substance as reflected in the Soviet press during the second half of the Thirties, there has been a tendency to suppose that writers willingly accepted the Party's new line in literature. And, now, with a certain degree of hindsight, we become aware of how uncompromisingly and in what an atmosphere of terror the new approach was dictated. The insistent official demand in literature was for the application of socialist realism to the creation of positive heroes drawn from what was essentially an idealized version of contemporary Soviet life. Actually, many authors evaded these prescriptions or only partially adhered to them, and the few superior works published were largely devoid of them.

One novel that seems to have entirely met the official demand and enjoyed a huge propaganda, if not artistic, success was Nikolai Ostrovsky's *How the Steel was Tempered* (1935). Something of the popularity of this autobiographical novel may be attributed to the fact that its half-blind, bed-ridden author, waiting for death, became a national hero because of his amazing courage and zest for life and work. The story of the novel is entirely that of its hero, Pavel Korchagin, a poor Ukrainian boy, whose whole life during the Revolution, Civil War and the reconstruction period is one of unswervingly dedicated service to the exacting tasks and political ideology of the Party. In the end, hopelessly crippled by wounds and illnesses incurred in the line of duty, and aware that he has not long to live, he turns by a relentless exercise of will to writing in order to continue his life of service to the cause. Though his story has the usual appeal of that of the man who overcomes impossible odds to achieve a well-deserved success, it loses credibility because the world in which Korchagin struggles is portrayed as one of unbelievable blacks and whites. And Korchagin himself emerges as something less than human, a monolithic man who translates all experience in terms of the intolerant, ruthless moral code and political values of his personal faith in communism.

Here at last the Party had its perfect positive hero, the Soviet Sir Galahad of socialist realism, and though the image of Pavel Korchagin exercised an influence on later fiction, the best novels in the second half of the Thirties failed to reproduce it. Yury German's well-received first novel, *Our Friends* (1936), is the interesting story of the trials and tribulations of an unfortunate girl during the NEP period. And Venyamin Kaverin's very popular *Two Captains* (1939) is a tale of adventure concerning prerevolutionary Arctic explorations. Nor did the other works appearing in the second half of the Thirties, which have already been commented on, capture anything of the special crusading flavour of *How the Steel Was Tempered* or the kind of communist internal burning of its hero.

In drama during this period the burden of socialist realism tended to weigh down and enervate plays dealing with contemporary Soviet life, such as in Vasily Shkvarkin's *A Simple Girl* (1937) and *The Spring Revue* (1938). However, there was an amiable sort of dullness in *Aristocrats* (1935), a successful play of the well-known dramatist Nikolai Pogodin. The action is centred in the construction of the White Sea–Baltic Canal by political prisoners and ordinary criminals under the watchful eyes of the GPU, an operation in forced labour that was widely propagandized as an effective method for reforging lawbreakers into useful Soviet citizens. This, too, was regarded as a fit topic for socialist realism and was much written about, for example, in Mikhail Zoshchenko's *The Story of One Life* (1935). In *Aristocrats* the racy dialogue and unconventional activities of bandits and prostitutes are realistic and at times amusing, but the transformation of these 'socially hostile elements' into zealous Stakhanovite labourers through the psychological sleight of hand of their GPU bosses is quite unconvincing. Some of these prisoners idealize their bondage, and their enthusiasm about being re-educated recalls that character in *Doctor Zhivago* whose account of acquiring maturity in gaol was like listening to a horse describe how it broke itself in. Later, like many writers of the Thirties, Pogodin seemed to prefer to retreat to the comparative safety of the past for subjects, where the challenge of socialist realism lost its exacting immediacy, as in his two plays on Lenin—*The Man With the Gun* (1937) and *The Kremlin Chimes* (1941). There is more of Chekhovian than socialist realism in Alexander Afino-genov's play on a contemporary theme, *Distant Point* (1936), and its sequel, *The Second Track* (1939), but when the score sheet is drawn up at the end by the dying Red Army commander, the answer is the approved Soviet moral—that any lowly citizen who performs his job with socialistic zeal and sincerity, no matter how humble it is or how remote from the centre of things, makes his own contribution to the well-being of the fatherland.

Like so much of Leonid Leonov's writing, his two plays in the Thirties on contemparory themes, *The Orchards of Polovchansk* (1938) and *The Wolf* (1938), employ life as it is as a mere frame-work for a concentrated study, often symbolically involved, of the moral and emotional conflicts of his characters. Events do not define the character, the customary emphasis in socialist realism, the character defines the events. That is, Leonov's interest is primarily in the psychological analysis in depth of his imagin-ary men and women, and in the course of their development, the political or ideological message becomes tangential or even muted. This is true of both these plays which are essentially dramatic presentations of family conflicts.

Of all the genres, poetry adapts itself with most difficulty to literary theories, especially to one such as socialist realism. Verse is somehow too intimate, too subjective to share its content with doctrinal messages imposed from without. As Pasternak put it in a speech to poets at the Writers' Plenum in February 1936: 'Stakhanovite promises . . . are capable only of depressing us.' And he pointedly declared later in this talk: 'Art is unthinkable with-out risk and the self-sacrifice of the soul.' His own capacity for risk worried his close literary friends, some of whom were swept away in the purges. He fearlessly refused to sign the public state-ment, in March 1937, condemning Marshal Tukhachevsky and other Soviet generals who were soon brought to trial, but a Party hack signed his name anyway. Pasternak's feelings about the purge years were probably accurately expressed by his hero in *Doctor Zhivago*: 'To conceal the failure [of collectivization], people had to be cured, by every means of terrorism, of the habit of thinking and judging for themselves, and forced to see what didn't exist, to assert the very opposite of what their eyes told them.' Though several collections of Pasternak's poetry were published during the Thirties, they contained almost entirely his earlier verse and attracted very little favourable attention from official critics bent on searching out instances of socialist realism. In fact, by 1937 he had begun to desert original poetry and to turn to translations.

Yet most poets of the Thirties cut their risks, quarrelled much among themselves about the relation of socialist realism to verse, and wrote poems in traditional forms and on subjects which, for the most part, offered no problems of comprehension to the literate masses. The older poet Aleksei Surkov continued to stress martial themes inspired by his Civil War experiences; Nikolai Tikhonov still concentrated on romantic realism and chiselled diction in a volume of verse concerning his foreign travels (*The Shadow of a Friend*, 1935); Nikolai Aseyev brought out his long socialist 'elegy', *Mayakovsky Emerges* (1940), in vigorous verse but yet a pale imitation of the master; Stepan Shchipachev contributed poems in his familiar vein of philosophizing weakly on simple themes; Alexander Prokofiev, however, changed his usual emphasis in a series of poems, somewhat influenced by folk songs, on the commonplaces of life. The traditional Russian folk songs no doubt helped to inspire a group of poets (Mikhail Svetlov, Vasily Lebedev-Kumach, Viktor Gusev, Mikhail Isakovsky, Aleksei Surkov) to turn out a series of popular lyrics intended to be sung—military marches, army songs, or sentimental lyrics on love.

Among the younger poets, Semyon Kirsanov's *Cinderella* (1935) is a modernization of the old fairy tale, the humour and fantasy of which are in no sense spoiled by the interpolation of unobtrusive social implications. Evgeni Dolmatovsky's volume, *Far Eastern Poems* (1937), successfully mingles patriotic verse with tender love lyrics. Of the other younger poets who began to publish in the Thirties such as Alexander Tvardovsky, Konstan-

tin Simonov, Margarita Aliger and Olga Berggolts, it was Tvardovsky who achieved the most notice by his long narrative poem,
The Land of Muravia (1936), for which he was later awarded a
Stalin Prize. The hero, Nikita Morgunok, refuses to join a collective farm until he has first searched for the peasants' never-never
land where he will be freely allowed to have a farm all his own.
After disillusioning and often amusing adventures on this quest,
experience and the advice of a mysterious old man teach him
that there is no Muravia Land and hence he must join a collective
farm. Here the element of socialist realism is in no sense offensive, for it is effectively combined with the logic of events in what
appears to be a believable experience. Tvardovsky thoroughly
understands the psychology of the peasant and his age-old hunger
for his own land, and at times the author seems to sympathize
with Nikita's dream. The subtle interweaving of folklore devices
and the flavour of peasant speech contribute to the convincing-
ness of the characterization of the hero and the authenticity of
his experiences. *Muravia Land* is the outstanding narrative poem
of the Thirties.

IV

Two of the most distinguished and frequently criticized fellow-
travellers of the Twenties, Konstantin Fedin and Leonid Leonov,
who had succeeded in contributing important artistic works in
spite of the Party but not necessarily in opposition to it, attempted
in the Thirties to write novels that would reflect a growing belief
in the socialist future of their country. Profoundly influenced by
the great tradition of nineteenth-century Russian realism, their
contemplation of the present is always caught up in a web of
memory of the past which they have renounced. In many respects
communism has been the agonizing problem of their spiritual
and creative life, and the struggle between the will to believe and
doubt and disillusion became the central factor in their artistic
development.

The basic plan of Fedin's two-volume novel, *The Rape of
Europe* (1934–35), is to contrast and compare the deteriorating
social and economic existence of the West under the influence of
the depression years following 1929 with the full employment and
economic upsurge in the Soviet Union during the first two Five-
year Plans. Neither picture is entirely objective, but curiously

enough that of the West, which Fedin knew well because of his long stays and extensive travel there, is more convincing in its verisimilitude and far more interesting in its artistic grasp of character and action. Philip van Rossoem, head of a wealthy Dutch family with a timber concession in Russia, is sensitively and most attractively delineated in the course of the first volume. It is a portrait superior to that of Ivan Rogov, designed to represent the captivating image of the new Soviet intellectual—a man of inner richness and complexity. In reality, beneath the varnish of Soviet idealism one plainly discerns in Rogov the grain of the old Russian intellectual of nineteenth-century fiction. The second volume, where the action shifts to the Soviet Union, contains the answer of Soviet socialism to the economic defeatism of Western capitalism, but the answer fails to compel belief as an artistically embodied contrast of two ways of life. In this second volume Fedin risks satiric jibes at commonplaces connected with the propaganda of the Five-year Plans—Soviet greatest-in-the-world boastfulness and undiscriminating reverence of the more material achievements of American industry.

Though *The Rape of Europe* was quite superior, artistically, to the average Soviet novel of the Thirties, Fedin himself regarded it as something of a failure. It appears to have been an effort on his part to write a political novel that would identify him, after much previous uncertainty, with the socialist hopes and aspirations of the Soviet regime. The new doctrine of work and the successes of the Five-year Plans, which contrasted so strikingly with the economic depression of the capitalist West, undoubtedly contributed to his growing convictions in this respect, as they did in the case of other writers among the former fellow-travellers. Yet Fedin's novel bears frequent testimony to his unwillingness to accept, as a good socialist realist should, the simplified values and antiseptic moral code of the literary image of the new Soviet man. Interestingly enough, he later explained his failure in the characterization of Rogov as compared with his success in the case of Philip van Rossoem in these words: 'I did not discover for my novel the "counter-balance" of Philip, though I confess that the creation of a Soviet hero, bearing, so to speak, an "individual" impress, the impress of his Western European antipode, is still the problem of our literature.'

Even more so than Fedin in *The Rape of Europe*. Leonov

attempts to embody in *Road to the Ocean* (1935) the dream cur-
rently propagandized that the communist Utopia was realizable
in the not-too-distant future. But this romantic vision is viewed
from the realistic vantage point of the end of the First Five-year
Plan with its achievements, its labour heroes and heroines and its
socialist discipline. In parts of the novel Leonov looks backward
to the prerevolutionary past, but with a sterner comprehension
of its inadequacies than was evident in his earlier fiction, and
forward to the future great destiny of his country which the
Soviet present would make possible. In fact, the *Road to the Ocean*
was perhaps the first attempt to write a large and authentic novel
about the age of the new Soviet man.

Road to the Ocean is essentially the story of the old Bolshevik
Kurilov, an obvious response to the insistent demand, expressed
at the 1934 Congress of the Union of Soviet Writers, for communist heroes whose lives would faithfully reflect the achievements and optimism of the present, dignify the new Soviet morality, and symbolize the approaching birth of a new world. The
stern, gray-haired Kurilov, with 'the shoulders of a stevedore
and the forehead of a Socrates', fulfils this demand in a memorable way. Yet the utter aridity of his personal and emotional life
over years of relentless self-sacrifice and self-denying for the sake
of the cause have fashioned a man who seems like an allegorical
personification of idealized communist virtues rather than a
flesh-and-blood human being.

Leonov, however, was too fine an artist to settle for sheer
monumentality, as Ostrovsky did in the portrait of Pavel Korchagin. He insists that Kurilov is 'an ordinary human being' and
he endows him with some pleasant traits which are more asserted
than revealed in action. But after Kurilov's discovery that he is
afflicted with an incurable cancer, he enters upon an exploration
of those pleasures of life which he had willingly abdicated because of his devotion to the cause. Now, however, it is too late
and his unconsummated enjoyment is filled with nostalgic sad-
ness. His favourite escape is self-indulgence in fantasy, his dreams
of Ocean, the city of the socialist future.

Leonov does not shirk the lesson implied in Kurilov's wholehearted sacrifice of all his private yearnings for the sake of what
he considers the universal good. On the other hand, Leonov does
not look beyond the rim of ruthless allegiance to estimate the

tragic cost in suffering involved in any such violation of the human personality. Perhaps he failed in this respect because he could not do otherwise—the solution had to be sought in the banal spirit of socialist realism. Kurilov did not fear death, Leonov explains, but true to his notion of communist service he regretted that he could not end his life 'in a more intelligent way', that 'he was not fated to screen a great leader with his body, or fall before a firing squad so that his death might serve as an example to others'. How many old Bolsheviks, like Kurilov, were falling before firing squads at that time, victims of their 'great leader's' paranoia!

It was some measure of the importance attached to *Road to the Ocean* that it was discussed at a meeting of the presidium of the Union of Soviet Writers. The judgements were rather harsh, especially when one considers that hardly any Soviet novel on the contemporary scene at this time could be compared favourably with Leonov's work in expansive design, comprehensive sweep and mature artistry. Further, he had skilfully fused ideological correctness with the living reality and complexity of Soviet life. The intricate design of the novel irritated critics, but their chief disappointment was with the characterization of Kurilov. He was not a typical, well-rounded communist hero, they declared, and he was too much of an individualist who never succeded dynamically in identifying his personality with that of the collective. This critical constant betrayed the weakness of socialist realism in the Thirties—failure to recognize the fundamental incompatibility between the heroic and the collective. The essence of the truly heroic is individualism, and the trouble with Kurilov in the eyes of non-Soviet readers, as was true of nearly all the so-called positive heroes of the Thirties, is that he was not individualistic enough.

v

But all these nagging concerns of socialist realism were largely submerged in the mighty wave of patriotism that swept the land upon the invasion of the Nazis in June 1941. The Party was fully aware of the propaganda value of literature in the struggle and encouraged it in every way, even exempting writers from active military service and wisely refraining from excessive interference in what they wrote. At that time, Ehrenburg recalled, in a *Pravda* article on 1 May 1962, 'we could communicate with our readers much more freely than in 1939 . . .' In fact, imprisonments, executions, and strict control of literature continued right up to the German attack on the Soviet Union. Writers in any way opposed to the Nazi–Soviet Pact were in danger. In his memoirs Ehrenburg tells of Stalin personally threatening Avdeyenko, Leonov and Katayev at a meeting of writers which he called in 1940, and Ehrenburg's *Fall of Paris*, which excoriated the Germans, could not be published until after their invasion in June 1941. However, once the country was attacked, the patriotism of writers required no planned stimulation; the mobilization of literature on behalf of the war effort was spontaneous and nearly everything written between 1941 and 1945 was dedicated to it.

Literally hundreds of Soviet writers became war correspondents and not a few of them perished in the performance of this task. Naturally, then, the bulk of published material consisted of reporting on fighting at the front or on partisan activities in the rear of the enemy. Nearly all of it was ephemeral, but a few volumes of the best pieces by the most talented authors have a lasting quality than transcends their documentary value. Among them may be mentioned Ehrenburg's two volumes, *War* (1941–42), Aleksei Tolstoy's two volumes, *Motherland* (1942) and *What We Are Defending* (1942), Evgeni Petrov's *Front-Line Diary* (1942), Fadeyev's *Leningrad in the Days of the Blockade* (1944), Vera Inber's *Almost Three Years: A Leningrad Diary* (1945), and Petro Vershigora's *People With a Clear Conscience* (1945).

An author's response to actuality in the turmoil of war can hardly be expected to embody those attributes that make for enduring art. There is no time for calm contemplation of the human mystery, for perspective, for infinite pains and polishing, and in general these deficiencies are patent in most of the war novels. Only the poetic muse is suited by its very nature to respond artistically to the burning immediacy of war and to capture its tragic moments in significant content and imperishable form, especially in the lyric. Poetry is a natural emotional outlet for the grief and anger of combat, and over these catastrophic years an incredible amount of verse was published in the Soviet Union. Much of it was jingoistic and sentimental, but many fine lyrics, full of deep love of country and hatred for the enemy, were written by Simonov, Surkov, Prokofyev, Dolmatovsky, Shchipachov and many others. For example, such poems of Simonov as *Do you Recall, Alyosha . . .* , evoking sad memories of the Russian retreat in 1941 *Kill Him*, a chilling indictment of the Nazis and *Wait for Me*, in which the soldier at the front implores his beloved to remain faithful to him, were enormously popular. Millions of copies of *Wait for Me* were said to have circulated among soldiers at the front and civilians in the rear. The two rising young poetesses, Olga Berggolts and Margarita Aliger, contributed a number of sensitive war lyrics, and a small sheaf of them also came from the pen of Pasternak, whose many-sided devotion to his country had always been the central focus of his verse.

Of the narrative poems that appeared, perhaps the best were two concerning the long, ghastly siege of Leningrad—Vera Inber's *The Pulkovo Meridian* (1943) and Nikolai Tikhonov's *Kirov Is with Us*; Aliger's *Zoya* (1942), the widely popular and emotional story in verse of a communist girl who had fought in the underground and was caught, tortured and hanged by the Germans; and Tvardovsky's *Vasili Tyorkin* (1941–45), a portrait of the typical Russian soldier that became almost legendary among the men of the ranks during the war. Tyorkin's tragic and comic adventures, his resourcefulness in every situation and his engaging 'philosophy' of war are narrated in that homely style which Tvardovsky had employed so effectively in *Muravia Land*.

Drama, like lyric poetry in a time of tremendous national ferment, achieved immense popularity because of its direct appeal to people through the spoken word. The stage was given over to a flood of war plays. And the theme of at least one of them may well have been prompted by a suggestion from high Party leaders. For example, only official action could have inspired and then secured the publication in *Pravda* of Alexander Korneichuk's widely acclaimed *The Front* (1942), a play that exposed the out-moded tactics of famous old generals of the Civil War and, in effect, justified to a confused public their replacement, after the early reverses of the Red Army, by younger commanders well versed in modern streamlined fighting. Another hugely success-ful play was Simonov's *Russian People* (1943) which chronicles the fierce patriotism and bravery, in the face of death, of a group of simple unassuming civilians and soldiers. The emphasis upon 'Russian people' in the title and characters of the play is in

keeping with a propaganda motif during the war which was denounced as bad taste after it, when 'Soviet patriotism' once again
became the Party's slogan. Of the large number of plays produced at this time. Leonov's *Invasion* (1942) and *Lyonushka*
(1943) were not only among the most popular, but almost among
the very few that have any value as art. Both deal with the grim
struggle of Russians under German occupation, but the conflicts
between good and evil are resolved from the vantage point of a
deeper, more universal understanding of human nature and with
a command of dialogue beyond the capacities of most Soviet
playwrights.

Many plays were an outgrowth of the nationalism which the
Party, in anticipation of a conflict, had emphasized in the years
immediately preceding the war. All great Russian military commanders and their resplendent victories in wars of the past were
celebrated on the stage. To mention only a few of the most successful: Vladimir Solovev's *Marshal Kutuzov* (1940), I. Lukovsky's
Admiral Nakhimov (1941), O. Litovsky's and K. Osipov's *Alexander Nevsky* (1942), I. Selvinsky's *General Brusilov* (1943), and
G. Mdivani's *Pyotr Bagration* (1944). In this outpouring of
patriotism, liberties were often taken with history as playwrights
strove to interpret these triumphs of the past in terms of the
propaganda clichés of the current struggle with Germany. The
will to victory of these famous leaders was somehow always connected with their great love for the masses.

Though the announced official position of the Union of Soviet
Writers was that literature should serve one purpose only—victory over the enemy—it also agitated against the ephemerality
implicit in this kind of writing. At a conference of the Union in
April 1942, the emphasis was on psychological rather than on
socialist realism because literature, one speaker declared, should
have an intense interest in man's inner world and in the changes
brought about by the war. And in the best fiction authors avoided
old stereotypes of Marxian dogma in their interpretations of Russian character and history at a time of great national peril. Their
heroes were often non-Party men, and their responses to the awful
problems of life and death encountered in mortal combat with
the enemy were filled with new feelings for the common cause,
the solidarity of the people and the triumphant destiny of Russia,
feelings which were inner-directed rather than Party-directed.

Few of these traits are evident in the stream of short stories, although there are some exceptions in the tales of Leonid Sobolev, Konstantin Paustovsky, Venyamin Kaverin, and Pyotr Pavlenko. Several of the younger writers, however, produced novels of unquestioned literary merit, such as Vasili Grossman's *The People Are Immortal* (1942), a story of the early days of the war that avoids jingoism in its bare realism, and Boris Gorbatov's more romantic *The Unconquered* (1943), which is concerned with the fate of a family in the Kuban after it had been occupied by the Germans. Simonov's *Days and Nights* (1944), which won considerable acclaim in the Soviet Union and abroad, hardly does full justice to one of the great stories of the war—the heroic defence of Stalingrad—but it is adequate perhaps because the author does not attempt to transcend his limitations as a novelist.

The efforts of older writers were superior. The ancient dullness that infects so much war fiction is avoided in Leonov's short novel, *The Taking of Velikoshumsk* (1944), because of his unyielding concentration on the main theme, the story of a tank and its crew, and his unusual restraint in the use of the fictional sinews of war—descriptions and emotions. The symbolism of the tank and its crew, representing the unity and qualities of the Soviet armies, is handled with deft simplicity and stark economy. Another short novel, *The Son of the Regiment* (1945) by Katayev, again reveals this author's remarkable psychological understanding of children in the story of an orphan adopted by a regiment. Perhaps the most celebrated of these novels by older writers was Fadeyev's *The Young Guard* (1945), which later, in the postwar period, was substantially revised by the author in answer to official criticism then that he had failed to stress the role played by adult Party members in the story's action. The novel is based on a real underground conspiracy of boys and girls in the Young Communist League, which is designed to make life intolerable for German occupiers of a Ukrainian town. In the end the youngsters are betrayed and brutally executed. The work is a moving and convincing account of the idealism, self-sacrifice and devotion to country of these young people, and at the same time is reasonably objective in portraying the cruelty of the enemy and the backsliding of Soviet citizens. Often, however, the suspense and exciting action are encumbered by excessive detail; Fadeyev never seems to have learned thoroughly the fine art of selection in fiction.

Sholokov, the most famous of the older fiction writers, disappointed numerous admirers by his failure to produce the great novel of the war, a work comparable in scope and excellence to his *Quiet Don*. Actually, he began such a novel, apparently a trilogy, tentatively entitled *They Fought for Their Country*, and a few initial chapters were printed in *Pravda* in 1943 and 1944. Though he stated in 1950 that the first volume was finished, no more of it seems to have been published. From the early chapters it appears that the war is to be a kind of crucible in which the qualities and values of the new Soviet man, formed by years of socialist existence, receive their final testing.

As in the case of drama, the historical novel was also used during the war to continue and intensify the nationalistic fervor, so frequently expressed in an exaltation of the martial glory of the Russian past. Eloquent testimony of this intention was the publication, in beleaguered Leningrad, of Leo Tolstoy's *War and Peace*, in an edition of 500,000 copies, to encourage the defenders' morale. Biographies of great generals, occasionally somewhat fictionalized, such as Suvurov, Kutuzov, Bagration and Brusilov, appeared. In a huge three-volume novel, *Ivan the Terrible* (1941–45), Valentin Kostylev attempted to justify the cruel ways of the tsar by portraying him as a far-seeing Russian statesman, as Aleksei Tolstoy had done in his two plays on this subject. Novikov-Priboi contributed another novel on the Russo-Japanese War—*Port Arthur* (1944). On the theme of the first world war, which had a special relevance for Russian readers in the present struggle, Sergeyev-Tsensky wrote three novels: *Brusilov's Breakthrough* (1943), *The Guns Emerge* (1944), and *The Guns Have Spoken* (1945). They are really part of a vast epic of Russian life, under the general title of *Transfiguration*, which the author had begun in the 1920's. These works are old-fashioned in technique, but the material is objectively handled. They are well-planned, highly interesting, and perhaps superior artistically to the many historical novels during this whole period, with the exception of Aleksei Tolstoy's *Peter I*.

On the whole, the relaxation of censorship and overt Party dictation during the war encouraged a sense of freedom among writers comparable in some respects to that which prevailed in the early years after the Revolution. But by the end of 1943, when the extreme peril to the country appeared to be surmounted, the Party once again began to manifest its concern with ideological orthodoxy. The Party's claws were first revealed in connexion with the serial publication, at the end of 1943, of Zoshchenko's *Before Sunrise*. Though he described the work as a novelette, it is really a collection of autobiographical fragments which he analyses in a serio-comic manner in an effort to discover the cause of his melancholia. Critics on the presidium of the Union of Soviet Writers and in the pages of the official Party magazine *Bolshevik* sharply attacked the work as a piece of unpatriotic, vulgar philistinism, and the publication of further instalments was dropped.

The Party next struck at the distinguished writer Fedin. When his *Gorky Amongst Us* appeared in 1943, the first of a three-volume collection of literary memoirs dedicated to a great author who had influenced him, the work was widely praised. However, when the second volume came out in 1944, it was just as widely condemned. The vituperation culminated in an official reprimand in *Pravda*, and the last volume of the memoirs was cancelled. Though Fedin's unbiased appreciation of certain older literary figures out of sympathy with the regime provoked most of the denunciations, no doubt his own creative faith, which he expressed in the second volume, aroused the special ire of Party critics. Art may be tendentious, he asserted, but the artist himself, since he creates unconsciously, is not tendentious. The jibes of the critics represented a kind of forewarning of the new Party line in the making in literature : Fedin was accused of objectivity, scepticism, defending the contemplative artist and apolitical art, preaching toleration of reactionary ideas of the past, and the sacrifice of socialist individuality in an effort to restore individualism in general. Though he was also accused of remaining outside politics at a time when his country was fighting for its very life, actually he had seen much service at the front as a correspondent and had written a war play. Apparently undaunted by this attack, Fedin began the serial publication, in 1945, of *Early Joys*, the first volume of his brilliant trilogy, in which the hero, Kirill Izvekov, is one of the very few believable representatives of the new Soviet man.

However, by the end of the war in Europe in 1945 the Party

was already swiftly moving toward a reassertion of its position of absolute control in all the arts, even though writers seemed determined to regard the freedom they had enjoyed as something more real than an opportunistic adjustment to the war emergency. For at their postwar conference in May 1945, some of them boldly spoke out against any resumption of interference in literature and argued that a miracle could not be organized in art. But the resolution of the Central Committee on 14 August 1946 made it plain that the Party was determined to 'pass a miracle' in literature, and that all Soviet writers would once more be expected to become organization men.

6

ZHDANOVISM (1946–53)

Walter N. Vickery

The years 1946–53 must be ranked among the bleakest and most sterile in Soviet literature.[1] During these years literature appeared to be operating in a vacuum; not only were contemporary trends in Western literature almost completely ignored, but the comparatively vigorous Soviet Russian literature of the Twenties was more or less consigned to oblivion. The free, creative spirit of the Soviet writer, which at the best of times labours under the disadvantage of severe restrictions, was imprisoned in a straight-jacket so confining as to make it a matter of wonder that, along with all the substandard stereotypes masquerading as literature, there were produced some works of literary merit. It is not my intention here to examine these works—either individually or collectively—from the literary viewpoint. Instead I prefer, as have others before me, to focus attention less on the literary product than on those events, often extra-literary in their origin, which forged and fashioned the literature of Stalin's last years. It is possible that a systematic, detailed, literary study of the many indifferent and the few respectable works of this period would yield dividends in the form of new or modified insights into its dynamics. But dividends must be weighed against investment, and it is extremely doubtful whether such Herculean labours would substantially alter our view of events. Furthermore, Soviet literature during the years 1946–53 remains completely unintelligible without reference to extra-literary factors. Therefore, the examination of these factors is probably the most fruitful and economical means of undertaking a survey of the period.

1. Some of the materials covered in this paper have appeared in a slightly different form in my book, *The Cult of Optimism*. My thanks are due to the Indiana University Press for permission to reproduce them here.

Surely one of the attractions in studying post-war Soviet literature has been to speculate, to the best of one's ability, as to the
true meaning of different events, to look beyond the printed word
in an attempt to see what was going on behind the scenes. As far
as the main lines of development of the 1946–53 period are concerned, the pleasures of this type of inquiry have now been
severely curtailed—thanks to increased contacts with Soviet intellectuals and thanks, above all, to the various revelations printed
in the Soviet Union which have cast the light of day on many
questions which remained shrouded in darkness during Stalin's
last years. Nevertheless, some minor questions still remain un-
answered and it is my hope that the following survey will answer
a few of these and at least give an airing to others.

First, a word about Andrei Zhdanov. He was active on the
Soviet literary scene as far back as 1934, and he died in 1948.
So that to speak of the 1946–53 period as the years of Zhdanovism
serves only to underline the fact that it was in these years that
the hard-line political orthodoxy represented by Zhdanov's name
reached its apogee. Zhdanov himself was scarcely responsible for
the repressive atmosphere that characterizes the period. Nor can
Stalin, though he undoubtedly bears a greater burden of responsibility, be held solely accountable. The 1946–48 decrees, which
Zhdanov so energetically bolstered and which bear the unmis-
takable imprint of Stalin's personality, have outlived their spon-
sors. Attempts made since the Twentieth Party Congress to dis-
credit these decrees have been rebuffed, and the third volume of
the Academy of Sciences history of Soviet literature, published
in 1961, speaks of the decrees as 'retaining in principle their significance even today'.[2]

Obviously the prerequisites for Zhdanovism are to be
found in the conditions which prevailed in the Soviet Union
during and at the end of World War II. During the war
years the struggle for national survival and the need to bol-
ster the morale of an embattled people had been paramount.
Under these conditions the role of the Communist Party had
been somewhat diminished and, in particular, its control of literature had been relaxed; the niceties of ideology had seemed relatively unimportant while cities were falling and people dying.

2. T. K. Trifonova, 'Literatura poslevoennogo perioda', *Istoria sovetskoi
literatury*, Moscow, 1961, III, 56.

And Soviet writers, no less patriotic than their fellow citizens, had taken advantage of the relaxation. The war's end radically altered this situation. First, it brought to a close a wartime alliance with the capitalist West—an alliance which had been viewed by statesmen on both sides as a necessary and temporary expedient—and led to a resumption of 'the struggle between the two systems'—a struggle in which ideology is deeply involved. Second, it confronted the Soviet leaders with the problems of a country that had suffered appalling devastation. A vast construction and reconstruction effort would be required to set the Soviet economy back on its feet. Fresh efforts and fresh sacrifices must be demanded of a people that was war-weary and had already sacrificed so much. To whip up flagging spirits for the new effort —to mention only one reason—the Communist Party must be restored to its dominant role so as to become an effective instrument of power. To achieve this and at the same time to focus the attention of the population on the urgency of construction tasks, the need for ideological orthodoxy must be stressed anew. Undoubtedly such considerations weighed heavily with the Kremlin and had immediate repercussions in the field of literature.

The 1946–48 Central Committee Decrees

14 August 1946 was an all-important date for Soviet literature and marks the beginning of the period under review. It was on this day that the Central Committee passed the decree which for years to come laid down the direction that post-war literature was to take.[3] The decree took the form of an attack on two Leningrad journals, *Zvezda* and *Leningrad*. It complained that many of their publications were 'devoid of ideas, ideologically harmful'. The editors of these two journals were taken to task for having forgotten the basic Leninist tenet that Soviet journals cannot be apolitical:

The Soviet system cannot tolerate the education of youth in a spirit of indifference to Soviet politics, to ideology, with a couldn't-care-less attitude. The strength of Soviet literature, the most advanced literature in the world, consists in the fact that it is a literature in which there are not and cannot be interests other than the interests of the people, the interests of the state. The task of Soviet literature is to help the state to educate youth correctly, to answer its requirements,

3. See *Pravda*, 21 August 1946 or *Bolshevik*, No. 15, 1946, pp. 11–14.

to bring up the new generation to be strong, believing in its cause, not fearing obstacles, ready to overcome all obstacles.

Lack of political orientation had, it seems, led to the publication of works 'permeated with longing, pessimism and disillusionment in life'. The journals were guilty on two further counts: their servile idolization of contemporary bourgeois culture, and their disparagement of Soviet life and Soviet people.

The Central Committee proceeded to drive home its point by taking disciplinary action. *Leningrad* was ordered to cease publication. *Zvezda* was ordered to mend its ways. And to make sure that the mending was successfully accomplished a Party propaganda bureaucrat was put in charge. The Deputy Chief of the Propaganda Administration of the Central Committee was appointed editor-in-chief with full responsibility for the journal's ideological-political orientation. *Zvezda* was further ordered to banish from its pages the two most blameworthy authors, Zoshchenko and Anna Akhmatova, 'and others like them'.

It is a time-honoured Soviet practice to make a point of general application by singling out individual culprits and holding them up to nation-wide censure. That the city of Leningrad was here selected for this honour is not entirely fortuitous. By geography and tradition Leningrad had for a long time been accustomed to look to the West. And looking to the West in any shape or form was precisely what the Soviet leaders were striving to prevent. The fortunes of war had afforded many Soviet citizens a glimpse of the West. Further, the war-weariness of the Soviet reading and theatre-going public was finding an outlet in a certain enthusiasm for Western bourgeois writers. These had an obvious advantage over their Soviet counterparts. While the latter were supposed to implant in the reader an unflagging awareness of his civic responsibility, the former aimed rather to distract and to entertain. And entertainment was just what the weary public needed— or thought it needed. It was, however, mistaken. What it needed was to be purged of corrupting Western influences and to be reminded that Soviet culture was the most advanced culture in the world. Under these circumstances Leningrad was the logical place to attack. But the lesson was intended for the Soviet Union as a whole.

Nor was the singling out of Zoshchenko and Anna Akhmatova as the two most reprehensible Leningrad authors a fortuitous choice. Zoshchenko was formed as a writer on prerevolutionary models and had for many years experienced difficulty in accommodating himself to Soviet ideological requirements.[4] Anna Akhmatova had made her name before the Revolution and in the early Twenties. The two main themes of her poetry had been love and religion. Her highly personal style of writing had not been calculated to find favour in the Thirties and she had not published for several years before the outbreak of war. The war years had temporarily released her from a silence which was now to be reimposed. Thus, in attacking two 'prerevolutionary' authors, who were patently off key from the ideological viewpoint, the Central Committee was making it clear that there was to be no return to the laxity and ideological 'confusion' of the Twenties and that wartime relaxations were very definitely at an end.

The 14 August decree should not be seen as a bolt from the blue. Actually the process of re-tightening the ideological reins had started back in 1943, after Stalingrad had marked a decisive turning point in the tide of war. Zoshchenko had come under attack at that time, and during 1944, 1945, and the first half of 1946 there had been other warning signals—gradually increasing in intensity.[5]

That the Central Committee decree was no mere routine order of the day but rather was intended as a major policy decision was made doubly clear by the fact that it was reinforced by a report by Zhdanov—the regime's ideological custodian, at that time regarded by some observers as Stalin's heir apparent. His personal intervention in what might have been regarded as a purely literary matter served to emphasize the importance attributed to the affair by the Kremlin.

Zhdanov's report was more virulent than the Central Committee decree in its attack on Zoshchenko and Akhmatova.[6] He

4. See Rebecca A. Domar, 'The Tragedy of a Soviet Satirist, or the Case of Zoshchenko' in *Through the Glass of Soviet Literature*, ed. Ernest J. Simmons, New York: Columbia University Press, 1953.

5. This has been demonstrated by H. Swayze in 'Soviet Literary Politics, 1946–1956', Harvard University, 1962; also by Avrahm Yarmolinsky, *Literature Under Communism* (Russian and East European Series, Indiana University, Vol. 20), pp. 1–15.

6. A condensed version of reports made by Zhdanov at a meeting of a Party *aktiv* and at a meeting of Leningrad writers may be found in *Bolshevik*, Nos. 17–18, 1946, pp. 4–19.

spoke of Akhmatova as 'part nun and part harlot, or rather both
harlot and nun, in whom harlotry is mingled with prayer'. He
claimed that 'moods of loneliness and hopelessness, alien to
Soviet literature, run through the whole history of Akhmatova's
"creative" work'. He berated Zoshchenko for turning out all the
seamy sides of Soviet life in order to paint an anti-Soviet picture
and to ridicule Soviet people. He attacked bourgeois culture. He
called on writers to 'show these new fine qualities of Soviet people,
to show our people not only in its to-day, but to look forward
to its tomorrow, to help to light up with a searchlight the road
ahead'. Basically Zhdanov's reports added little on the ideological
plane to what had already been stated in the decree of 14 August.
His intervention was, as already indicated, none the less important for that.

The blackballing of Zoshchenko and Akhmatova and the
vicious manner in which this was done were probably partly motivated by a desire to remind writers of the not so distant ugly
past, of the purges of the Thirties which had claimed as victims
several men of letters. The attack on the two writers could be
calculated to strike fear into writers' hearts and so to prevent the
formation of anything approaching a cohesive body of opinion,
a feeling of solidarity among intellectuals; to prevent the emergence of anything remotely resembling an opposition intelligentsia; to sow fear and mistrust; to divide and so to rule.

The 14 August decree was shortly followed by two further
decrees devoted respectively to the theatre and to the cinema.[7]
These two hewed to the same rigid ideological line. All these
decrees, reinforced by the Zhdanov report, were designed not
merely to warn writers of what they should not do or to set limits
to their freedom; rather they were designed to tell writers precisely what they should do. The writers were to 'help the state to
educate youth correctly'. Their efforts were, in fact, to be
geared meticulously to Kremlin requirements. They were to illustrate and endorse in literature the prevailing Kremlin propaganda line: the vilification of all things bourgeois and the exaggerated glorification of all things Soviet, Stalin in particular.
Above all, their writing was to be ruthlessly optimistic.

7. For the 26 August decree on the repertoire of dramatic theatres and
measures to improve it, see *Bolshevik*, No. 16, 1946, pp. 45–49. The 4 September
decree on the motion picture *Bolshaya zhizn* is in the same number, pp. 50–53.

The effect of Zhdanovism, as this official attitude came to be called, was to castrate completely a literature which had during the war years been groping for its erstwhile virility. I have already mentioned that the years immediately following the 1946 decrees did witness the publication of some works which were not without literary merit.[8] But they produced a majority of colourless, stereotyped works of the type which was later to be associated disparagingly with the name of Babayevsky.[9] The general tendency was to idealize Soviet life and Soviet people, to gloss over the ugly and harsh facts of this life, to reduce conflict to a minimum; any attempt to paint a more or less realistic picture was sure to be decried as a 'slander' against Soviet reality. And the general atmosphere of the time was manifest in the fact that the critics based their judgements almost exclusively on ideological content, paying little or no attention to literary quality. The 1946 decrees ushered in the darkest chapter in the history of Soviet literature.

The main obstacle to the development of a healthy literature, it hardly needs to be said, was and was to remain the ideological controls imposed from above. But to recognize this fact would have been to undermine the whole concept of literature's educational role. Therefore, other explanations had to be found: the writers or the critics had failed to interpret correctly the wise directives of the Party; some arts committee had been negligent in its attitude; the 'creative sections' were not giving sufficient aid to writers, the work being done on aesthetic theory was inadequate. Always some scapegoat had to be found to mask the true reason.

The Anticosmopolitan Campaign

Perhaps the most flagrant example of the scapegoat technique was provided by the 1949 anticosmopolitan campaign. The poor quality of Zhdanov-inspired literature had become especially noticeable in the field of drama where half-empty houses left little possibility of self-delusion. This fact received official recog-

8. e.g. *Neobyknovennoe leto* by Konstantin Fedin, 1948; *Sputniki*, 1947, and *Kruzhilikha*, 1948, by Vera Panova; *Zvezda*, 1947, and *Dvoe v stepi*, 1948, by Emmanuil Kazakevich; *Ivan Ivanovich* by Antonina Koptyayeva, 1949.

9. S. P. Babayevsky, Stalin prize-winning author of *Kavaler zolotoi zvezdy*, Moscow, 1949, and *Svet nad zemlei*, Moscow, 1951. *Babayevshchina* became a synonym in literary circles for the naively rose-coloured portrayal of Soviet life.

nition of a sort in a Council of Ministers decree of 4 March cur-
tailing state subsidies to theatres. Articles began to appear commenting on the sorry state of affairs. Typical of such comments
was one critic's complaint that 'the main defect of our drama
is the quite unjustified attempt on the part of writers to smooth
out the conflicts which manifest themselves in life, to make a
play less sharp-edged, and to make the hero into a "mouthpiece
for ideas" who loses the traits of a living character'.[10] Another
writer, playwright and critic, whose views normally came close
to reflecting the views of officialdom, insisted that 'we must not
forget that character is the basis of drama, clearly delineated
character and a well-developed, vital conflict. But many of our
plays possess neither conflict nor character, they have only
comedy-type situations'.[11] These and other articles expressed
genuine concern at the lowering of artistic standards brought
about by the need to whitewash and varnish reality.

Toward the end of 1948 a two-day conference was held jointly
by the Union of Soviet Writers, the Committee on Affairs of the
Arts and the All-Russian Theatrical Society. The weaknesses of
Soviet drama were again deplored. One critic, Borshchagovsky,
noted, according to the *Literaturnaya gazeta* report of the meeting, that in recent plays it was impossible to feel the personal
experience of the writer and that there was much that was pure
abstraction.[12] He stressed the lack of genuine conflict. But he and
others, here and elsewhere, must have been considerably more
outspoken than reports indicate. For at this point the story takes
an unexpected twist. Up to then criticism had been, logically
enough, levelled against the drama itself. But at the next plenary
meeting of the Board of the Writers' Union on 15 December, an
attack was opened not on the writers of bad plays but on certain
of their critics. The attack was initiated by no less a person than
Fadeyev, Secretary-General of the Writers' Union. Fadeyev had
at the time greater influence than anyone else in the Writers'
Union and constantly acted as the Party's mouthpiece. The basis
of his attack was that the critics in question had directed their
criticism 'not against the genuinely harmful and worst phenom-

10. I. Altman, 'Dramaturgia v 1947 godu', *Oktyabr*, No. 3, 1948, pp. 177—91.
11. A. Sofronov, 'Neskolko slov o komedii', *Oktyabr*, No. 12, 1948, pp. 167-
80.
12. 'Razgovor o sudbakh repertuara', 4 December 1948.

ena in the field of drama, but against the advanced and the best ... Critics like Malyugin and Borshchagovsky, instead of unmasking bourgeois ideology, servility to Western bourgeois culture, laboured formalistic works, or works which grossly distort Soviet life and Soviet men, are seeking first and foremost to strike down those Soviet playwrights who are portraying the new in Soviet life.' Fadeyev based his attack on stenographic reports of other meetings 'which made it possible to judge what people really think' in spite of the 'façade' they present when speaking 'from this platform'.[13] The drama critics found themselves thus manœuvred into an invidious position. For now their criticisms of the drama would no longer be dealt with on their merits, but treated as attacks on Soviet prestige. This is precisely what happened. They were accused of having formed an antipatriotic group, disloyal to the Soviet Union.[14]

On 28 January 1949, *Pravda* came out with an unsigned and therefore authoritative editorial entitled 'On an Antipatriotic Group of Theatre Critics'. The *Pravda* article sounded the alarm in the style typical of the time: 'Nests of bourgeois aestheticism, camouflaging an antipatriotic, cosmopolitan, corrupt attitude toward Soviet art, have maintained themselves until recently in the field of theatrical criticism.' It repeated Fadeyev's charge: 'The sting of aesthetic-formalist criticism is directed not against the really harmful and inferior works but against the advanced and best ones which depict Soviet patriots. It is precisely this which attests to the fact that aesthetic formalism merely serves as a camouflage for antipatriotic substance.' And it laid down that 'the top-priority task of Party criticism is the ideological crushing of this antipatriotic group of theatre critics'.

This article, frequently cited in the days to come as an authori-

13. See *Literaturnaya gazeta*, 22 December 1948.
14. Indeed this attack by Fadeyev at the Twelfth Plenum really marked the beginning of the anticosmopolitan campaign in literature. H. Swayze gives reasons (see 'Soviet Literary Politics, 1946–1956', Chap. II) for his belief that this may not have been the deliberate intention of Fadeyev and those who joined in the attack at the Plenum. Konstantin Simonov would seem to be confirming Swayze's view in his 1956 'Literaturnye Zametki', where, after pointing out the injustices perpetuated at the Twelfth Plenum, he goes on to remark: 'But soon the situation was aggravated by the *Pravda* article "Ob odnoj antipatrioticheskoj gruppe teatralnykh kritikov".' See *Novy Mir*, No. 12, 1956, p. 249. The exact moment of the launching of the campaign is not in any case of primary importance.

tative pronouncement (yet not even mentioned in the chronicle of literary events in the third volume of the Academy history), was the signal for a full-scale anticosmopolitan campaign in literature, a campaign of hate, with all the trappings of repetitious editorials, obsequious quotations, 'subversion' and 'plots'.

Confessions from the errant critics were elicited. For instance, *Literaturnaya gazeta* on 26 February, reporting a Moscow meeting of playwrights and critics, had the following to say:

Instead of telling from the platform—truthfully, without evasions—of their guilt before the Soviet people, of the forms and methods of the antipatriotic group, they twisted and turned like snakes, lied and used previously prepared crib-sheets to try and represent themselves as in no way connected with each other, and they tried to represent the chain of consciously committed crimes as 'chance errors'. The facts refuted them. Driven to the wall, they found themselves obliged, reluctantly and incompletely, to admit the existence of a group, of agreement, of co-ordinated acts which had been prepared in advance.

And the report goes on to give some individual 'reluctant' confessions. The 'rootless cosmopolitan' critics, some of whom lost their posts in the theatre world, had been disgraced on a national scale.[15] And the mandatory laudation of all things Soviet had been re-emphasized for the benefit of writers in general.

It should, of course, be mentioned that December 1948 did not mark the beginning of postwar Soviet anticosmopolitanism. Anticosmopolitanism had been expressed in the 1946 Central Committee decrees. It was implicit in the whitewashing techniques demanded of Soviet writers. It provided the ground on which Nusinov was attacked in 1947 for having given too much credit to Western influences in the development of Pushkin.[16] It was on the same ground that Aleksandrov was attacked, also in 1947, for his views on Western philosophy—an event which produced

15. Kron, for instance, lost his position as chairman of the drama commission. On 11 February 1949, a *Pravda* report speaks of him as 'former' chairman. The same report, devoted to a two-day Party meeting, calls on the Party bureau to examine the membership and candidate-membership of others of the accused. The casualties in literature produced by the anticosmopolitan campaign were numerous. Most writers and critics, Kron among them, subseqently won their way back into print.

16. e.g., A. Fadeyev, 'O literaturnoi kritike', *Bolshevik*, No. 13, 1947, pp. 20–35.

yet another personal appearance and report by Zhdanov.[17] Anti-cosmopolitanism was very much the order of the day. December 1948 and January 1949 merely marked the launching of the anti-cosmopolitan campaign in literature.

Why was this done? After all, others outside the 'cosmopolitan' group had voiced their dissatisfaction at the state of affairs in the field of drama; there had been general agreement that all was not well. Later, in the decidedly liberal atmosphere of 1956, Simonov had the following observation to make about the views of 'cosmopolitan' theatre critics: 'Their statements did contain elements of snobbishness and aestheticism, and sometimes there even did creep into these statements an unjustifiable opposition between literature's educational role and its artistic standards.' [18] It is clear that the drama critics had, by pointing out the harmful consequences for literature of the rigid ideological requirements then in force, called in question, if not the whole concept of controls, at least the system of controls as it was then being exercised as well as the entirely unrealistic ideological orientation of those days. To see, as Simonov's remarks suggest, an incompatibility between the educational pretensions of literature and artistic quality was to strike at the very roots of official thought.

It would be hard to find a more authoritative assessment of the entire incident than that given by Simonov. In this same article in 1956 he expressed shame over the hounding of the 'cosmopolitans', in which incidentally he had himself played no small part.[19] His remarks afford valuable insights and are therefore here reproduced at some length:

At the plenum of the Board of the Union of Writers, which took place at the end of 1948, critics who had been calling attention to the genuine weaknesses of our drama were completely routed. It was asserted that critics who had noted weakness in our drama did not

17. See *Bolshevik*, No. 16, 1947, pp. 7–23. For similar expressions of sentiment see also, for example, 'Protiv burzhuaznogo liberalizma v literaturovedenii', *Kultura i zhizn*, 11 March 1948, or the editorial 'Protiv kosmopolitizma v nauke o literature', 20 March 1948, which attacked Veselovsky.

18. K. Simonov, 'Literaturnye zametki', *Novy Mir*, No. 12, 1956, pp. 239–57.

19. For instance, K. Simonov, 'Zadachi sovetskoi dramaturgii i teatralnaya kritika', *Pravda*, 28 February 1949, in which he proclaims: 'The criminal work of the group of anti-patriotic critics has been exposed by the Party and the Party press. . . . One of the most pernicious aspects of its activity lies precisely in the fact that they were a group, that they supported each other in their activities, activities hostile to Soviet drama.'

S.L.—9

hold its fate dear; that they wanted to undermine it and were allegedly by their statements impeding its growth; that they were criticizing it from alien, hostile standpoints and that, though there were indeed shortcomings in our drama, we would be able to criticize these from our standpoint only after we had routed all those who were speaking about drama from alien standpoints. The theory of 'first-things-first' (*ocherednost*) in criticism, consisting in the idea that we would criticize our own shortcomings only after suppressing criticism from allegedly alien or genuinely alien standpoints, was ridiculous, for Bolshevik principles of criticism and self-criticism demand that we should have dealt with both at the same time. But the affair did not stop short at this theory. Unscrupulous, demagogic methods were employed at the plenum to create the impression that the standpoint of a number of critics was 'alien'. Among these the principal method was that all critical remarks addressed to this or that hero in a play were re-addressed, re-directed against the whole of Soviet society. If the author of a critical article had ironized over the unsuccessful, platitudinous representation of a Party organizer, he was directly accused of mocking at the Party. If he said that a play had resolved poorly, in primitive fashion, the theme of servility, he was himself accused of being servile and cosmopolitan. If he stated that characters in a play pronounced high-flown didactic speeches about the motherland and the people, then he was accused of lack of patriotism. The plenum did also produce true comments on the elements of aestheticism in the articles of a number of critics, on the weakness of their positive programme in the field of drama. But these reasonable comments were rendered worthless by the general orientation of a number of unscrupulous statements by people who wished to guard drama from criticism, to gloss over its obvious weaknesses, to defend the honour of their uniform, falsely interpreted and sometimes interpreted in terms of personal interest. The character of this plenum alone had a negative influence on the development of our drama, but soon the situation was aggravated by the *Pravda* article, 'On an Antipatriotic Group of Theatre Critics'. Above all, this article emphasized one-sidedly the task of Soviet literature as a literature devoted to the glorification of our achievements and successes. The list, showing what should be the sources of inspiration of Soviet literature and what it should write about, did not even include the word 'struggle'.

Simonov's revelations serve to emphasize not only the depths to which Soviet literature had been reduced by the 1946 decrees but also the impossibility under prevailing conditions of remedying the situation. For in this case authorities, writers and critics

alike were all agreed on the inadequacy of Soviet drama. But
when certain critics came forward with some common-sense sug-
gestions, the top leadership was unable to look the truth in the
face and diverted the public's attention back on to the nearest
target.

The anticosmopolitan campaign is connected in some people's
minds with anti-semitism and brief mention should be made of
this problem. There is no doubt that anti-semitism was to some
extent involved in the anticosmopolitan campaign. Many of the
critics under attack had been writing under 'Russian' pseudonyms; and during the campaign these pseudonyms were in some
cases printed alongside their true names, revealing their Jewish
origin. Further, it became known after Stalin's death that the
Jewish poet, Feffer and other Jewish writers who disappeared
from literature at this time, had perished in a concentration
camp. Nevertheless, anti-semitism seems in the sphere of Russian
literature (as opposed to Yiddish literature, where anti-semitism
was directly responsible for the imprisonment in 1948 and subsequent execution of a number of writers and intellectuals) to
have been of less significance than purely ideological factors.
Many Jewish writers and critics never came under attack.[20]
Furthermore, it has been pointed out that not only were there
non-Jews among the critics under attack but also there were Jews
among their accusers.[21] In view of these considerations it would
seem wrong to think of anti-semitism as a prime mover in the
anticosmopolitan campaign, more accurate to think of the campaign as having anti-semitic overtones.

The Campaign Against Bourgeois Nationalism

One more campaign in this sombre period deserves mention.
Less vicious than the anticosmopolitan campaign but equally
designed to maintain ideological purity was the campaign against
bourgeois nationalism. It was launched by a *Pravda* article of
2 July 1951, 'Against Ideological Distortions in Literature', and
the object of the attack was a poem by the Ukrainian writer V.

20. See Bernard J. Choseed, 'Jews in Soviet Literature', in *Through the Glass
of Soviet Literature*, ed. Ernest J. Simmons, New York: Columbia University
Press, 1953.
21. See Gleb Struve, *Geschichte der Sowjetliteratur*, Munich: Isarverlag, 1957,
p. 412.

Sosyura, *Love the Ukraine*.[22] The poem was labelled 'an ideologically defective work'. 'It produces', *Pravda* complained, 'a
feeling of disillusionment and protest ... What Ukraine is V.
Sosyura glorifying? Is it that Ukraine which for centuries groaned
beneath the yoke of the exploiters? .... Or is it the new, flourishing Soviet Ukraine, created by the will of the people under the
guidance of the Bolshevik Party? Outside of time and epoch—
that is the Ukraine depicted by the poet.' The poem had been
written back in the relaxed atmosphere of 1944 and it concentrated on the 'eternal' Ukraine of field and sky and nature—not,
as *Pravda* pointed out, the Soviet Ukraine with its giant plants,
socialist industry, construction projects, etc. Sosyura had failed to
condemn the old or to praise the new. Further, the poem gave
evidence of a specifically Ukrainian patriotism, failing to show
the Ukraine as one member in the family of Soviet peoples. It
was thus a manifestation of bourgeois nationalism, not of Soviet
patriotism.

The Russian translator, A. Prokofyev, was also taken to task
for his irresponsibility in translating and publishing the poem.

The *Pravda* article was followed by a flurry of other articles
in various newspapers and journals. In writers' meetings throughout the country traces of bourgeois nationalism, hitherto un-
suspected, were now assiduously uncovered. Sosyura and Prokofyev saw their errors and recanted.[23]

The campaign launched on 2 July 1951 did not of course, any
more than in the case of the anticosmopolitan campaign, mark
the beginning of official hostility to so-called bourgeois nationalism. Also, both this specific campaign and the general mood that
produced it had their origins outside the field of literature. Hostility towards bourgeois nationalism made itself felt in other
fields, notably history, where some historians were criticized for
works glorifying the non-Russian national heroes who had re-
sisted tsarist Russian advances in the nineteenth century. These
heroes were now seen to be feudal brigands, reactionaries, and
Anglo-Turkish agents; and annexation to tsarist Russia was seen

22. Also under attack was the libretto, written by V. Vasilevskaya and A.
Korneichuk, of K. Dankevich's opera *Bogdan Khmelnitsky*.
23. Sosyura recanted at a plenary session of the Board of Ukrainian Writers,
reported in *Literaturnaya gazeta*, 4 August 1951. Prokofyev admitted his error
in a letter printed in *Pravda*, 30 July 1951.

to be a progressive phenomenon.[24] In the strictly political sphere
the campaign was, in essence, the other side of the medal of anti-
cosmopolitanism. One of the chief arguments in the anticosmopolitan campaign had been that American imperialism was pro-
pagating cosmopolitan ideas in order to make other nations forget
their pride in their national heritage and thus become more
pliable, more amenable to American domination. This same procedure of which America had been accused was now being
applied, *mutatis mutandis*, to all peoples of the Soviet Union
other than the Great Russians. Soviet patriotism demanded that
they condemn the past and praise the new. They must never
forget their place in the great Soviet family of nations, nor their
debt to the great Russian people. In place of the old 'feudal'
heroes, who had fought the Russians, new heroes were now to be
found for them, men who had seen the importance of close ties
with Russia and, if at all possible, had had some sort of contact
with members of the Russian nineteenth-century progressive
intelligentsia. Within the Great Russian people, the same sort of

24. The view once held, later disparagingly associated with Pokrovsky's name,
had been that annexation to tsarist Russia was enslavement, and therefore an
'evil'. This theory of 'absolute evil' was superseded by the 'lesser evil' theory,
according to which annexation to Russia had been a 'lesser evil' than the
alternatives—internal feuding and annexation to reactionary Turkey or Iran.
This rather grudging recognition of Russia's positive role was later seen to be
inadequate. It was pointed out with a certain Marxist logic that: (1) Russia,
by drawing precapitalist countries into the 'maelstrom of the world economy',
had historically played an objective-progressive role, and (2) annexation had
brought these people into contact with the Russian working class—the revolutionary vanguard. This statement of the three views is necessarily over-
simplified (for instance some evil results of colonialism were admitted, but were
regarded as being outweighed by the positive results). But it will be seen to be
essentially correct by reference to, e.g. M. Mustafyev, 'O formule "naimenshee
zlo",' *Voprosy istorii*, No. 9, 1951, pp. 97–101, or to M. D. Bagirov, 'K voprosu
o kharaktere dvizhenia myuridizma i Shamilya', *Bolshevik*, No. 13, 1950, pp.
21–37. It is interesting to note, as indeed Bagirov does with some regret, that as
recently as 1947 Shamil's movement had been regarded as 'a liberating and
progressive phenomenon'. *Voprosy istorii*, No. 11, 1947, in an article entitled
'Diskussia o dvizhenii Shamilya', reported that Kh. G. Adzhemyan, advancing
at a meeting the theory that the struggle of the Northern Caucasian hillmen
under Shamil was a negative phenomenon, ran into heavy opposition from
other historians, who maintained that Adzhemyan was idealizing tsarist colonial
policy and reviving old colonialist viewpoints. However, by 1951 Adzhemyan's
views had become official. After 1956 the whole question was reopened and
seems still to be in doubt. See Lowell R. Tillett, 'Shamil and Muridism in Recent
Soviet Historiography', *American Slavic and East European Review*, Vol. 2,
April 1961, pp. 253—69.

logic was applied to discourage regionalism; Leningrad writers, for instance, were accused of regionalism.[25]

The lessons for literature were obvious. There was to be no glorification of outmoded ways of life, no nostalgia for an 'eternal' Russia, no idle dreaming on the beauties of nature; the eye that scanned the steppe was to take note of the combines and the construction projects. All possible stress was to be laid on the transformations which had taken place, were taking place and would take place under the Soviet regime. Thus the campaign against bourgeois nationalism, which was in conformity with the spirit of the 1946 decrees, was designed to stifle once again any manifestations of apolitical literature and to reaffirm the need for ideological purity.[26]

Fadeyev and the Young Guard

The predicament of the Soviet writer at this time was difficult indeed. And of the many sores that plagued him one of the worst, undoubtedly, was the complete lack of any feeling of security. That the first publication of a work had evoked no criticism or had even elicited praise was no guarantee of its fate in the future; a shift in the ideological climate or even Stalin's caprice could be enough to reverse the official evaluation of the work overnight. Sosyura, as has been noted, was in 1951 called on to make amends for a poem written in 1944. But the classic example of such re-evaluation was provided when Fadeyev was called on to rewrite *The Young Guard*. Fadeyev was by no means the only writer who was obliged to rewrite, but his case was, perhaps, the most sensational for two reasons: first, Fadeyev in his capacity as Secretary-General of the Writers' Union was a power among writers and frequently acted as hatchet man and spokesman of the Party; second, *The Young Guard* had in 1946 been hailed as a success and awarded a Stalin Prize. In December 1947, Fadeyev was informed by *Kultura i zhizn* and then by *Pravda* that his novel, which described the heroic underground struggle waged against the Germans by the young Komsomols of Krasnodon, had omitted 'the main thing which characterizes the life, growth

25. In particular, of course, Prokofyev. See the *Pravda* editorial 'Ob oshibkakh v poezii Aleksandra Prokofyeva', 25 July 1951.

26. Worthy of mention among other measures designed to reinforce the Zhdanov line is the Central Committee decree of January 1949, criticizing *Znamya* for its lax editorial policy. See *Literaturnaya gazeta*, 15 January 1949.

and work of a Komsomol—the guiding, educational role of the Party and the Party organization'.[27] He was also taken to task for describing Soviet disorganization in face of the advancing German army. Fadeyev repaired these omissions, bringing out a revised version in 1951—just before the celebration of his fiftieth birthday, on which occasion another *Pravda* editorial expressed the view that after revision 'a good book has been made still better'.[28] Perhaps owing to the good grace and alacrity with which he accepted the 1947 criticism, Fadeyev appears to have been in no way penalized because of his 'error'; he retained his position in the Writers' Union, continued to preside at meetings and head delegations, and played, as noted, a leading and semi-official role in the anticosmopolitan campaign. The article specifically devoted to Fadeyev in the third volume of the Academy history of Soviet literature (which, in general, by its format and tone has something of the unreality of a college year-book) attempts to represent the chore of revision as more self-imposed than imposed from without; Fadeyev is described as being himself dissatisfied with his first version and needing only the gentlest of nudges from *Pravda*, which as it were echoed his own thoughts, before going back to work on a new version. However, this view of the matter is scarcely credible.[29] Greater reliance can, in this particular instance, be placed on the testimony of Simonov who in 1956 maintained that the task of revising the novel had been imposed from without—by none other than Stalin.[30]

27. ' "Molodaya guardia" na stsene nashikh teatrov', *Pravda*, 3 December 1947. See also *Kultura i zhizn*, 30 November 1947. Actually, as pointed out by Avrahm Yarmolinsky (*op. cit.*, p. 66), in the 1947 edition 'the picture of fear and confusion during the evacuation of Krasnodon was somewhat toned down'; also a favourable review in *Pravda* as early as 11 March 1946, did contain the criticism that the role of the Party was not adequately portrayed in the novel.

28. See 'Novoe izdanie romana A. Fadeyeva "Molodaya gvardia" ', *Pravda*, 23 December 1951.

29. *Op. cit.*, p. 177. The article refers to a speech made by Fadeyev in early 1947 in which he admitted that, from the artistic viewpoint, there were too many characters in the book, but maintained that truth and respect for the dead had compelled him to put them all in. However, a look at the speech in question, 'Vstrecha s chitatelyami', in Aleksandr Fadeyev, *Za tridtsat let*, Moscow, 1957, pp. 931–35, reveals that Fadeyev is speaking not of the Party members, whose role he was to be called on to inflate, but of the Komsomols already in the first version. Nevertheless, given Fadeyev's alleged concern for truth, it was, according to the Academy history, impossible for him to ignore documentary evidence which conveniently came to light after the writing of the first version and which allegedly established beyond doubt the important role played by the Party in the Krasnodon underground.

The Appeal for Satire and Fuller Characterization

Up to now attention has been concentrated exclusively on
events which show the Party using its authority to stifle literary
freedoms. There had also been times when the Party used its
influence to curb some of the worst excesses engendered by its
own policies.[31] But, by and large, it was not till 1952 that the top
leadership became sufficiently conscious of the hopeless situation
in literature to be willing to take a step which might ultimately
be calculated to provide a more favourable climate for the writers.

Enough has already been said to render superfluous any further insistence on the difficulties confronting the writer. It should
be remembered that, though it seems not unfair to picture the
regime as basically indifferent to literary values, the regime too
had its difficulties. The regime's dilemma lay in the necessity of
insuring ideological orthodoxy without entirely alienating the
reading public and thus defeating its own purpose. On the side
of the regime were advantages it would not have enjoyed in the
West. First, the public was more recently literate and more avid
for reading. Second, it was not able, as in the West, to take refuge
in paper-back thrillers which were non-existent in the Soviet
Union. Finally, the Soviet public, more politically aware and
more politically indoctrinated than its Western counter-part and
often deprived in its reading of purely literary pleasures, was willing to find a sort of vitiated substitute pleasure from observing
the way in which various authors handled various politically
pregnant situations. These advantages notwithstanding, the
Soviet public expressed such choice as it had in preference for
translations of world classics and the classics of nineteenth-century Russia. Soviet literature, 'the most advanced literature in
the world', was being neglected. Its trite problems and pat 'solutions' evoked no enthusiasm. The campaign for satire, instituted

30. See 'Literaturnye zametki', *Novy mir*, No. 12, 1956.
31. The following examples may be mentioned: (1) After the rout of the
'cosmopolitans' some of their criticisms of Soviet drama were taken into account
by those very people who had joined in the campaign against them. See H.
Swayze, 'Soviet Literary Politics, 1946–1956', Chapter II: (2) The critic A. Belik
was criticized in *Pravda*, 30 March 1950, in an article entitled 'Protiv oposhlenia
literaturnoi kritiki'. Belik had written an article 'O nekotorykh oshibkakh v
literaturovedenii', *Oktyabr*, No. 2, 1950, pp. 150–64, which in effect suggested
that the method of socialist realism presupposed a uniform socialist realist
style; (3) Stalin's 1950 article on linguistics seems to have made for a slightly
more relaxed atmosphere.

in 1952 from above, may be seen as an attempt, half-hearted though it was, to re-inject a little life into literature. Here again the original impulse probably came from outside the sphere of literature: the campaign was almost certainly connected with a more general desire to counteract the evil effects of a widespread official complacency—itself the product of the official postwar Kremlin line. The 1952 campaign for satire went hand in hand with the debunking of the so-called 'no-conflict' theory.

It is, of course, true that throughout the entire period from 1946 there had been talk of conflicts within Soviet society between the new and the old, the advanced and the backward. During all this time there had also been talk about the 'remnants of capitalism' in men's minds. There had been talk of the bureaucrats, liars, toadies and swindlers in 'our' midst. There had, we have seen, been talk of the need for conflict in drama and of the need for satire. But the arrogant self-satisfaction and official complacency of the regime, the anticosmopolitan campaign and, to a lesser extent, the campaign against bourgeois nationalism had created an atmosphere which warned the writer that he must tread with extreme caution if he was to present a 'conflict' which would not be a 'slander' against Soviet reality.

The restrictions created by this atmosphere had been rationalized in various ways. Going the rounds for some years had been the idea that under the Soviet order the old-type conflicts could no longer occur; and the new-type conflict often enough centred on advanced production techniques versus backward ones. There was also the notion that conflict in the Soviet Union did not occur between the good and the bad, but between the good and the better, or the good and the excellent; there had even been attempts to maintain that the new art would centre not around conflicts but around 'misunderstandings'. These various rationalizations and attitudes had come unofficially to be known as the no-conflict theory. This 'theory', in one or another of its variations, had from 1946 on occasionally appeared in print. It had never received official sanction and had from time to time been dismissed as incorrect. It was now held up to the ridicule it deserved.

The debunking of the no-conflict theory took the form, which we recognize as customary in Soviet letters, of an attack on specific individuals. The main victim in this case was the Stalin Prize-

winning playwright, Nikolai Virta. It has been his misfortune
to have made one of the then most recent no-conflict statements.
Attacked by a fellow playwright, Virta immediately recanted.
His recantation *Let Us Speak Frankly*, is of interest for the intimate light it sheds on the headaches plaguing the writer during
this period. He explains that his mistake in adopting the no-conflict theory

arose as a consequence of 'cold observations of the mind' on the
manner in which those of our plays which contain sharp life conflicts passed through the barbed-wire obstacles of the agencies in
charge of the repertoire. As I have already said, everything living,
true to life, sharp, fresh and unstereotyped was combed out and
smoothed out to the point where it was no longer recognizable. Every
bold, unstereotyped word in a play had to be defended at the cost of
the playwright's nerves and the play's quality.[32]

This article was the most outspoken and damning indictment
of Soviet literary politics to be written in the period between 1946
and Stalin's death. Virta's frank speaking was applauded by the
poet I. Selvinsky in an article entitled *Poetry Requests the
Floor*.[33] But a few days later Surkov, a more or less official spokesman in the Writers' Union, came out with an article *In Debt
to the People*, which not only rightly demolished the no-conflict theory but made a vicious and unfair attack on Virta.[34]
The latter was berated as cynical, unprincipled, lacking in
modesty, ideologically unstable. He was taken to task for having
attempted to lay on others (the bureaucrats and critics) the blame
for his own mistakes. His frankness had not been appreciated.

Meanwhile *Pravda* had chosen the occasion of the centenary
of Gogol's death to proclaim the need for satire, announcing that
'we need our Gogols and Shchedrins'[35]. All was not well in the
Union of Soviet Socialist Republics; there were still many shortcomings; it was the duty of writers mercilessly to attack and
expose them. These points *Pravda* again emphasized in a
lengthy, unsigned editorial, 'Overcome the Lag in Dramaturgy',
on 7 April 1952.[36]

32. 'Pogovorim otkrovenno,' *Sovetskoe iskusstvo*, 29 March 1952.
33. 'Poezia prosit slova', *Sovetskoe iskusstvo*, 5 April 1952.
34. 'V dolgu pered narodom', *Literaturnaya gazeta*, 8 April 1952.
35. 'Nikolai Vasilevich Gogol', *Pravda*, 4 March 1952.

It goes without saying that there were limits beyond which the writers were warned not to go. Gogols and Shchedrins may have been needed; not Zamyatins and Zoshchenkos. The criticism contained in satire was to scourge the old, but it was to affirm the new. It was, in fact, not a call to freedom, merely an autocratic diverting of writers' energies into new channels. But it did, whatever the Kremlin's intent, however confining the written and unwritten limits of satire may have been, give writers some chance to touch on the less admirable but more interesting sides of human nature.

At the same time, a demand was voiced for fuller and more true-to-life characterization. The same *Pravda* editorial of 7 April which had called for Gogols and Shchedrins had also set the lead in criticizing works in which the heroes were depicted as entirely absorbed in production problems. Articles began to appear on this subject. 'Plays', wrote one playwright and critic, 'must portray the working man in a comprehensive and detailed manner. To portray a worker does not mean to bring a turner onto the stage at the moment when he is turning out a mold. We must get to know his inner world, his loves, his friendships, the whole range of feelings and passions which possess him, and embody all these in clear characters which make an impression on the audience. But of late the characters in many of our plays and films have lost the ability to love, to be jealous or indignant or to hate . . . For example, in Aleksandr Bek's *New Profile* the heroes, Shumeyko and Nina, confess their love while collating analyses of a metal—without taking time off from work, so to speak.' [37]

Many similar comments began to appear. For instance, on 28 August 1952, *Pravda* complained in an editorial on motion pictures: 'Not infrequently the authors of scripts subordinate the rich material of life to a set scheme, depicting the workers and collective farmers in a one-sided way as persons entirely absorbed in technical interests.' To show characters only at the work bench was to fail, it was now revealed, to do justice to the rich and many-sided nature of Soviet man.

Critical articles sought to expose the ridiculous lengths to

36. 'Preodolet otstavanie v dramaturgii'.
37. A. Sofronov, 'Za pravdu zhizni', *Literaturnaya gazeta*, 27 May 1952.

which authors had been driven by the overemphasizing of production problems. In one play the conflict centres around which
crop should be sown. The wife, who favours the 'advanced' crop,
leaves her husband, a collective-farm chairman, who still clings
to the 'backward' crop. Eventually the right crop is sown, he
sees the error of his ways, she returns, the play ends happily. But,
it is discerningly pointed out, this is an artificially contrived plot
and, though intended to glorify Soviet people by showing how
seriously they take their production problems, actually has the
effect of belittling them. If a wife is going to pack her bags on
every occasion of disagreement with her husband over a production problem, what price Soviet marriage? And what confidence
can the husband have when sowing time comes around next
year?

Another story apparently described the heroism of a collective
farm worker who fell ill from exhaustion during harvest time.
Rather than lay off for a few days he disregarded the doctor's
advice and went right on working. Some days later he keels over
and dies. It is again pointed out that this highly unlikely story has
the effect not of glorifying but of diminishing the Soviet people.
If the worker in question had had an ounce of common sense,
he would have survived to gather in many future harvests. Furthermore, his foolhardy attitude belittled Soviet medicine!

In yet another work the young hero makes a rendezvous with
his girl in the woods. She gets there ahead of time and begins
to wonder why he wanted to meet her. Perhaps to discuss production problems, she thinks! [38]

The demand for fuller characterization, though here too there
were prescribed limits, could be accounted a partial step in the
direction of greater freedom. Though writers were undoubtedly
aware that this was one more tightrope to walk, they would at
least be spared the necessity of loading their books with unnecessary and intensely boring technological details. And indeed from
1952 on attempts were made to invest characters with more individual personality traits than previously.

Tipichnost ('typicalness')

At the Nineteenth Party Congress in the autumn of 1952 it was

38. Dm. Shcheglov's 'Gde sosny shumyat' was thus criticized in the above-
mentioned *Pravda* editorial which also pointed out that production problems
provided the main topic of conversation even at a wedding feast.

Malenkov who gave the keynote speech.[39] He devoted little space
to literature—a sin of omission for which he was later criticized,
after he had been ousted from the Party presidium and relegated
to the management of an obscure hydroelectric station. His
brief remarks did little to change the situation. He followed the
prevailing line in stressing the need for satire. And he re-emphasized the concept of *tipichnost*. *Tipichnost* is, of course, an elastic term. 'The typical', Malenkov said in part, 'is not only what is
encountered most frequently but that which most fully and vividly expressed the essence of a given socio-historical phenomenon.
In the Marxist Leninist interpretation, the typical does not at all
mean some statistical average.' Thus *tipichnost* does not necessarily by any means involve an invitation to the writer to describe
what he most often sees in everyday life. The essence of a given
phenomenon is, according to the Hegelian or Marxist-Leninist
dialectic, the new which is coming in to oust the old. Thus the
demand for *tipichnost*, at its most restrictive, comes close to
Zhdanov's 1946 exhortation 'to show our people not only in their
to-day, but to look forward to their tomorrow'. Why did Malenkov thus emphasize *tipichnost*? A *Kommunist* editorial written
at the end of 1955 rejected the idea whereby 'the typical is reduced to the essence of a given socio-historical phenomenon'. It
discredited too the idea of a close tie-in between *tipichnost* and
partiynost, also posited by Malenkov in 1952 when he spoke of *tipichnost* as 'the basic sphere of the manifestation of *partiynost* in
realist art'. It further denied that the problem of *tipichnost* was
inevitably a political problem and spoke glowingly of the 'typical'
characters created by such obviously non-Marxist 'reactionary'
writers as Balzac and Tolstoy.[40] That this liberal *Kommunist* editorial was undoubtedly aimed at Malenkov need not concern us
here. Of immediate interest is its confirmation of the thesis
that Malenkov's pronouncements on *tipichnost* were restrictive
rather than liberal in intent. It is true, as has been pointed out
by Yarmolinsky, that shortly after the Nineteenth Party Congress the concept of the typical was expanded to include negative
phenomena.[41] Nevertheless, I am inclined to think that the

39. *Pravda*, 6 October 1952.
40. 'K voprosu o tipicheskom v literature i iskusstve', *Kommunist*, No. 18,
1955, pp. 12–23.
41. See Yarmolinsky, *op. cit.*, p. 144. Yarmolinsky does not, of course, interpret this as a step in the direction of liberalism.

re-emphasizing in 1952 of *tipichnost*, for what it was worth (and the whole question is no more than a footnote in the history of the period), was motivated by the desire to provide some sort of vague counterweight to the call for satire and for fuller characterization.

This raises a further question. Was any counterweight needed? Can anything remotely approaching liberalism be read into the 1952 appeal for satire and fuller characterization? I have already described this appeal as an autocratic diverting of writers' energies into new channels. But I would not go so far as to label the clamour for satire 'empty phrases' [42]. This is a period in which all the colours are so sombre that one may be forgiven for trying to distinguish black from dark grey. Though certainly the call for satire and for fuller characterization was not liberal in intent (liberal is anyway too strong a word), the regime must have been aware that writers would respond by writing otherwise than they would have written, had the call never gone out. It is difficult to escape the conclusion that, confronted with the dilemma of reader apathy, also probably motivated by considerations lying outside the domain of literature, the regime had taken a very small but deliberate step to facilitate the writer's task.

It is idle to speculate what would have happened, had Stalin not died in March 1953. The incident of the 'doctors' plot' indicates clearly that the whole country, to say nothing of its writers, still lay in the grip of a paranoiac and unpredictable personality. The far-reaching changes that took place after his death have overshadowed and rendered insignificant the minor shift that, I believe, took place in 1952. That some shift did nevertheless occur is, in my opinion, borne out by the response of various writers. A good example is provided by Kazakevich's *Heart of a Friend*, published in January 1953, in which both war and sex are described with a degree of realism which was noticeably lacking in his 1949 *Spring on the Oder*.

In looking back over the period, the main events which stand out are: (1) the 1946–48 decrees; (2) the anticosmopolitan campaign; (3) the campaign against bourgeois nationalism. The close connexion between them has already been pointed out; they are, in fact, only different links in a single chain. But in the 1952 call for satire and fuller characterization may possibly be seen the first

42. See Yarmolinsky, p. 140.

faint harbinger of a slightly different policy, no less orthodox, no less authoritarian, but freed perhaps of some of the grosser absurdities and crasser excesses of the preceding years.

The effect of Zhdanovism on Soviet literature was devastating. What, it may be asked in conclusion, was its effect on Soviet men of letters? The effect varied, of course, with the individual and it is quite impossible to know how each individual reacted. I would nevertheless like to hazard a few general conjectures. That Zhdanovism restricted the writer in his work as a writer there can be no doubt. The point is, rather, how did he feel about these restrictions and how was he able to live as writer and human being—with these restrictions? Some writers undoubtedly hewed more or less willingly to the official line under the impulse of fear or cynicism. But any such explanation can never be more than partially valid. Soviet writers are not a particularly cowardly or cynical lot and many of them have displayed a great deal of courage. The fact has to be faced that many writers, though no doubt frustrated by the restrictions, derived enjoyment from their work and genuinely felt that they were serving the Soviet cause.

One reason for this accommodation lies in the fact that there was no way out. It was not a matter of setting one's courage on the line, not a matter of the courage of one individual; in its wisdom the regime had made ideological orthodoxy a collective responsibility, and consequently an unacceptable piece of writing brought trouble on the head not of the author alone but also of the editor, the editorial board, the 'creative section', the Writers' Union and any other person or body involved. Under these circumstances the choice was simple—silence or accommodation; and when there is no escape, most animals will choose the path of accommodation. But how could these men, sensitive intellectuals as many of them were, live at peace with themselves and preserve their self-respect, knowing, as most of them knew, that what they wrote was not the whole truth and was sometimes the reverse of truth? The answer lies, I believe, in a sort of conspiracy of silence reminiscent of the situation depicted by Dostoevsky in his *Legend of the Grand Inquisitor*. The feeding to the people of myth and distorted truth can easily be thought of as a tactical necessity—of benefit to the people. So that a certain amount of falsehood becomes not incompatible with devoted, patriotic service. This sort of silence, conspiracy of silence, is thus not only imposed; it is also self-imposed. And restrictive and frustrating thought it often must be, it does contain some small element of self-flattery, for it puts one in a position of superiority relative to the less enlightened people, the backward flock. One acquires, as it were, the Hegelian freedom of understanding necessity.

This attitude—this complicity in myth, this conspiracy in silence and half-truth—was, I believe, by no means confined to Soviet writers. It is difficult to judge just how widespread it was, but most Westerners who spent time in the Soviet Union during the period under review and had even cursory contact with intellectuals will surely attest the fact that the 'sophisticated' view which rather condescended toward the people and saw the people as being capable of absorbing only so much truth—for its own sake—was by no means a rare phenomenon. For these people, including the writers, the end of the Stalin era and, in particular, the de-Stalinization policy of 1956, welcome though it was for most, must have presented some complicated moral and psychological problems. Pomerantsev's insistence in 1954 on sincerity in literature and the demand in 1956, expressed by the more idealistic writers, for the whole truth and for truth whatever the cost are, in my view, sure indications not (as was sometimes naively maintained in the Western press in 1956) of any desire to upset the Soviet regime, nor yet merely of an overly eager desire to support the line laid down at the Twentieth Party Congress (though this weighed heavily). They were also indications (and this is the point I wish to stress here) of the grim and complicated hoops of psychological and moral adjustment and accommodation through which many Soviet writers were obliged to jump between 14 August 1946 and 5 March 1953.

7

SOVIET LITERATURE
DURING THE THAW

George Gibian

What the Thaw Was

It may be time to take another look at the Soviet literary
situation between 1954 and 1960, or, in the narrower sense,
1954 and 1957. More recent literary works and later social
and political developments in the USSR help to cast some light
on the Thaw, which perhaps appears to our hindsight arranged
in a slightly different configuration than it did originally.

The general outlines of the literature of the Thaw will by now
be well known to the readers of *The Times* of London or New
York, not to mention *Survey, Encounter*, or the various
monographs and general studies of Russia since Stalin. There
would be little point in rehearsing once more lists of authors,
works, apologias and attacks, recantations and stubborn silences,
manuscripts smuggled abroad, awards of Lenin Prizes, Writers'
Congresses, Khrushchev's literary exhortations, Pomerantsev on
'Sincerity', and the post-mortems on *Not By Bread Alone* and
Literary Moscow, volume II. The literary politics of the period,
in particular, in the sense in which the sadly appropriate term
has come to be used technically, have been more than adequately
described in several works, the most recent of them being the
study by Harold Swayze.

What justification there may be for returning to the subject
rests in this question: in what ways does the literature of the
Thaw appear differently to us now, in contrast to those of its
aspects to which we were alive when it was being published? We
ought to know more about the subject than we did eight or five
years ago. Studies have been published in the West; inside Soviet
Russia, too, a temporary entombment of the period has been
effected in a few chapters of the last volume of the three-volume

Academy of Sciences *History of Soviet Literature*. The major
works are now fairly widely known. The passage of time has
bestowed on us the freedom to change emphases through com-
parisons now made retroactively possible: we can trace in the
period tendencies leading to landmarks erected only in recent
years. As always in history, we give slightly more emphasis to
those elements of the past, which, we now see, were harbingers
(or ancestors) of what was to follow—those authors who still interest us (which may mean continued to write and drew more
attention to themselves, or became better writers, or came to
stand for something—as, for example, did Evtushenko, Kazakov,
Tendryakov). A story such as Kazakov's *Blue and Green* was considered remarkable by only a few observers in 1957; in retrospect
I would attribute greater importance to it.

A further contribution to our image of the literature of the
Thaw has been made by Soviet literary authorities, who, after
months of vacillation, drew at least some lines of demarcation
for us—consisting mainly of a list of works which are no longer
to be both attacked and defended (as happened in 1955–56 and
early 1957), but may only be used, henceforth, as deterrent examples. In 1956 it was possible to wonder how far the Thaw would
continue to melt Stalinist glaciers. Now, despite some continuing
vagueness, limits have emerged. There is a canonical list, an outline index, consisting, beside other taboo works, of a few works
in *Literary Moscow* (volume II), Granin's *Opinion of One's Own*,
Dudintsev's *Not by Bread Alone*. One of our tasks later will be to
attempt to define what in the view of Soviet officials is special
about these works, why they have been declared beyond the pale
(although their authors may continue to publish other,
approvable works), whereas other writings, to some extent similar,
are not condemned. What are the *differentiae* of these rejected
books?

One reason why the label 'Thaw' has become widely accepted
for the period is that Ilya Ehrenburg's novel of that name expressed cogently a whole set of attitudes and problems which
many people in Russia had dimly sensed, but which had not been
comprehensively expressed in print. Another reason for the
vitality of the label is the appropriateness of its image. It con-
notes the objects of the hopes of many Russians in 1954 and by
implication suggests the situation before Stalin died. Soviet Russia

had been frozen, rigid, cold. The thaw suggests a melting, the approach of warmth and spring, general improvement, a lightening of burdens, a softening of rigidities—or an unfolding—or the resumption of growth, a rejuvenation, rebirth, a general easing. All these rather vague words, rich in connotations, will later have to be translated into more concrete terms—as they were expressed in literature. But a thaw can certainly not last indefinitely and will hardly have a prolonged duration. The term suggests a process, a becoming, not a static condition. It is a transition—how long can a transitional period last? Can it become fixed at a certain point within the flux, and not thereby cease to be itself, a thaw, and become something else? Is this not what has happened with the Soviet Thaw of 1954–58? Our discussion may suggest that the term Thaw, appropriate as it was to the process which began in 1954, is misleading and inadequate as a description for the new bounds and rigidities which supervened later. The trouble with metaphors used for elucidation is that at a certain point they begin to break down.

A fruitful approach to sketching a map of the literary scene, with equivalents for the four points of the compass, within which to locate various Soviet writers, may be made by reference to their attitudes towards, and representations of, two poles: ideology and reality. In any culture, there is a gap between the ideal image of what its present situation, values, vitalizing principles, mission in the world and ultimate future are or will be. and between the realities of its concrete existence. In the United States, for example, in the last 150 years, an important fact useful in studying American thought and writing has been the discrepancy between the view of America as an innocent, pastoral land, unlike the workshops of Europe, and the real conditions of life in a country bent on undoing its innocence as well as other qualities similar to those of a Garden of Eden and on 'catching up with and surpassing' the industrial, mechanistic life of the Old Word.

In the Soviet Union of the 1950's we can distinguish two groups of relationships. The first is that between a writer's view of the reality of Soviet life and the official interpretation of that reality. This includes: literary representations of individual characters and the official versions of what Soviet people are; the writer's attitude towards their being such as he represents (approval, condemnation, neutral acceptance); his interpretation of

the causes which produced them, their typicality or excep-
tionality, their projected future; and the relation between such a
judgement and the official views of where they 'belong' historically, morally and socially.

Secondly, there is the relationship between the official ideology,
with its partially Utopian view of present day Soviet Russia and
its totally Utopian projection of its future development, and
whatever in a work of literature, openly or by implication, may
be read as a comment upon these views. There is very little open
contradiction of official ideology by writers, except in literature
'for the drawer' and in *Doctor Zhivago*. A few essays published
in 1956 came close to questioning Party control in matters of
culture. But there are books in which elements of plot, character,
or attitude seem tacitly to contradict parts of official Soviet
ideology. Here it is essential to pay attention to the nuances of
views expressed by what character, under what circumstances; to
the extent to which his opinions are refuted or left suspended; to
whether other elements of the book (themes, mood, outcome)
reinforce or nullify those views. Sometimes the divergence may
take the form of merely implicitly setting forth an alternative
ideology—a set of values which serves as the tacit norm of reference within the work, different from the official Soviet ideology,
without ever coming into overt conflict (or even any direct contact) with it.

Major Topics

From the literature of the Thaw it is possible to abstract a set
of subjects to which the writers were particularly attracted. Some
of them are political, others social or individual; it is difficult at
times to separate the ethical reflection from the specific, concrete
observation. They include wishes for change; new areas of life
to depict in a book; expressions of shifts in attitude. The following is a partial list of enlargements of scope in subject matter and
of changes in the directions in which the writers' tendentiousness
was pointed—one way of summing up the general shift which
occurred in Soviet literature in the late 1950's. These topics and
preferences were on the whole given more emphasis during the
Thaw than previously:

(1) Admissions of the gulf between reassuring slogans and press
reports on one hand and the realities of Soviet life on the other.

Economic and social abuses are shown to exist on a large scale.

(2) The demand for more truthfulness in public and private life; less mere propaganda, greater openness in conceding inadequacies, failures both of Soviet institutions and men highly placed in them: frankness in referring to the seamy side of material conditions.

(3) Hopes for an end to political repression and witchhunting; less petty tyranny on all levels of life, in industry and in political organizations.

(4) Fewer privileges for highly placed officials; an almost Marxian analysis of social inequalities in Soviet Russia.

(5) Greater flexibility (adjustment to the concrete situation at hand), less red tape, more individual initiative.

(6) More attention to concrete, material improvement of life, as opposed to lip-service to abstract ideals and goals.

(7) More confidence and respect in dealing with human beings, who are regarded as needing a sense of personal dignity.

(8) Greater tolerance and forgiveness for suspects—former prisoners of war, inmates of labour camps, people with foreign associations.

(9) Presentation of characters (not necessarily as positive heroes) who express cynical views about human nature and particularly about Soviet slogans; depiction of selfish, suspicious, greedy individuals in such a manner as to show that not everybody had been re-educated into a New Soviet Man.

(10) Related to the previous point, a shift in the kind of 'villains' or 'negative characters' presented. More of them were now depicted as highly placed bureaucrats, not isolated cases, but members of a numerous group, sometimes even, it was suggested, typical products of Soviet (Stalinist) conditions rather than unregenerate survivors of prerevolutionary conditions.

(11) Increasing concern with emotional, private experiences of individuals; a more sympathetic attitude in the representation of divorces and love affairs.

Hopes for the changes such as those listed above were probably shared by a substantial proportion of the population at large. Some of them were also adopted by the Party leadership after Stalin's death. In furthering them through the didactic influence of their writings, some of the authors, then, were doing the work the Party wished them to pursue. Some Western

observers were inclined to read into the Thaw goals which their
own compatriots might have been expected to hold in comparable circumstances: the desire to shake off Communist Party
controls, to escape the confines of socialist realism, a thirst for an
Open Society, a movement towards some approximation of a
pluralistic ideology and possibly a bi- or multiparty political
system. Such an interpretation is consciously or unconsciously
based on regarding the institutions and ingrained habits of
Britain, or France, or the United States as the poles towards
which any movement with a 'liberal' tendency is likely to move.
Only a very small section of Soviet writing has given support to
such a view. The aspirations of most writers were more limited
in scope, being confined within the basic boundaries of the Soviet
social and political structure.

Some Categories of Literary Works

There are many ways of classifying the literature of the Thaw,
none of which is completely satisfactory; yet some grouping is
necessary. Admitting the eclecticism of our criteria, as well as the
fact that some of the works could be fitted into several categories,
which to some extent overlap, we may mention the following
groups:

I. *Late Works of Established Writers.* Books published by
authors who had made their reputations considerably earlier:
Leonid Leonov's *Russian Forest*, a revised version of *The Golden
Chariot*, and a new version of *The Thief*; Kaverin, parts of *The
Open Book*; Sholokhov, *Man's Fate* and later the second volume
of *Virgin Soil Upturned*; Fedin, *Fire (Kostyor)*; books by Panfyorov, Gladkov, Fadeyev and others. Two other works which
could be listed here are Ehrenburg's *Thaw*, which, although also
a work by an author prolific in the 1920's and 1930's, thematically
fits better into a later category; and Konstantin Simonov's *The
Living and the Dead*, a novel published in 1960, but written between 1955 and 1959. In some of its themes it speaks not only for
the Thaw but also the 'Settlement' which followed the Thaw.

Two observations suggest themselves here. One is that to a
surprising extent these older authors were attuned to the changes
in the atmosphere. Many of their works show deviations from
their authors' previous writings, in the direction in which the

times were moving. Leonov's *Russian Forest,* for example, among other things conforms to the new concepts of the villain to be represented in literature, the predilection for scientific-scholarly topics, and the stress on personal themes. But the new topics can be better studied in the works of some younger men.

The second point is that most of the significant works, characteristic of the Thaw, were written by members of the younger generations—not by the Grand Old Men of Soviet literature. The literature of the Thaw is the product of writers who emerged during and after the war—except for Ilya Ehrenburg's important role.

II. *Works Remarkable for their Psychological Method,* primarily Nekrasov's *Home Town* and Nikolayeva's *Battle on the Way.* In some passages in both works we see something like a 'New Realism', which may be a way of saying 'a representation of human behaviour faithful to the way in which our own literature has led us to view it'. This is not to claim, as some Soviet critics did, that Nekrasov can be reduced to definable Hemingway factors. There are, in his story of former soldiers returning to ruined Kiev, pages describing the numbness of the main characters which convey superbly the sense of postwar shock, of being wrenched out of one's normal contact with conventions, social life, human beings. The novel is based on a direct rendering of experience, unadorned, unvarnished, brutal, such as could rarely be found in Stalinist literature.

Battle on the Way similarly, conveys with accuracy psychological states seldom studied in Soviet literature of the preceding years. Among these are the state of mind of a dedicated communist whose husband is falsely accused and arrested, the loss of one's faith in the Party, and the paralysis which ensues:

Life presented a puzzle to her. People built new machines, changed the course of rivers, dug canals, built gigantic dams and hydroelectric stations and rejoiced in that. Even she could not fail to see and perceive the greatness of those works and the purity of that joy. How could she reconcile all that with the blackness that tore into her life? A physiologist friend of hers had once told her about an experiment with dogs. In order to produce artificial neurosis in dogs, it was necessary to train them to be fed and petted when a bell was rung, and to receive blows when a light was turned on, and then to turn on the bell and the light at the same time. Two such simultaneous, opposed, incompatible stimuli put before the brain a task beyond its strength, and lead to a deathlike jamming of all reflexes. The dog ceases to drink and eat, loses mobility and receptivity. For hours it sits by itself, rigid, indifferent, ignoring shouting and petting. Tina reminded one of such a dog. Life put before her the task of reconciling the irreconcilable. Her soul, oppressed by the unbearable difficulty of this, fell into a deathlike paralysis.

Another passage describes the effect produced on a young boy by the disorderly, cramped life of his parents:

In good moments, his father sat down on the bed alongside his mother, stroked her face and shoulders, and, delighting in her beauty, said, 'My good one, my beautiful one, best one of all.' But if his mother as much as stirred, he shouted, 'Don't move!' For many years these words stayed in Dmitri's ears, the tender 'mine, mine', and the loud 'Don't move'. The parents' love was sometimes more horrible than the parents' fights. The son saw it all. Father, mother, and other drunken couples sometimes rolled on the floor, right then and there, in the small room. From childhood on, he was filled with loathing for that repulsive thing they called love. When he grew up, he avoided girls. What the girls were suggesting in their subconscious girlish play arose before him in its naked and coarse form.

The two novels could be studied for several other important characteristics (Nikolayeva's concern with agricultural and industrial production; their presentation of the personal lives of their characters), but it is their direct undidactic treatment of situations such as those cited above which is their outstanding strength.

III. *The Large Category of Works Most Characteristic of the Thaw.* These are works which present new themes and touch on subjects in a manner different from that prevalent in Stalin's days. They can be subdivided into:

(a) *Problems of Youth Group.* In retrospect, in view of the fact that books about the younger generation have acquired particularly great importance in the early 1960's, I am inclined to attribute greater significance to those published in the 1950's than they seemed to have at the time of their appearance. This group includes Volodin's *Factory Girl*, Rozov's *Good Luck*, and, somewhat later, Kuznetsov's *Continuation of a Legend*. Human beings, the authors show, are more complex than the black and white schemes would have us believe. Rozov's play shows young people choosing careers, wondering what to do after finishing secondary school, one set of choices being whether to strike out for oneself in the world of employment or to study in a university or institute. Another antithesis is between cynical, self-seeking considerations and idealistic, selfless service to the community and the future generations.

Kuznetsov's *Continuation of a Legend* later set the pattern for stories of young people going out to Siberia, their reactions to the journey and the new environment, meeting with fellow workers (some cynical, some idealistic), the exposure of their own ideals to the fire of hostile views, derision, even crime; and the emergence, in the end, of a chastened or, more accurately, tempered determination, shorn of highflown phrases and resting on a solid basis of principle—now matured, cleansed of unfelt, bookish slogans.

Aksyonov's *The Colleagues* and *Ticket to the Stars*, during the post-Thaw period, were to carry further this line of books about youth. The works in this category as a whole have this in common: an interest in the generation just reaching adulthood and choosing their first employment: confrontations between parroted ideals, empty Komsomol and school moralism—and cynical, sometimes nihilistic contradiction; and a sense of the Soviet Union as an expanding universe, with opportunities, areas being settled, industries developing—a forward looking, open country. It is probably the last point, as much as the two previous ones, which is responsible for the great popularity of such works in Russia.

(b) *Personal Issues Group. Works dealing problematically with Marriage, Love and Divorce.* In Pogodin's *Petrarch's Sonnet*, for instance, a sympathetic picture is given of a girl's friendship with a married man, which, the end of the play suggests, may eventually develop into love. The characters pilloried are the Mrs. Grundys and dishonest Party moralists, whereas the feelings of the hero and heroine are endowed with poetic tenderness and sincerity.

Alyoshin's *Odna* (Alone) focuses on the problem of divorce. Both the loneliness of a woman on the downward path and the disintegration of a marriage are the topics of primary interest to the playwright. Here, too, official communist institutionalized interference in personal affairs is presented unfavourably. The stress is on the situation as it affects the individuals involved, not on its relevance to broader society.

An Armenian poet translated by Evtushenko also questions the adequacy of organizations in understanding the complexity and subtlety of personal relations. He juxtaposes the two realms in his poem:

> The meeting lasted
>   for some five hours.
> They considered everything
>   They came up with the decision:
> I must
>   'interrupt relations' with you.
> What sort of a name—is that—
>   'relations'!
> They explained to me ardently and clearly
> That one must avoid
>   Family dramas.

The poet's attitude is one of dismay over the insensitivity, lack of understanding and arrogance of the 'group' which, after a bureaucratic conference, gives him directions, couched in clichés and jargon, concerning his private emotional life. A similar issue is one of the themes of Tendryakov's story *Unsuited* (*Ne ko dvoru*).

(c) *The Central 'Thaw' Group.* Works with subjects and attitudes belonging in the mainstream of these years. This group centres on Ilya Ehrenburg's *Thaw*. It raises topical issues and vigorously opposes the various abuses and rigidities understood under the name 'cult of personality and its consequences'.

In many respects these works are socialist realism turned upside down. They are committed, public spirited works, primarily didactic and moralistic. They are fiction utilized to unmask, attack—and to propose alternatives.

Here belong, besides Ehrenburg's *Thaw*, most of the stories of Ovechkin and Kalinin; Zorin's *Guests;* some of Tendryakov; Korneichuk's *Wings*, and other works. Their common trait is the profusion of the topics about which they take strong lines. Among the targets of this problem-literature are: bureaucrats more interested in their record and the outward appearance of success than in the welfare of the workers dependent on them and the real achievements of their factories or farm districts; self-satisfied workers and administrators who pay little attention to the people's needs; artists who have exchanged their integrity for truckling to the market; men who take advantage of suspicions about others to persecute them and advance themselves. The positive goals (ideal human institutions and beings) can be deduced by supplying the opposites of the qualities which these books attack.

There is much overlap, of course, between works in this group and those in the previous two, as well as in what might be called the general 'Problem Story' subgroup (into which many of Tendryakov's somewhat overvalued stories belong) and the 'Pseudo-Heterodoxy' or 'Orthodoxy in Unorthodoxy's Clothing' Group (works trying to sound like bold innovation or iconoclasm, which, however, in reality follow the Party's policy of wishing to awaken lethargic bureaucrats and to encourage improvements in planning methods and personal boldness. What is safer than to strike the pose of a courageous throne-shaking rebel, and yet be sure of a pat on the back by the occupant of the throne?). *Battle of the Way*, for example, in some respects belongs to this 'Central "Thaw" Group'. However, the distinction I am making is based on two points of difference: the principal claim to attention of the works in the Central 'Thaw' Group lies not in the excellence and originality of their psychological or other observations, as it does in the group to which I have assigned Nikolayeva's novel, nor in dealing with some one dominant theme (as do the works in the Problems of Youth or Personal Issues categories), but rather in their grape-shot at an entire list of targets, which they show to be inter-related. They create a whole climate of opinion and a set of ways of behaving, instead of delivering a sharp, concentrated blow at one topic.

IV. *The Taboo List*. These works (Dudintsev's *Not by Bread Alone*, Granin's *Opinion of One's Own*, some of those in *Literary Moscow*, volume II, and a few others), after a certain amount of controversy, were finally relegated to a short list, to be referred to on suitable occasions, of writing of the kind not to be permitted—examples of writers who went too far in the direction of revisionism, and endangered the spirit of *partiynost*. They are useful as marking the limit where criticism and proper initiative are deemed to have ceased and excess begun.

How do these works differ from those in the previous category? In what special ways have they offended? One clear

difference is their wider diffusion and greater intensity of gloom.
In Granin's story, for example, defeat, injustice, impotence lie
over the action like a heavy pall. The chief character's entire life
is blighted; he will never be courageous. All his dreams are vain,
it is made clear—no matter how high he rises, he will always feel
insufficiently secure or powerful to live up to his pristine dream
of courageously defending justice. The prevailing atmosphere of
sad resignation is a point of distinction between the accepted,
never outlawed Central 'Thaw' Group and the works on the
Taboo List.

The second difference is a matter of degree. In a Taboo work
like *Not By Bread Alone*, or Zhdanov's *Trip Home*, injustice in
high places is presented—sometimes explicitly, sometimes by implication—as very widespread. The men to whom one can appeal,
the authorities to whom to have recourse, are few. Weakening
of moral fibre, corruption, time serving, cowardice, the 'empire'
of the log-rolling, back-scratching bureaucrats, the conquest of
insititutions by the men who have sold out and seem traitors to
Soviet ideals are presented by the Taboo works as overwhelmingly
ubiquitous.

The third point, related to the second, is the outcome of the
action. Sometimes the difference seems limited to this: the acceptable story ends well, with a victory of the previously persecuted
man, the outsider who is critical of bureaucrats and engages them
in a struggle which at first may seem hopeless. (But, it must be
said, the end need not always necessarily be 'happy'. Tendryakov's *Unsuited*, for instance, refrains from patching everything
up in the conclusion. There are other ways in which the story
justifies itself from the official point of view despite the absence
of a cheerful ending).

Fourthly, the Taboo works contain passages in which a character expresses objectionable ideas not later adequately cancelled
through being contradicted by some other, positive character
or refuted by ensuing action. Such are some parts of *Not by
Bread Alone*, which disagree with the official picture of Soviet
reality. They claim that lonely men exist in Soviet Russia, that
original creative men may find themselves alone, that it may
even be desirable, or inevitable, that they be lonely, and affirm
that the life of the imagination and emotions is of such high value

that it should not have to need to wait until some kind of a 'foundation' of the economic structure is laid. Feelings and the arts are not merely 'pictures' or 'curtains' to be hung later after the important material construction is completed. Some of the passages even point at what we might consider the existence of a class structure in Soviet Russia. The literary authorities are sensitive to what may look like a step in the direction of a Marxist critique of Soviet social relations, similar to a fictional counterpart of Djilas's analysis in *The New Class*.

On the other hand, it must be admitted that on rereading, some of the works which caused a great stir in 1956 and 1957 seem, in their literary manner, more stilted, schematic, naively didactic, than they had earlier. Except for certain passages, these works seem interesting only for their 'message'.

V. *The 'Conservative' Group.* Antithetical to the Taboo List, these works during the years of the Thaw were mainly essays of literary criticism and polemics, particularly those of Sofronov, Sobolev, and so forth, and later the works of Kochetov, who was to acquire great importance with *The Brothers Ershov* and *Secretary of the Obkom*. They are marked by distrust of the intellectuals as a class; opposition to the prevalent nostalgia for the 1920's; warnings against the dangerous lengths to which liberalizing or revisionist tendencies might lead (as one of Kochetov's characters says in *The Brothers Ershov*, the relaxations might bring what happened in Hungary, where they hanged Party members from lamp posts); stress on writing about 'real heroes' —important men high in the Party and government bureaucracy, showing them as essential men, leaders beneficial to society, stalwart martyrs; calls for maintaining vigilance against internal and external enemies; the ridiculing of interest in what they consider decadent, subjective, psychological topics, as well as formalist tendencies, symbolism, myth, fantasy, abstraction, surrealism, especially in poetry and the plastic arts.

VI. *The World of Feelings Group.* All the categories of works mentioned thus far had one characteristic in common: they continued to convey 'messages' about how to live and how not to live, primarily with implications as to how society ought or ought not to be organized. It was polemical literature, argumentative and didactic. Among the lessons inculcated was the importance (or the right to autonomy) of the personal, emotional realm of life;

it was always a moral which was being preached. Even when some
of the works (*Not by Bread Alone, The Thaw*) stressed integrity
in the sense of honesty to one's artistic vision of the world, the
works themselves reported this idea, instead of applying it.

Yet a few works were written which were not mere argument. Vera Panova's books, for instance, create a world of personal relationships in which the unfolding and crossing of
human destinies is the main concern. Sholokhov's *Fate of Man*
is similar. Yuri Nagibin, who in many of his stories merely presented official Soviet pieties, wrote a few during the period of the
Thaw (and later) which are devoid of public commitment. In
these stories, he did not, in an explicit, didactic way, make an
effort to mould human minds; nor, like the writers of the Thaw
or Taboo groups, did he reverse the goals aimed at by socialist
realism while continuing to use literature as a means to a peda-
gogic end.

In a sketch called *In the Streetcar*, for example, Nagibin merely
describes a young girl accompanying a somewhat older friend,
who is about to join a man in order to live with him, without
registering as his wife. The younger girl is the observer of the
action, as well as the emotional chorus commenting on the story.
Her reaction is a combination of admiration for the courage of
the older girl who is about to take a dangerous 'adult' step, and
of trepidation at what her friend is doing. The story ends when
the older girl leaves the streetcar, and the younger girl glances
after her with concern and fear. Nagibin shows not the least
interest in moralizing about his incident: he is neither preaching
that girls should beware of such dangerous behaviour, nor exhort-
ing them to follow suit. He does not turn his subject into a social
problem. He is presenting a human situation: a relationship between two girls. The attitude of one of them towards the other is
to him a sufficiently worthy topic, in itself, without any further
involvement with work, industry, agriculture, the collective and
so on.

Kazakov, Nagibin, and Tendryakov in prose, and Evtushenko
and Voznesensky in poetry, are among those authors active during the Thaw whose works seem to us in retrospect of still greater
importance than at the time of their publication.

If works of the Thaw and Taboo groups continue to interest
us for reasons of 'content' (in Soviet literature, at least, the dis-

tinction between 'form' and 'content' is valid—content meaning primarily themes, attitudes, hortatory pictures of human conduct) but seem threadbare and schematic apart from their historical-social-political value, then the stories of Kazakov, from our vantage point, are exceptional in their artistic excellence. They show a keen literary sensitivity and the desire to innovate (even if, as in Kazakov's *Blue and Green*, the 'innovation' may limp considerably behind Joyce, Proust or even Ivan Bunin and Yuri Olesha). They are efforts to study human behaviour in its fleeting moments and to extract the essence of our emotional response to the world around us in seemingly trivial (or sad) moments. Kazakov is the writer of the bittersweet, the squalid, of glory in defeat, the coruscation of the semi-defeated. Personal, seemingly trivial and frequently depressing subjects have preoccupied him.

In *Arcturus* Kazakov presented the heroic, but also pathetic, life and death of a blind hunting dog, who followed tracks of animals in solitary sallies through the forests. The dog dies and establishes the duality of his life—its epic glory and pitiful vulnerability. Kazakov conveys a sense of wonder at the mystery, complexity and ambiguity of life; not for him any facile optimism in sorting and filing away the phenomena of our existence.

The term 'world of feelings', applied to these writers, was used by Kochetov, newly named editor of *Oktyabr*, in a programmatic editorial statement in that monthly (in February 1961). He attacked sarcastically those who thought the 'road to communism' lay in the same direction as Ilya Ehrenburg's views on Chekhov and Stendhal, formalistic painting, and 'that world which they call the world of feelings'. During the years of the Thaw, only the beginnings of this school of writing were beginning to emerge. Now we see that they were to develop into a significant movement. These works, concentrating on the simple events of emotional life, pay little attention to public questions and the macrocosm of industry and agriculture. They do not engage in controversy. 'Usefulness', didactic involvement, are of no consideration in them. Their authors neither disagree with nor propagandize the official values of Soviet ideology. For all we know, their authors, as individual citizens, may be enthusiastically loyal to the Communist Party (Yuri Nagibin has assured us of this in print); but in their works, they are concerned with the small events of individual feeling. Compassion for unfortunate creatures, intense passion, the trivial data of the kaleidoscopic dance of life, often with an inconclusive and sad end, merge particularly in the stories of Kazakov. Thus literary treatment of private life began to reclaim some of the ground lost under Stalin. VII. *Works of Fantasy*. An exception to the prevalent prosaic dullness of socialist realism was children's literature and writing bordering on children's literature, particularly the work of Marshak and Shvarts. During the years of the Thaw, Shvarts wrote *The Ordinary Miracle* (1954) and *Tale of the Man and Wife* (1955). His plays are genuine creations, endowed with humour, whimsy and flights of the imagination.

Another work of fantasy was Dudintsev's *New Year's Tale*, far from completely successful artistically, but of great historical importance. It is the first work published in post-Stalin Russia which, with the exception of children's literature and science fiction, moved from realism into fantasy. In some ways it is close to the stories later published in France under the name of Tertz and the play by 'Ivan Ivanov'. It has an aura of Poe, Kafka and earlier Soviet writers of fantasies. Set in a strange world, the *New Year's Tale* uses symbolism and allegory, and mixes fantasy and reality. One cannot doubt it is a parable. Some of the features of the story (the Doppelgänger relationship between the hero and the chief of the bandits, the mysterious owl hovering around) are a little obtrusive, over insistent and irritating. Yet despite its contrived air, and other artistic failings, the *New Year's Tale* is a landmark. VIII. *A Few Words on Two Genres*. (a) *Poetry*. There is not time to go at length into the history of Soviet poetry in these years (a separate paper is devoted to this subject), but Evtushenko and Tvardovsky ought to be at least mentioned. Tvardovsky wrote extensively and successfully before, during and after this period, and gained great popular favour. His discursive, reflective and narrative poetry belongs firmly in the centre of the 'Thaw' group of attitudes: loyally Soviet, patriotic, firmly anti-Stalinist, thirsting for truth, demanding justice staunchly but un-shrilly, hoping for an order among men based on dignity and self-respect.

Evgeni Evtushenko, who caused a stir with his early poems (for example *Station Zima, Oktyabr*, No. 10, 1956), has become a major institution in recent years. Like Tendryakov, he has grown in stature. By a retroactive reassessment, his early works loom larger now. In my opinion, the boldness of his ideas, which his poetry occasionally expresses, is less important in making him a favourite of the Russian audience than his spontaneous passion of feeling and exuberance. Russians respond to his longing for the fiery, intense, exotic and varied experiences of life.

(b) *Literary Criticism.* Topical literary reviewing and polemics reached the level of genuine literary criticism only on rare occasions, in some lines and paragraphs. Outstanding were the essays of Mark Shcheglov, whose death was a great loss. Kron's essay in *Literary Moscow*, volume II, was bold. Of particular importance were some of the prefaces to new editions of rehabilitated authors, such as Ilya Ehrenburg's to Isaac Babel.

IX. *Unpublishable Literature.* This group (also called Underground Literature or Literature for the Drawer) is composed of works written by authors who had no hope for their publication within the Soviet Union, at least in the near future. Naturally such a state of mind is unusual in a writer: the strange psychological situation of writing for a very limited public of friends (and readers of typed and mimeographed copies), for a very vaguely visualized public of the future, or for no public at all, is likely to affect the work written in ways other than the obvious opportunities which it affords for free expression of one's opinions.

Some of the authors who wrote such 'unpublishable' works, we know, also wrote very different acceptable poems and stories for the Soviet publishing houses. Some of the 'unpublishable' works reached the West and have been printed: the poems and a hasty and unrepresentative 'tract' by Esenin-Volpin; poems by several authors published in *Problems of Communism* and elsewhere; the works of 'Tertz' and 'I. Ivanov'; and of course *Doctor Zhivago*.

Doctor Zhivago (although Pasternak early in the Thaw apparently held hopes for its publication in Russia) is typical of the other 'unpublishable' works inasmuch as it contains paragraphs and sentences which conflict head on with official socialist, Marxist and Soviet principles, as well as with basic policies, such as collectivization of agriculture (for example: 'Marxism is too uncontrolled to be a science. . . . I don't know a movement more self-centred and further removed from the facts than Marxism.') But still more important is its general, pervasive spirit, which it would be very difficult, perhaps impossible to eradicate, in any project to bowdlerize the novel in order to make it fit for publication in the USSR, since it is utterly individualistic and, in its basic values, antithetical to the very assumptions of Soviet ideology—as in the following passage:

Reshaping life! People who can say that may have lived through a lot, but have never understood a thing about life—they have never felt its breath, its soul . . . they look on it as a lump of coarse raw material that needs to be processed by them, to be ennobled by their touch. But life is never a material, a substance. If you want to know, life is the principle of self-renewal, it is constantly renewing and remaking and changing and transfiguring itself, it is infinitely beyond your or my obtuse theories.

In the works of Esenin-Volpin, of the authors of the clandestine periodical *Syntax* and others, we also find attitudes never encountered in such intense form in published Soviet literature: revulsion at existing conditions, pessimism, a feeling of the artist's or chosen individual's superiority to 'the crowd'. *The Fantastic Stories* of Tertz go beyond Dudintsev's *New Year's Tale* in abandoning realism and embracing the methods of Kafka, perhaps Poe and others. They apply in practice what Tertz had urged in his essay on socialist realism—its replacement by 'a phantasmagoric art, with hypotheses instead of a Purpose, an art in which the grotesque will replace realistic descriptions of ordinary life. Such an art would correspond best to the spirit of our time. May the fantastic imagery of Hoffmann and Dostoevsky, of Goya, Chagall and Mayakovsky . . . teach us how to be truthful with the aid of the absurd and the fantastic.'

If works like Tertz's *Fantastic Stories* should indeed some day become acceptable in publishable Soviet literature, if fantasy, allegory, symbol, and general immersion in the mainstreams of Western twentieth-century art (with its implicit ideology—in epistemology as well as in attitudes towards man's position in the world) should be regularly permitted to appear in Soviet print, then a very important departure in Soviet life will have taken place.

What the Thaw Did Not Melt

In the above survey of the chief themes and categories of literature written during the Thaw, we have noticed the central points, as well as the limits, of the Soviet Russian writers' interests. We

have seen that they have failed to question the institutional structure of the Soviet Union, and its possible connexion with the
various failures in private and public life which they depict,
though they occasionally suggest by implication that official
Soviet ideology may not be the sole, perfect, all-sufficient body of
doctrines applicable to all of human existence.

However, if we leave out of account some of the poets, the
authors of unpublishable literature, and the writers of fantasy, a
striking feature of the literature of the Thaw, which emerges
more clearly in retrospect than it did at the time, is the sameness
rather than the variety of what was being written. Whether we
read what we have called the authors of the Taboo, 'Conservative'
or Thaw groups, they seem very much alike in their basic approach to life and literature, even if their conclusions on specific
issues may differ. Their works make the impression of being composed not by individuals, but by a committee or a workshop of
interchangeable ghost writers.

What are the reasons for this apparent homogeneity of most of
Soviet literature of these years despite the thematic differences
within it? One is probably the determination of the writers to be
understood by a wide and to some extent unsophisticated, often
newly or barely literate public, acquainted with only a narrow
literary fare, unaccustomed to and incapable of responding to intricacies or idiosyncracies of style and personal vision. Hence a
prevalence of a similar, clear, impersonal, simple style.

Another reason may be an agreement about the nature of
reality (or if not an agreement, then at least the perhaps unconscious habit of writing as if the writer did hold such basic assumptions about the world and man's knowledge of it) as being solid,
material, knowable. There is only one reality, the truth, one
correct way of seeing it, if one is sane, educated and enlightened
—this is what most of Soviet literature seems to be saying. If
different people disagree about the same situation one of them is
right, the others wrong (unless all of them are wrong); the correct
view of reality can be explained, argued, and is amenable to
rational proofs. Only diseased, imperfectly seeing and ignorant,
unenlightened minds can fail to be persuaded of the validity of the
one correct explanation of reality. Such optimistic and simple
faith in reason and human understanding is endearing, but it
easily leads to dull and uniform writing.

Much of the sameness of Soviet literature is also due to the writers' considering writing and publication a privilege and a sacred duty. Their aim is not the creation of a world, or the delving into subjective, idiosyncratic areas, or the presentation of an individual vision of an aspect of life. They—whether Dudintsev, Kochetov, or Ehrenburg—concentrate on showing how people should live and think and how they should not. Their works are a series of How to Do It, and How Not to Do It handbooks. This is how we must read them, if we want to see them on their own terms. That does not mean that some writers, for instance Ehrenburg, are not very well aware of other ways of conceiving of the functions and possibilities of literature or that they would not be capable of writing (or have not done so in the past) in a different manner, with different aims in mind. In their particular historical situaton, however, they cannot or do not wish to do so. They have chosen to be pedagogues; and Soviet literature in the Thaw has continued to be a gigantic, collective *paideia*.

A related consideration is that some of the writers may be conscious not so much of having to write in a certain way to be published (although that of course is a crucial test), as of wishing to reach, among others, a public whose language and attitudes they must at least in part adopt if they are to be granted a hearing. One such important segment of the reading public, which is most influential and hence desirable to write for, is the younger members of the Party and bureaucratic officialdom—the rising, new leaders and leaders to be. In order to persuade the members of this group that to hold certain views is reasonable and not necessarily heterodox and dangerous, a writer must convince them that he is really talking the same language as they, stands on the same side of the barricades, is basically solid, orthodox, trustworthy—and then he can go on to try to present and advocate certain novel views which are the main purpose of his writing. This may account for the sameness of outlook, the monotony of stereotyped categorizations of life, the concern with the same issues, the occasional reassurance that the author is reliable and trustworthy. By demonstrating that he shares the presuppositions and ultimate goals of his public, the writer may purchase his reader's willingness at least to hear his advocacy of some other views, such as, for example, the defensibility of local disobedience to wrong orders from the higher level of the Party, the need for flexibility in administering agriculture, a plea for mercy for former collaborators.

The flight away from the eccentric and individual towards what is held in common leads to the dominance of types. In themselves, types are not to be automatically condemned. As Apollon Grigoryev wrote a hundred years ago,

Literary works that are serious and grasp life in its types are a good thing. Not only are they good in themselves, positively good, but they have a negative utility as well: once they have grasped certain types and have immortalized them artistically and strikingly, they eliminate the desire to repeat those types. . . . Now one only has to agree on the general type of substantial men of the former era, depicted strikingly and at the same time good naturedly by the late Aksakov, and only note the differences and exceptions, and there you have a portrait which, if not drawn by myself, can easily be drawn by the reader.

But unfortunately, in Soviet literature, reliance on types leads to stock responses and stereotypes. We find the same recognizable, unindividualized factory managers, Party secretaries on various levels, chairmen of collective farms, subdivisible into a few 'good' and 'bad' groups, the same monotonous problems, typical scenes and situations—Party and *Komsomol* meetings with predictable agenda, visits to superiors to solicit their support, summonses to receive reprimands, plenary conferences.

It is a mistake, however, in commenting on Soviet literature to concentrate exclusively on the analysis of the main characters, the ideas they embody or express and their actions. The special quality of the books with which we have been dealing—and to some extent the sameness which we have been deploring—are due also to formal characteristics: to similar methods of narration, dialogue, 'point of view', changes from dramatic account to comment and panoramic scene, the manner of reporting the characters' thoughts and feelings. There was very little variety in artistic method during the Thaw.

In the years with which we are concerned, it became a platitude in Russia to complain about the neglect of the artistic side of literature. Kaverin, at the Writers' Congress in 1954, for instance, said that many books showed so little form and mastery of technique that if the pages were scattered, they could not be put together again. Fedin also demanded more 'aesthetics'. He distinguished formalism, 'the negation of the ideological nature of art and the repudiation of the principle of the unity of form and content', from 'the refusal of critics to analyse form' which 'is formalism upside down' and 'causes harm to the idea content of Soviet literature'. Yet in Soviet literary criticism, little attention was paid to the formal side of literature, nor can one find much variety of styles, creative originality, or imaginativeness in Soviet literature (with the exceptions already noted). The title of one of Pisarev's essays *The Destruction of Aesthetics*, describes accurately the razing which has taken place.

One of the cardinal causes for the discouraging sameness of Soviet fiction is the nature of the narrator. Whether he is a participant in the action, or an impersonal narrator, he is usually an interchangeable, stock viewer and interpreter. He is sober, rational, and sees the action clearly. He is not confused; he suffers from no astigmatism and very little hesitation and uncertainty. The characters may be swayed by emotion, but not he. Whether we read Ketlinskaya, Koptyaeva, or Dudintsev, we know we are in the hands of the same fictional narrator with crystal-clear sense perception, level-headed evaluation.

The exceptionally fresh angle of vision of the narrator in some passages in Nekrasov's *Home Town* and some stories of Nagibin and Kazakov is responsible for their originality and aliveness. There we feel the narrator is an imaginative, living mind—sometimes confused, tentative, provoked, changeable—in short, a unique, imperfect centre of consciousness, rather than the generalized, scientifically impersonal, common denominator of a mind who is at work in most of the other novels and stories of the period. A good example of an original narrator is found in Kazakov's *Blue and Green*. The young man who relives his love for Lila, in an eternal present, from the first meeting with the young girl through the growth of his love, until her marriage to someone else, registers the fleeting data of the passing moment of his sensuous and emotional life. He is in a state of wonder, rather than stolid, retrospective, analytic calm. He jumps from one point to another; there are shifts of focus, various areas of life are in close proximity. The faculties of reason and will are not given the time or opportunity to process the materials of experience.

More significant than the thematic differences between this and the run-of-the-mill Soviet story (the fact that *Blue and Green* concentrates on an individual's private emotional experience without any reference to social concerns, for example) is its individualization through selection of details and use of an unusual narrator.

The rarity of such works as Kazakov's story may be due also to other factors than those already suggested. The Soviet people are indeed greatly occupied with the material demands of everyday life. The demands made on one's time and mental energy by outward life in the USSR (personal, industrial, political) are engrossing, even to those who are not 'activists'. Public and social matters do absorb much of the attention of many people. As a result of all these involvements, not much leisure and spare energy is left for an inner life—for delving into the intricacies of the self and one's immediate, individual life, the problems which concern many English, French and American writers, of one's identity, subjective nuances of feeling, ways of relating oneself to other individuals. To some extent then, the Soviet writers who give little scope to what Kochetov ridiculed as 'the world of feelings' may merely be giving an accurate picture of the concerns of their fellow citizens, who live 'simple lives', what Tendryakov in his recent *Short Circuit*, called an existence limited to 'earning money, buying things, amusement'. The effort of the Party to induce the population to identify itself with communal, large scale undertakings, one would also expect, must have been at least in part successful and hence would be reflected in literary works describing what the Soviet people pay attention to.

In Western Europe and the United States, some authors do study social and public themes, but a greater number of the significant and best authors concentrate on the fate of the individual, outside politics, office, factory—ignoring his links with society, delving into inter-personal and intra-personal matters. This may be a symptom of the depoliticalization of the intellectual-artistic classes in the West; it may also be connected with the sense of purposelessness and loneliness of which our writers complain.

The complementary and antithetical situations in the Soviet Union and some Western countries are reflected in the excessive dedication to social involvement and purpose in Soviet Russia, and in the sense of drift and inability to concentrate resources to eliminate social evil in the West; in the lack of artistic originality and interest in man's private, individual life in the USSR, and in excessive preoccupation with the subjective complexities of socially irresponsible individuals, in the West. (One cannot forever gnaw at one's own vitals. As soon as one's self becomes one's commodity, it tends very quickly to diminish', an American critic wrote recently.)

In Yuri Olesha's story *Love* (1929), Shuvalov, falling in love with Lelya, complained: 'I'm beginning to think in images . . . Laws are ceasing to exist for me. . . . I am becoming an idealist . . . I am seeing things that don't exist.' He made 'many imaginative discoveries'. 'It comes from love,' Lelya explained. When Shuvalov was about to fall asleep, 'close to childhood sensations, he did not resist the transformation of familiar and lawful forms,' but on awakening, he reflected: 'I am a materialist . . . and yet suddenly, in front of my eyes, a criminal, antiscientific deformation of elements, of matter, begins to occur.'

However, when a young man whose senses convey 'a correct picture of the world' offers to give his scientifically correct view of the outside world in exchange for Shuvalov's wild, 'useless' vision rich in pathetic fallacies, fantasies, and 'criminal, antiscientific deformation of elements', Shuvalov sends him packing.

The bulk of Soviet literature in the years of the Thaw was written by authors similar to Olesha's young man, rather than by Shuvalovs. Whatever their personal ways of looking at the world may be, when they sit down to write, they adhere to a plain, factual, logical ideal of vision. Whimsy, pathetic fallacy, imaginative flights, momentary disturbances of perception, all the fleeting, undigested, colourful details of our lives are not the proper subjects for their art. If someone were to suggest to them that for some French, British and American artists, there seem to exist various kinds of reality, depending on one's perspective; that the individual may be changeable and incoherent; that the search for one's own identity, through memory and other avenues, is the major theme of many Western works; that the creation of one's own, beautiful, unique artistic world is the chief or sole goal of many Western artists—they might find this alien, decadent, or at least impossible to consider for their own guidance in their work, with its social and rational categories. The view held by Joyce of artistic creation as an individual, creative quest is basically incompatible with Soviet ideology.

Am I judging Soviet literature by 'culture-bound criteria? Have I been taking Salinger, Hemingway, Butor, or Beckett (or Proust and Mann) as standards and judging every degree of the arc of deviation from their norm to be an aberration? To some extent I plead guilty. Yet I have tried to look at Soviet literature within its own setting, even if I have concluded by noting the gulf which separates the achievements of Western literature from those of Soviet literature during the Thaw. One cannot point to the differences between the Western and Soviet social settings and then disclaim the relevance of any comparison of the value of the achievements. Soviet literature, even during the Thaw, seems monotonous not merely when measured against the great Western achievement of the twentieth century—or the Russian authors of the nineteenth: it also fails in a comparison with Isaac Babel, Yuri Olesha, and other authors of earlier Soviet decades.

8

THE REPERTOIRE OF THE FIFTIES

François de Liencourt

'In a communist organization of society the subordination of the artist to local and national narrow-mindedness—a subordination which results simply from the division of labour—in any case disappears. In such a society the subordination of the individual to his specific art also vanishes—a subordination which made him exclusively a painter, a sculptor, etc., and which by its very name sufficiently expresses the narrow limits of his economic development and his dependence on the division of labour. In a communist society there are no painters but, at most, people who, among other things, paint.' [1] Thus Karl Marx.

If we apply this idea to Soviet playwrights, we should first note that the CPSU does not claim that a communist society has already been established in the USSR, and that Marx's opinion is irrelevant for art in a 'socialist' society, whether we consider Stalin's period or the years since. In both cases, at the height of Zhdanovism as well as during the best periods of the post-Stalin thaw, the Soviet theatre has not put an end to 'the subordination of the artist to local and national narrow-mindedness'; it has been and still is marked by many essentially national characteristics.

If we consider the second part of the quotation, i.e. the prophecy according to which in a communist society there will no longer be painters, but at the most 'people who, among other things, paint', then the Soviet playwrights are often not so very far from Marx's idea. If we apply it to Stalin's time, there would be much to support the definition that there were no longer Russian dramatic authors, but at the most men who, among other things, wrote plays. It would be closer to the truth to say that the playwrights were not so much men who, among other things, wrote for the theatre, but rather that they were 'engineers of the

1. Karl Marx, *Die Deutsche Ideologie, Marx-Engels Gesamtausgabe*. Erste Abteilung. Band 5, p. 373. Berlin, 1932.

human soul', very often political journalists, who, with due obedience, did, among other things, write plays. The quality of the Stalinist repertoire was not high as Soviet critics today admit quite openly. Nowadays, in spite of the move towards the 'construction of communism', we note a step towards a better division of labour. There are more professional playwrights who come from the theatre and not from the Party press, more Soviet authors who are first and foremost intellectuals and writers.

The changes can be established by comparing two periods: the high tide of Stalin's rule (that is mainly the 1946–52 period), and the years 1954–61 when, in spite of some zigzagging in the party line, the theatre benefited from a 'thaw' to an extent which did not exclude the possibility of creating really good plays. As an attempt to measure the changes which occurred in the character of Soviet dramatic production, in the repertory of the theatres, and in the situation of the playwright, and at the risk of being schematic, I should like briefly to consider three items:

(a) the changes in the policy of the Soviet authorities as regards control of dramatic art, and in the organization of the theatre,
(b) the changes in the *content* of the repertoire, content (*soderzhanie*) being understood mainly in political, moral and sociological terms,
(c) the changes in the aesthetic, literary and dramatic quality of the repertoire.

The Soviet theatrical repertoire might be compared to a cart pulled by three horses, the first horse being the regime, the second the theatre-goer, and the third the tastes and desires of the professionals—writers, actors, producers and directors. This third horse was very strong and restive in the first years of the Soviet regime, was broken in and tamed under Stalin, and is now starting a new life. The first two horses often pull in opposite directions.

The first attempts of the Party to get the theatre completely under its control can be traced back to 1927. In order to fight the 'bourgeois influence' which had flourished under NEP, a meeting convened by the Central Committee *Agitprop* department decided to reinforce Party control over the theatre by appointing communists as directors, by establishing 'artistic councils' within the theatre, and by emphasizing the role of 'activist' groups (Party, *Komsomol*, and trade unions) in order to wage a 'civil war in the theatre' and to put an end to the kind of 'spiritual NEP' which had developed in the Twenties.

In 1929 a committee to deal with the theatre repertoire was set up in the People's Commissariat for Education; this *Glavrepert-kom* was a department of the newly-established *Glaviskusstvo*, the section of the Commissariat dealing with art and literature. Stalin's stranglehold on literature became tighter after 1932, with the dissolution of RAPP, and even more after 1934 with the foundation of the Union of Soviet Writers. In the name of 'social-ist realism', as defined by Zhdanov at the 1934 Congress of Soviet Writers, more than half of the new plays or dramatic productions presented during the 1936–37 season by the main theatres of the Soviet Union were forbidden by *Glavrepertkom*.[2] In 1936 control was transferred from the Commissariat to the newly-founded Committee for Art Affairs.

At the same time, many organizational measures were taken against the theatres accused of 'formalism'. In February 1936 Studio D of the Moscow Arts Theatre, run by Mikhail Chekhov, was closed, and in September the Leningrad Theatre of Young Workers (TRAM) was also suppressed. The Committee for Art Affairs decided to 'merge' theatre troupes which had nothing in common with each other; the Kamerny Theatre of Tairov for instance, famous for its intimate and refined symbolism and its neo-classic stylization, was amalgamated with the Realistic Theatre of N. Okhlopkov, a disciple (at that time) of Meyerhold.[3]

Nor did physical terror spare the theatre. Its most famous victim was Meyerhold. His theatre was closed in January 1938 after a violent attack in *Pravda* by Kerzhentsev, then chairman of the Committee for Art Affairs,[4] who reviled the theatre as 'alien' and accused the famous producer of having staged plays by 'enemies of the people' such as Tretyakov and Erdman, play-wrights who were taxed with 'slandering Soviet reality'. Meyer-hold was arrested and died in prison or in a camp in 1941. Playwrights like Erdman and Tretyakov met the same fate; even Kirshon, a rather pro-Stalinist author, was arrested after having

2. B. A. Nazarov and O. V. Gridneva, 'On the backwardness of drama and the theatre', *Voprosy Filosofii*, 5, 1955, pp. 85–94.

3. A. Sverdlin, 'In search of a new path', *Teatr*, 10, 1956.

4. Kerzhentsev, 'An Alien Theatre', *Pravda*, 17 December 1937.

been denounced in the *Literary Gazette*[5] for having 'worked with Trotskyists' by his colleague and rival, V. Vishnevsky, the author of *The Optimistic Tragedy,* then starting on his career of sycophantic and fulsome praise of Stalin.[6]

This despotic and arbitrary rule was softened by the outbreak of war, when the theatre recovered some measure of freedom, and it became possible for good writers such as Leonov and Paustovsky to write plays and have them staged. This relaxation of control was part of the effort of the Soviet leaders to enlist the support of all loyal citizens, an effort which entailed concessions not only to the peasants and churchgoers, but also to the intelligentsia. Because of the alliance with the West, many theatres included British, American and French contemporary plays in their repertoire. The tendency to seek in the theatre some escape from the grim realities of war encouraged the staging of light and amusing plays, Soviet or foreign, although patriotic drama got a good showing.

Once the war was over, there was a reaction in all fields to ensure the purity of communist ideology against alien influences. The Zhdanov era opened in the summer of 1946 with three decrees, of which the second dealt specifically with 'the repertoire of dramatic theatres'. The decree stiffened the regulations already in force and the powers of *Glavrepertkom,* and added the stipulation that theatres were obliged to stage annually 'at least two new spectacles of high ideological and artistic quality on Soviet contemporary themes'. The structure of the theatres was also reorganized. Up to 1946 the director, the administrative chief of the theatre, was also charged with political responsibility; the artistic manager (*khudozhestvenny rukovoditel*) was his subordinate. This was not enough for Stalin and Zhdanov. A third man was brought in, the 'deputy artistic manager in charge of literature', the *Zavlit,* to take charge of the repertoire. In 1949, the functions of the artistic manager came to an end. He was replaced by the chief producer, explicitly subordinate to the director, usually

5. V. Vishnevsky, 'A reply is needed', *L.G.*, 26 April 1937 (Quoted by E. J. Brown, *The Proletarian Episode in Soviet Literature*, New York, 1953.

6. After the war Vishnevsky wrote one of the most Stalinist plays of the Soviet repertoire, *Nezabyvayemy 1919*, in which the history of the fight against Yudenich near Petrograd was rewritten. *Sovetskaya Dramaturgia 1949*, Moscow, 1950.

a political boss with little or no knowledge of the theatre.[7] At the same time Stalin decided to spend less money on the theatre. Many theatres were closed. The total number of theatres in the Soviet Union, a little over 960 in 1941, fell to about 500,[8] the victims being mostly the non-Russian theatres. From 1941 to 1953 their number was reduced by half, and from 1948 subsidies were cut; theatres had to be self-supporting.[9]

The situation of the theatre managers had never been so difficult. They were not allowed to choose their repertoire, which had to be planned and approved by *Glavrepertkom*; they were supposed to stage at least two new contemporary plays of high ideological (and, supposedly, also artistic) quality every year; they were also obliged, in the same way as the factory managers, to fulfil their financial plan without subsidies—a difficult task if they could not satisfy the consumer, i.e. the theatre-goer! This seemed to be the case more often than not, although the average theatre-goer was not too fastidious.

That a reaction had begun to set in even before Stalin's death is shown by an article in *Pravda,* published at the end of 1952; three journalists united their efforts in writing it.[10] They questioned the value of centralized planning by the Committee on Art Affairs; the result of the state-commissioned repertoire had been a squandering of state funds, and at the same time a weakening of the sense of responsibility of theatre directors, who often took refuge in classical drama and declared that it was not their fault if they had no decent contemporary plays to stage.

After Stalin's death, the Committee on Art Affairs disappeared, its duties being transferred to a department of the newly founded Ministry of Culture, the 'Chief Administration for Art Affairs'. During the first year of the new 'collective leadership' the trend was towards relaxation of controls; after setbacks in 1954–55, the trend was continued, especially after the 1956 CPSU congress. This was of course followed by a fresh reaction after the October-November events in Poland and Hungary, but on the whole the

7. Cf. the debate on 'Directors and Producers' in *Teatr*, 2, 1957.

8. Cf. *Kulturnoye Stroitelstvo SSSR*, Moscow, 1956, p. 293.

9. T. I. Cayan, 'Against the Spirit of Parade', *Teatr*, 1, 1954; E. Botvennikov, 'For a Theatre of Unanimous People', *Teatr*, 2, 1954.

10. V. Zaleski, V. Kuznetsov, V. Mlekhin, 'Do away with Bureaucratic Obstacles to the Development of the Theatre', *Moskovskaya Pravda*, quoted by *Current Digest of the Soviet Press*, Vol. 18, p. 21.

movement towards greater freedom (or less standardization) for the theatres and playwrights has persisted and has achieved limited but noteworthy results.

The first improvement made for decentralization. More responsibility was given to the theatre directors; members of the Union of Soviet Writers were allowed to submit their plays *directly* to the theatres, and could also send them to the publishing houses and to the editorial boards of the literary periodicals. Of course the plays were still subject to rewriting, but the job was done in the theatres and not in the centralized repertoire committee. At the Ministry of Culture plays were now examined after they had been accepted by the theatres (actually by the *zavlit*) or published in periodicals. Once plays had been approved by the Ministry, they could be 'recommended as good to be played everywhere'.

These reforms were not welcomed by the conservative elements, nor were they considered sufficient by genuine playwrights.

In 1955 the Deputy Minister of Culture, V. Kemenov, one of Zhdanov's lieutenants, complained that the theatres had misused their newly-acquired autonomy concerning the choice of the repertoire and that most plays were of a low ideological and artistic level; the *glavrezh* (Chief Producer) should be considered the 'ideologist' of the theatre, and should use a veto when necessary: he bore full responsibility for the plays which were produced.[11]

On the other hand Aleksander Kron, in his *Notes of a Writer*, published in *Literaturnaya Moskva*,[12] disclosed that in all contracts between a theatre and a playwright a provision was included in which the author undertook to accept any modification or correction required by the director of the theatre; the playwright was not allowed to withdraw his work if he disagreed with the theatrical direction. Any campaign (as for instance against alcoholism) was a pretext for imposing changes even in plays already performed; the texts, even those which were only duplicated, were edited by *redaktors*, whose names were always given beside that of the author. 'It seems that for every book there is an officer and a political commissar. Numberless "instructors"

11. The IX Congress of the All-Union Theatrical Society, *Teatr*, 1955.
12. *Literaturnaya Moskva*, Moscow, 1956, p. 789.

and inspectors were accustomed to give orders in a decisive manner as if they were preceptors or watchmen.' In 1956 the right of the theatres to choose, in the conditions described by Kron, their own repertory was limited to classical drama.

In the same year, the practice of state-commissioned drama was officially condemned in an order of the Ministry of Culture, and a further order assigned funds to the theatres for payments to playwrights, on the responsibility of the *glavrezh*; the rates fixed were quite high (up to 15,000 roubles).[13] The only information to be found on playwrights' fees before that date is that they were in proportion to the number of acts: a drama in four acts paid 33 per cent more than one in three acts.[14] The theatres were given greater autonomy, and the artistic councils (*khudozhestvennye sovety*) created in 1955 became partly elective in 1956, but their role remained consultative and in spite of the presence of the *glavrezh* the director remained the real chief.[15]

In 1956–57 the problem of director versus *glavrezh* was openly discussed. It was disclosed that many directors were utterly incompetent; many of them had been chosen from 'among party or government officials who had been a failure at their job', or among actors who had been active in local Party committees.[16]

The function of director was not abolished, but the Ministry of Culture undertook to choose more competent people. It is clear from the press, however, that up to now directors are mainly concerned with two problems: how to satisfy the political authorities, and how to fulfil their financial plan. The result is often a compromise between the tastes of the theatre-goer and the requirements of the Party authorities. To pretend that the two are always in conflict would be an over-simplification, especially at a time when the tasks assigned to the playwright are less exacting than formerly; nor are all theatre directors incompetent bureaucrats with no personal opinions. Political interference has not disappeared; it is now more decentralized, but the system is still burdensome and complicated. This provides the background for an examination of the changes which have occurred in the repertoire since Stalin's time.

13. *Teatr*, 1956, Nos. 4 and 5.
14. E. Kholodov, 'The Last Act', *Teatr*, 1, 1955.
15. 'Order of the Ministry of Culture', *Teatr*, 6, 1955; M. Lyachenko, 'Rights and Duties', *Teatr*, 2, 1957.
16. G. Georgievsky, 'How I became a theatre director', *Teatr*, 1, 1957.

To measure these changes the starting point must be Zhdanov's speeches and the Central Committee's decrees in 1946; then
the current Soviet repertoire can be judged by the standards they
established.

The 1946–48 Zhdanov 'purge' was the culmination of Party
attitudes towards literature and art which had their beginnings
in the Thirties under the name of socialist realism. Socialist realism, as defined by Zhdanov in 1934 at the First Congress of
Writers, can be briefly summarized: the word realism was not
opposed to romanticism. (Gorky was then praising revolutionary
romanticism.) By emphasizing the concept of realism, Stalin and
Zhdanov were making clear their hostility to any kind of
'modern' art, to all that was arbitrarily vilified under the name of
'formalism'. But the first word in the term was more important.
In Zhdanov's own words, literature and art had to be 'tendentious'. Writers were invited to show 'reality . . . in its revolutionary
development'. One of their tasks was to promote 'the ideological
transformation and education [of the public] in the spirit of
socialism'. Sholokhov remarked a few years ago that he never
understood what was meant by socialist realism; we shall not be
very wide of the mark if we define socialist realism as above all
subservience to the party line by the 'engineers of the human
soul'.

The main points in Zhdanov's 1946 decrees on the theatre
repertoire related to Western 'bourgeois' plays and to the Soviet
repertoire. Zhdanov not only condemned contemporary Western
playwrights like Somerset Maugham, who had become very
popular during the war; he also rejected nineteenth-century
Western plays as serving the interests of 'bourgeois culture'. They
distracted the public from the political struggle by concentrating
their attention on plays whose heroes were 'gansters and music-
hall girls' and by 'praising adultery and the exploits of all kinds
of adventurers'. As to the Soviet repertoire, it had to be purged of
all plays reflecting the author's concern to remain aloof from
politics. There were far too many light dramas, and authors who
claimed that the time had come to stage amusing plays were rebuked. Too much attention was paid to 'so-called psychological'
problems, which were devoid of all interest. On the other hand,
there had been too many historical plays idealizing the past.

Playwrights were urged to help raise the standard of political education of the young by writing optimistic works designed to inculcate a spirit of courage, devotion to the fatherland, and faith in the victory of communism.

The appeal to portray 'positive heroes' was reinforced by a stern condemnation of 'crude satire'. Zoshchenko, two of whose plays had been staged in Leningrad, was the main target of Zhdanov's attack. But many playwrights were accused of presenting 'caricatures', 'monstrous' portraits of Soviet citizens, and of choosing too many 'negative' heroes. In the same spirit, Zhdanov's decree on the cinema rebuked the author of a film on the reconstruction of the Donbas for portraying workers who lived in filthy, decayed hovels.

Zhdanov had invited the critics to be bolder in their support of 'the party spirit' in the theatre. After his death (August 1948) the drama critics themselves were taken to task. A 'certain group of anti-patriotic drama critics' was attacked by *Pravda* (28 January 1949); they were accused of 'having lately given refuge to a nest of bourgeois aesthetes, camouflaging their anti-patriotic, cosmopolitan, and rotten attitude towards Soviet art'. This monopolistic group, working mainly in the journals *Teatr* and *Sovetskoe Iskusstvo* had, among other sins, made frivolous references to such works as *Daleko ot Stalingrada* (Far from Stalingrad) by Anatoli Surov, *Pobediteli* (The Victors) by Chirskov, and *Moskovski Kharakter* (The Moscow Character) by Sofronov. The critic Gurvich, who had dared to praise Pogodin and to speak of his 'easy-going humour', in which the Russian spectator could see himself reflected, was accused of levelling 'a hateful accusation at Soviet man, to whom "easy-going" humour was deeply alien'. The 'perfidious and slanderous attacks' of this group were aimed mainly at Stalin Prize-winners, and often took the form of silence. 'The method of silence, as Comrade Stalin has rightly stated, was . . . a form of criticism, a stupid and absurd one, but still a form of criticism.' The most urgent task of party critics was to deliver a crushing ideological blow to this anti-patriotic group. This 'crushing blow', which was not only ideological, heightened the effects of Zhdanovism. How could playwrights simultaneously implement Party slogans and satisfy the theatre-goer? Many theatres resorted to the classical Russian repertoire; up to 1953 Alexander Ostrovsky was the most popular playwright. Virta, one of the 'accepted' playwrights, recipient of a Stalin Prize, advanced the idea that since negative characters were no longer typical, the only conflicts it was possible to represent on the stage were those between the 'good' and the 'better'.

This idea, known as 'the theory of lack of conflict', served the Party as a pretext to blame the critics for the failure of its own policy. The shift was marked by a *Pravda* editorial of 7 April 1952, which accused the anti-patriotic drama critics of having launched the pernicious theory of lack of conflict, and urged playwrights to resort to satire. At the 19th CPSU congress in October 1952 Malenkov said that 'The Soviet people . . . will not tolerate dullness, art that has no message, and falsity. . . . Our remarkable authors must scourge the faults, defects and sores still to be found in our society. . . . We need Soviet Gogols and Shchedrins who, with the fire of their satire, will burn away everything that is undesirable, rotten, and moribund, everything that retards our progress.'

The invitation to resort to satire was scarcely heeded by the playwrights, except by Sergei Mikhalkov, an author specializing in children's literature, who during the war had written the highly patriotic words of the new Soviet national anthem and had followed the Zhdanov party line in his extreme 'anti-cosmopolitan' plays. For instance, *Ya khochu domoi* (I Want to Go Home), published in 1949, described the efforts of 'British imperialists' and 'Latvian traitors' to prevent a young Soviet child, Sasha¹ Butuzov, from escaping from a DP camp in Germany. The Soviet authorities help Sasha to flee the imperialist yoke, and start a new life in the Soviet Union. When all is ready for him to fly to Moscow, the Soviet Captain Peskayev asks him: 'Do you want to go to Moscow?'

Sasha: I want to go home.
Peskaev: You will soon be home.
Sasha: (Looking at Comrade Stalin's picture) Stalin!
Peskaev: Yes, this is Comrade Stalin.
   (a pause)
Sasha: Is Stalin in Moscow?
Peskaev: Yes, in Moscow. You too will be in Moscow.
Sasha: I want to go home!

Following the new 1952 slogan, Mikhalkov wrote a satirical play called *Raki* (The Crayfish), its theme not unlike that of *Revizor*.

The trend towards satire became more marked after Stalin's death; Leonid Zorin's *Gosti* (The Guests) criticized certain defects in Soviet 'high society' which, originating as they did in bureaucracy and careerism, did not fit into the Marxist-Leninist category of 'remnants of the capitalist past'. After only two Moscow performances of the play, the collegium of the Ministry of Culture issued a communiqué stating that, as everybody knew, 'Soviet civil servants had no other aim than to serve the people and the fatherland'; they were 'the very embodiment of the people'. It condemned *Gosti* and similar plays, and reminded playwrights that 'Soviet art is strong in its truth, and cannot tolerate the slightest degree of mendacity ... "Write the truth"; this is the contant advice of the Communist party to Soviet writers and artists.'[17] Although backed by no formal resolution of the Central Committee, the statement nevertheless discouraged many writers who might have wished to try their hand at drama or revert to it. The result was a most severe crisis in the theatre. At the end of 1955, the Minister of Culture, N. Mikhailov, noted that the number of theatre-goers had sharply declined during the new season.[18]

Although it produced no clear directive on the theatre, the 20th CPSU congress encouraged greater boldness in the choice of repertoire. The proportion of Russian classical (i.e. prerevolutionary) plays fell from 26 per cent in 1953 (for the Moscow 'drama theatres'), to 17 per cent in 1956, and to 15 per cent in 1961. In 1953, Ostrovsky headed the list, with 274 performances (twenty different plays); by 1960 the number of Ostrovsky performances had fallen by 90 per cent to 25, and declined still further in the first six months of 1961. Maxim Gorky, who can be regarded broadly as a prerevolutionary writer, suffered a similar setback. The number of performances of Gorky plays was 127 in 1953, and 7 and 10 in 1960 and 1961 respectively. On the other hand, while in 1953 and 1954 no adaptations for the stage of Dostoevsky novels were presented in Moscow, performances of such plays

17. *Sovetskaya Kultura*, 5 June 1954.
18. Speech by N. Mikhailov at the conference of theatrical workers, *Vechernyaya Moskva*, 16 November 1955. Cf. also 'Novye gorizonty', by Georgievsky, *Teatr*, 2, 1956. The author speaks openly of the resolute strike of theatre-goers in the autumn of 1955.

numbered 35 during the first six months of 1961, not far short of
the figure for Tolstoy.

These figures, of course, do not show whether the theatre is full
or empty, but in March 1957 the journal *Teatr* published figures
showing the proportion of tickets sold in twelve Moscow theatres.
None of the plays performed to capacity audiences belonged to
the Russian classical repertoire.[19] Statistics on the plays most
often performed in all Soviet theatres since 1955 confirm that the
decline in poularity of the Russian classics is not confined to
Moscow.[20]

As to foreign drama, Zhdanov's strictures on 'Western bourgeois culture' appear to have been disregarded. In the Moscow
theatres, for example, the proportion of foreign plays in the repertoire has fluctuated from 22 per cent in 1953, to 34 per cent in
1957, and for 1961 was down to 29 per cent. Since 1957, there have
been official protests against too frequent performances of Western contemporary unpolitical drama, and these 'alien' influences
have been lessened though not suppressed. The problem for the
theatres seems to have been to choose progressive, left-wing
Western playwrights—though the meaning of the word 'progressive' has altered since 1953. In that year, the contemporary
Western playwrights whose works were performed in Moscow
were mainly writers like Howard Fast and Roger Vaillant, then
both orthodox communists; Shaw's *Pygmalion* was one of the
plays most often performed in Moscow—no doubt death makes
writers ideologically more acceptable to the Soviet Communist
Party.

After the theatre-goers' strike at the end of 1955, and still more
after the 20th congress, the definition of the word 'progressive'
became much more elastic. Among the living figured Jean-Paul
Sartre and Lilian Hellman, though their plays suffered severe
rewriting. In Sartre's *La Putain Respectueuse*, decently renamed
Lizzy MacKay, the ideologically reformed heroine ended by joining the ranks of the Peace Movement. But much less politically
engaged playwrights were soon to reach the height of popularity.
Priestly's *Dangerous Corner* and Eduardo de Filippo's *My Family*

19. Griboyedov's *Zamuzhnyaya nevesta* had a 98 per cent attendance, *Teatr*,
3, 1957.

20. See for instance *Teatr*, 6, 1956; 1, 1957; 6, 1961.

162 *François de Liencourt*

were among the plays most often performed; the repertoire even included detective plays by Agatha Christie and Frederic Knott (*Dial M for Murder*). They balanced the theatre budget, but were subjected to strong criticism by the Party.

Many contemporary Western plays are still successful today. Two works by Arthur Miller, for instance, *Death of a Salesman* and *View from the Bridge*, were produced in Moscow in 1961. The Satire Theatre recently put on Noel Coward's *Nude with Violin*. Maeterlincks's *Blue Bird* has always been popular, and plays by Oscar Wilde, John Galsworthy, Stefan Zweig, Gerhard Hauptmann and E.-M. Remarque have been performed, apparently without strong opposition from Party quarters.

A word must be said about the continued success of Western classics. A little-known comedy by Voltaire, *Monsieur du Cap Vert ou les originaux* was one of the best-attended plays of the 1956–57 Moscow season. The same holds good of Calderon's *Dama Duende*.

The popularity of Shakespeare has always been great. In 1954 he came second only to Ostrovsky (usurping the place previously held by Gorky) in the list of authors with the greatest number of plays being staged in Moscow at any given time. Nor has his popularity declined since—seven of his works were put on in Moscow in 1960, and his success is not confined to the capital. It may be noted that during the postwar 'anticosmopolitan' campaign certain critics were accused of 'Hamletism', and that neither *Hamlet* nor *Macbeth* was performed, at any rate in the more important theatres, until after the death of Stalin.

Changes in the contemporary Soviet repertoire are important if judged by the Zhdanovite yardstick. The proportion of contemporary Soviet plays has increased slightly, and in Moscow amounts to half the total.[21] Statistics relating to the Soviet Union as a whole show that practically all the most frequently-staged plays are by contemporary Soviet authors. But on the whole the *nature* of this Soviet repertoire is very different from what it was after 1946. Although playwrights are still urged not to remain

21. From 53 per cent in the first six months of 1943 it fell to 49 per cent in 1957, owing to the popularity of foreign plays. It was 58 per cent in the first six months of 1961.

aloof from contemporary political problems, most of their works
in fact deal with personal problems (*bytovye*), and Zhdanov's condemnation of 'so-called psychological' drama is completely
ignored. The same (despite official criticism) can be said of his
opposition to the 'light' repertoire. Since plays of this kind are
not usually forbidden, they go on being performed, with increasing success. During the first six months of 1960, for instance, the
very respectable Moscow Academic Theatre put on 35 performances of a light comedy entitled *The Road through Sokolniki*, by
the young Soviet playwright Razdolsky. The subject is remote
from politics: it is the story of a young student who has failed
his entrance to a university, becomes a servant in the family of a
wealthy writer, and falls in love with the latter's wife. The play
was criticized for its lack of ideological content at the conference
of theatrical workers held in October 1958. As the chief producer
of the Soviet Army Theatre wrote in 1957, 'the public reads the
critics back to front: if a play is praised, one must refrain from
going: if attacked, it has to be seen'.[22]

Generally speaking, light Soviet plays have become an important part of the repertoire, not only in Moscow but also in the
provinces. Some of the most 'conservative' playwrights have
turned to writing light works, a task which does not, of course,
prevent them from striving to raise the morale of the theatre-
goer, in accordance with Party doctrine. But the great majority of
Soviet plays that go on being produced, and not written with the
sole aim of winning a prize, are to a large extent unpolitical. They
can be considered, broadly speaking, as responding to the Party's
appeal for 'contemporary' themes, but more often than not are
contemporary only in the sense that the action takes place in the
present, and there is usually a happy ending to indicate the
author's loyalty to the Party and government.

This does not mean that the Soviet theatre-goer takes no interest in politics. On the contrary, playwrights have often dealt
successfully with politico-ethical problems in a way which would
have been considered 'politically alien' in Stalin's time, is still not
approved by the 'conservative' section of the party bureaucracy,
and meets with strong opposition from Stalinist critics.

Most illuminating in this respect are the attacks on the present
Soviet repertoire made by V. Kochetov in his 1960 novel, *The*

22. A Popov, 'Our responsibility', *Teatr*, 11, 1957.

Brothers Ershov. Nothing has yet been written that shows more clearly how far the average successful playwright has deviated from Stalin's and Zhdanov's concept of 'engineers of the human soul'. Kochetov's book is full of blame for contemporary plays—the authors are not named, but are easily recognizable—which denounce the inhumanities of the Stalinist past.

Here is a short quotation from Kochetov's book, a passage complaining about a successful anti-Stalinist play:

They saw the new play of an untalented but clever new playwright. He knew how to titillate the audience. In every single act all through the play a good man was being done down. Everyone was doing him down: the Party organization, the trade union, the factory management, some despicable individuals. He struggled through a flood of tribulations, rousing the audience's pity and even drawing tears from many female spectators.

Kochetov's book is a violent attack on the most popular trend among the young and even the older playwrights. It is notable that some of the works which have most boldly attacked the misdeeds and the bigotry of the Stalinist bureaucrats finally reached the stage, and met with great success, but in the teeth of stubborn opposition from the so-called right-wing faction.

Such was the case of *Odna* (Alone), by the young playwright Alyoshin. Though vigorously opposed for a long time by the Deputy Minister for Culture, it was performed in 1956 with great success—it was one of five plays in Moscow that were completely sold out. *Odna* tells the story of an outstanding engineer, a communist, who divorces his wife in order to marry the woman he loves. He protests his fidelity to communism, but at the same time argues that the Party has no right to interfere in his private life.

The Factory Girl, a play by another young author, Volodin, ridicules the almost unconscious falsity of a stupid Komsomol organizer, Bibichev. The heroine, a straightforward, plain-spoken factory girl, is very far from the 'positive heroes' of the recent past. She is proud of her critical mind and says bluntly: 'I do not care to pretend; here people say one thing and do another. If anyone tries to oppose such a state of affairs, that is his undoing.' In spite of much party criticism, the play was put on and had successful runs in 1957 and 1958. In Moscow it was even produced at the Army Theatre.

There are a great many such plays, either dealing with unpolitical, human problems, or criticizing with greater or less audacity some of the typical features of Stalinism (while never, of course, calling in question the basic tenets of communism). This is not to say that 'conservative' works, by playwrights strongly opposed to anything that smacks of revisionism, do not get written and acted. The fact that *The Brothers Ershov* was adapted for the stage and performed in many theatres can only mean that this tendency is still strong in the Party bureaucracy, to which many directors of theatres, especially in the provinces, belong. For the same reason Sofronov's new plays were among those most often performed in 1960. On the other hand, if plays by 'dogmatic' writers enjoy greater success with local Party authorities than with the public (and are often staged as an excuse to put on very light plays at the same time), there are some fields in which political slogans do not run counter to the public taste. This is true of patriotic plays dealing with the past or with what may be termed 'Soviet patriotism' (including the cult of Lenin). Plays about heroes who died in World War II are often popular: a case in point is *Ivan Rybakov*, by Gusev, which tells the story of the son of an officer in the Civil War who, after behaving badly, redeems his honour by fighting bravely against the Germans. But it is difficult to find a public to attend, or playwrights to produce, so-called anticosmopolitan plays. The same is true of 'production drama' and in general of plays dealing with factory workers. The absence or scarcity of such plays has often been deplored by official critics.[23]

The changes described concern the ethical and political content of Soviet drama. But the reaction against the Stalinist concept of socialist realism did of course embrace aesthetic matters as well. The main issue, and the first to be discussed, was that of the *mise-en-scène*.

The Soviet tendency to canonize famous persons after their death should be borne in mind. This happened in the case of Mayakovsky, of whom Stalin wrote that he had been, and remained, the most gifted poet of the Soviet era ('indifference to his memory and his works is a crime'). Despite this canonization,

23. Cf. 'Where are the plays about the working class?' in *Trud*, 11 December 1955. Cf. also A. Salinsky's speech at the conference of theatrical workers, *Teatr*, 12, 1958.

Mayakovsky's plays were completely ignored, at any rate in the
big cities, until the death of Stalin. The staging of *The Bathhouse*
and *The Bedbug* by the Satire Theatre in 1954 was thus an important event. The stage managers, among them the highly gifted
Vladimir Pluchek, put on modernist productions of both plays,
which enjoyed a great success; in Stalin's time they would have
been denounced as full of 'formalist stunts'. The main problem
was how to get free of Stanislavsky's 'system', or at least free of the
obligation to apply it strictly in all theatres. His methods were
and still are scrupulously observed by the Arts Theatre, of which
he was the director. The level of acting of the company is high,
and, like that of the *Comédie Française* and other theatres with
an established tradition, interesting to the foreigner; but in the
eyes of a great part of the Soviet intelligentsia, especially the
young, the Arts Theatre is looked upon as a museum. Under
Stalin, any attempt to criticize it was regarded as 'anti-patriotic
slander'. As the *Pravda* journalist Zaslavsky wrote in a book on
the Soviet theatre published in 1947:[24] 'The Moscow Arts
Theatre marked a turning-point, and not in Russian dramatic art
alone ... not one progressive theatre in Europe or America
escaped the influence of Russian *mise-en-scène*. The "Stanislavsky
System" won recognition wherever the theatre had not yet completely petrified into commercial enterprise, no longer in search
of a goal but only repeating the old saws.'

The rebellion against standardization of style became explicit
after the twentieth CPSU congress. Some drama critics began to
rehabilitate Meyerhold, at least partially, and also Tairov, whose
Kamerny Theatre was closed down after the war, shortly before
his death. The seventieth anniversary of Tairov's birth was celebrated at the beginning of 1956 at a meeting in the 'House of the
Actor', attended by such writers as Fedin, Ehrenburg and Olga
Berggolts. In winding-up a debate begun in 1957, the theatrical
director M. O. Knebel, a well-known elderly actress, said that
Stanislavsky was not responsible for the bureaucratic rule (*ad-
ministrirovanie*) common under the 'cult of personality'. 'Stanislavsky's system had often been introduced forcibly; his
authority had been used to suppress artists of other tendencies
who tried to go their own way ... meanwhile the name of Stani-

24. D. Zaslavsky, 'The world significance of Soviet art', *Sovetsky Teatr*,
Moscow, 1947, p. 26.

slavsky was the sole password for gaining admittance to the flock of "orthodox realism".' [25] Although Madame Knebel emphasized her belief in the value of the Stanislavsky system, she compared it to antibiotics, which should be used sparingly. As for Meyerhold, she said he was a great artist, neglected for twenty years. He should not be reviled as a formalist, though it would be irresponsible to call him a socialist realist. Her conclusion was supported by the editors of *Teatr*. In spite of Party criticism of that journal in 1957–58, the posthumous rehabilitation of Meyerhold has become more and more outspoken, although most critics have to add that he made mistakes. His influence on the best theatrical directors of the younger generation is very great.

Stalinism had encouraged bad taste in staging, and its harmful results were not limited to theatre-goers. At a meeting of the 'artistic council' of the Ministry of Culture held in 1958, the gifted director of the Satire Theatre, Pluchek, emphasized how important a task it should be to raise the standard of public taste. 'Clouds pass, rose-water flows, and the audience starts clapping wildly. Every time I hear them applauding I feel sad, because it seems to me we are perverting the taste of theatre-goers' (*Teatr*, 3, 1958).

Interesting efforts have been made to break away from the standardization in staging prevalent since the mid-Thirties. If some of the attempts at modernity were of doubtful value (such as the 1955 production of *Hamlet* by Okhlopkov,[26] a former disciple of Meyehold, now chief producer of the Mayakovsky Theatre), there have lately been some genuinely personal and interesting efforts. Ravenskikh's production of Tolstoy's *Power of Darkness* at the Maly Theatre (the director, M. Tsarev, is one of the best Soviet actors) was a big event in Russian theatrical circles. Ravenskikh's harshly realistic *mise-en-scène* (he is now chief producer of the Pushkin Theatre, Moscow), showed him to be a most gifted producer; the production was recently staged in Paris at the *Théâtre des Nations*.

25. M. Knebel, 'Is Stanislavsky's system universal?', *Teatr*, 6, 1957.

26. Okhlopkov headed the 'Realist Theatre' which was merged in 1936 with Tairov's. His present theatre was founded during the war as a result of a merger between the Theatre of the Revolution (formerly headed by Meyerhold) and another theatre. It was named *Mayakovsky* in 1952. Okhlopkov was one of the numerous pupils of Meyerhold who later became staunch supporters of the Stanislavsky system (see M. Knebel, loc. cit.).

Another chief producer who was in disfavour towards the end of the Stalin dictatorship is Nikolai Akimov, now artistic manager of the Leningrad Comedy Theatre. In 1931, his 'formalist' staging of *Hamlet* at the Vakhtangov Theatre, Moscow, incurred the wrath of the Stalinists. In 1956 he wrote that the profession of theatrical director should be chosen only by people who were not afraid of criticism.[27]

One of the most remarkable recent successes of Leningrad's Comedy Theatre was Akimov's production of E. Shvarts' enchanting play *The Shadow*, a fine and witty work on a subject borrowed from Chamisso's Peter Schlemyl and one of Andersen's tales. Written in 1940, it is one of the few Soviet contemporary plays of indisputable literary value.

It is still difficult to pass judgement on the quality of Soviet drama today. The interference of frequently incompetent authorities certainly does not encourage the best Soviet authors to begin writing for the stage or to revert to doing so. This does not mean that good Russian playwrights cannot be found today. The situation may improve, and there is no reason to exclude, in the sphere of drama, the possibility of work of the same quality as, say, Kazakov's novels appearing. The shortcomings of many young Soviet playwrights are to some extent survivals of the past: they are suffering from their twenty-year isolation from the outside world. Their style is often negligent, and they are tempted to pander to the tastes of theatre-goers which have been depraved by socialist realism. Moreover, the rewriting to which their plays are often subjected before performance makes their lot worse than that of novelists and poets, in spite of the very high royalties they receive.

There are, nevertheless, playwrights whose works do not have a solely documentary value. Such is the case of Victor Rozov, for instance, who has written several plays about young people. *Eternally Living*, the drama on which the film *The Cranes are Flying* was based, is of better quality than the screen play seen (and liked) by the Western public. It would not be surprising if better plays were on the way; there is at least a tendency in the Soviet leadership to admit the existence of artistic and literary values,

27. N. Akimov, 'Teatr i Zritel', *Teatr*, 4, 1956. His portraits of theatre people were reproduced in *Teatr i Zhizn*, Leningrad, 1957.

and to recognize that much has yet to be done in this respect. Most playwrights are no longer 'engineers of the human soul'. Whatever their shortcomings, they are first and foremost playwrights, not political journalists who happen to write drama.

9

THE YOUNG POETS

Pierre Forgues

Surely there is no country in which so much poetry is published as in the USSR. Everything there is a pretext for a poem: a decree of the Supreme Soviet, the visit of a foreign communist leader, indeed, any random cutting from a newspaper, and, it goes without saying, any congress of the Party. *Izvestia* and *Pravda* publish poems several times a week: the austere and boring *Pravda* regales its readers regularly with articles written in verse by Alexander Nikolayev, the Ukrainian Stepan Oleinik, or the famous Bezymensky, commenting upon events of internal or international politics.

And if we turn to the literary journals and reviews the importance of poetry seems to be greater still: every number of the *Literaturnaya Gazeta* publishes the poems of one or more, sometimes of as many as five poets. The list of contents of the journal *Yunost* for all twelve numbers of the year 1961 contains the names of 122 poets who have had one or several of their poems printed in the magazine during that time. *Yunost* is, moreover, far from being a review that specializes in poetry : it is subtitled 'a literary, artistic, social and political monthly'.

In comparison with Western countries, where poets, especially young ones, have so much difficulty in publishing far fewer works, and still more in finding a public for them, one is tempted to think of the USSR as a 'paradise of poetry'. But one has only to turn from the statistics of published works to the reading of them to see that this is unhappily not the case. In the domain of poetry the USSR has not yet made the leap from quantity to quality—a fact, moreover, to which Alexander Tvardovsky drew dicreet attention in his speech to the Third Congress of Soviet Writers in May 1959.[1] You could transpose the authors' names on the col-

1. A. Tvardovsky: *Statyi i Zametki o Literature*, Moscow, 1961, pp. 183-95.

lected poems of dozens of poets without anyone noticing it. The abundance is mostly that of interchangeable products, abortions that one is surprised to find under the title of 'poems'. The columns of verse that Oleinik and Bezymensky perpetrate in *Pravda* only present in an extreme form what Stalin wanted poetry to be reduced to: a discursive illustration of the main themes of governmental policy. Poetry was to be the servant of the Politbureau, an ornament, of the same order as a lick of paint, to the Marshal's speeches.

The Central Committee decisions of 14 and 16 August and 16 September 1946, striking at Anna Akhmatova among others and at the journals *Zvezda* and *Leningrad,* mark a decisive moment in the history of Soviet poetry. From that date, Soviet poetry was strictly confined to its function as an instrument of propaganda. From 1946 to 1953 verse was still published in the USSR, but poetry had disappeared.

The kind of embarrassment then felt by those who preferred to submit completely rather than keep silence is manifested in the extraordinary homage lately rendered by the old Stalinist 'poet' Aleksei Surkov to Anna Akhmatova, who was condemned to silence from 1946. In a postscript to the collection of her poems published in Moscow in 1961, this poet-policeman writes:

By the poems she wrote during the last fifteen years Anna Akhmatova has won a special personal position in contemporary Soviet poetry, a position she did not pay for by any moral or creative compromise.

The authors of the *History of Soviet Literature* were also highly embarrassed when they came to their third volume, covering the period from 1941 to 1957, and had to analyse the work of the outstanding writers of that epoch. With the prose writers they could get by; the authors could find eleven names worthy of a monograph apiece. For poetry they could find only five: Tikhonov, Marshak, Selvinsky, Surkov and Tvardovsky; and to help fill this awkward gap the authors analyse the work of Konstantin Simonov almost solely from the point of view of his poetic production. If we add that, of the above-named poets, Marshak is hardly known except for his verses for children and his translations, and that Surkov is only a literary official, we have a pretty good idea of the void into which Stalinism precipitated Soviet poetry after the war. Apart from the regularity of the lines, there was nothing to distinguish a poem from an article in *Pravda*.

The death of Stalin was at once felt by the writers as a possibility of deliverance. It was a woman poet who inaugurated the new era: Olga Berggolts, who had spent several months in prison under Stalin. She wrote (*Literaturnaya Gazeta*, 16 April 1953), that Soviet lyrical poetry was very nearly nonexistent, crushed as it was under the weight of description and objective analysis; the 'I' would have to be brought back into poetry. Olga Berggolts's own attempts to revive Soviet lyricism are of less importance than the clarity with which she raised what was then a vital problem: the poet's right to seek the sources of poetry in himself and not only in the universe of objects. Her love poems, though they are less academic and less discursive than those of Stepan Shchipachev, are, however, rather flat.

Although the era of the thaw had been thus heralded by a poet, the years 1954 to 1957 were marked by no great development in poetry; it was mainly in prose that the thaw produced the most interesting upheavals. Against a score of novels which, on one point or another, broke the tables of the law of socialist realism, one can cite only a very few works of poetry: *The Seven Days of the Week*, by Semyon Kirsanov (*Novy Mir*, September 1956);[2] *Station Zima*, by Evgeni Evtushenko, published in the review *Oktyabr* in October 1956; the poems of Julia Neuman published in the second volume of *Literary Moscow*, including the famous *1941*. Since that date, however, Neuman has not, to my knowledge, published anything but some translations into Russian from Soviet poets writing in Yiddish.

Like the novels and short stories of that period which diverge a little from the beaten tracks, these poems are works of social criticism; their content depends upon external contingencies as much as upon a predetermined poetic conception. The use of allusion, or periphrasis, of the symbol, and the search for the oblique word, are recommended by prudence as much as by poetic reflection.

It is after the 'interval of freedom' that a new Soviet poetry be-

2. Kirsanov was attacked as early as 1925–28 for petty-bourgeois tendencies, and had then cleared himself of the accusation by publishing conformist works such as *Pyatiletka* and *Comrade Marx*.

gins to hatch out—a fact, moreover, that casts some doubt on the
very notion of the 'interval of liberty'. This new poetry arises
plainly in reaction against the previous generation: that is under-
lined in Soviet criticism itself. In the May 1961 number of the
review *Neva*, the critic, V. Druzin, divides Soviet poets of to-day
into two groups: those who are 'free from all decadent influences',
and those who are 'under the influence of decadent ideas', otherwise classed as the 'good' and the 'bad' poets. Among the good,
Druzin lists N. Aseyev, M. Svetlov, S. Smirnov, A. Kovalenkov,
V. Kulemin, Margarita Aliger, N. Anfitserov, A. Mezhirov and
S. Podelkov. In the category of the decadent, 'led by the venerable
Kirsanov and the younger Evtushenko', Druzin places, besides
those two poets, Yuri Pankratov, Victor Bokov, F. Evseyeva,
D. Samoilov, Yuri Levitansky and E. Kotlyar. In the January 1961
number of *Novy Mir*, the critics Menshutin and Sinyavsky declare that 'in their combative ardour, the young are about to leave
their poetic elders behind', and the two critics are so conscious
of a division of Soviet poetry into two camps that they place
Andrei Voznesensky on 'the extreme left of the young poets of
to-day'.

These young poets are not emerging, however, in the midst of
a complete desert. Not to mention Semyon Kirsanov and Tvardovsky, N. Zabolotsky (who died in 1958) and Leonid Martynov
(born in 1905) have played the part of 'caretakers' in the domain
of poetry that Konstantin Paustovsky has played in prose. The
pantheist lyricism of the former and the fantastic lyricism of the
latter have often had rough treatment from the official critics,
who deplore such disregard of the canons of socialist realism:
their works have kept alive the idea of a poetry not necessarily
tied to the contingencies of political or social action. But
Zabolotsky has never rediscovered the satirical epic view of his
Triumph of Agriculture (1929), and Martynov's fantasy is very
thin and garrulous. Both have remained too subservient to the
traditional rhetoric of speech-making. One might, at a pinch,
add to these two names that of Shchipachev, who has hardly
ever ceased to write 'love' poems [3] which strike one as too calm
and cold not to be fabrications; still, they bear witness to the

3. His principal book of poems is entitled *Strophes of Love*, from which the
lines quoted below are taken.

truth that poetry need not be a political weapon or an ideological tool. After all, there are very few Soviet poems in which anyone tells us of a 'light and partly-dressed woman', of 'breasts', or 'caresses'! But after having written:

> In the shade the breeze caresses her,
> She is light and partly dressed. . . .

the poet goes on:

> Where is the kitchen, then? . . .

showing the solidly prosaic temperament which often takes pleasure in lines like these:

> In July the cool dews
> Moisten chilly the hands.
> There's a fragrance of roses
> In the blooms of potato plants. . . .

Zabolotsky, Martynov, Shchipachev, Kirsanov—all these did little to fill the gap left by the suicide of Tsvetayeva and the imposition of silence upon Akhmatova and Pasternak.

To the four names above, we might be tempted to add that of Alexander Tvardovsky. He is an institution in contemporary Soviet literature. Editor of *Novy Mir*, Lenin Prize-winner in 1961, delegate to the 22nd CPSU congress, he is already regarded as a classic of Soviet literature, and worthy of a monograph 41 pages long in the latest *History of Soviet Literature* published by the Academy of Sciences. The last edition of the handbook of Soviet literature for high schools, written by A. Dementyev, E. Naumov, and L. Plotkin, devotes a whole chapter to him, an honour that is bestowed upon only two other living writers: Sholokhov and Isakovsky.

Born in 1910, Tvardovsky is the youngest representative of the generation born before the first world war. In 1936 he published *The Land of Muravia*, the hero of which, Nikita Morgunok, symbolized the Soviet peasant in search of the land of happiness; in 1942 *Vasili Tyorkin*, a classic portrait of the Soviet soldier; in 1946 *The House at the Side of the Road*, and in 1960, after having been almost silent from 1946 until the death of Stalin, *Afar, Farther Yet*.

Tvardovsky seems to be the leader of the group of liberal writers, and it is true that, as editor of *Novy Mir*, he has published many works which are among the most interesting in Soviet literature; more, however, in the domain of prose than of poetry. The significance of the role Tvardovsky plays in the realm of 'sympathetic' ideas expressed in *Afar, Farther Yet*, and his courage, should not conceal from us the fact that he is, nevertheless, a very conventional and traditional poet. His *Vasili Tyorkin* is undoubtedly one of the best works of Soviet literature inspired by the war, ranking with Simonov's novel *Days and Nights*, and his poem, *Do you recall, Alyosha. . . .* But if the union of skill and emotion, if the lyrical density imposed by the sense of frightful danger then weighing upon the USSR, save *Vasili Tyorkin* from banality, the epic of peace, *Afar, Farther Yet*, labours on from worthy sentiments to generous ideas without ever rising to poetry. Tvardovsky is at his ease in the classical development, in the rhetorical amplification of simple feelings. His works abound in pages that never rise above the level of this recent poem (*Novy Mir*, 1961, No. 10).

> Towards the century's heroic deed,
> In the name of universal happiness,
> The land of the sickle and the hammer
> Leads its daughters and sons.
>
> Fatherland of peace and liberty.
> What of it if enemies should threaten you?
> Your peoples will always stand beside you,
> Friend beside friend,
> Brother beside brother.
>
> Our might is unconquerable;
> Under the red banner
> It has opened new roads for the world
> And points to the reaches of the stars.
>
> Stream aloft, the banner of Lenin,
> Spanning our road ahead.
> Half the world is marching beneath it already,
> The day will come when the whole world will march.

The May 1962 number of *Novy Mir* contains a poem by Tvardovsky, *A Word about Words,* which ends with this gnomic
stanza, and it would be an error to think that the translation
exaggerates its platitude:

> [the word]
> It is no ossified sound,
> Nor just some raw material.
> Oh, no—the word is also a deed
> As Lenin oft reiterated. . . .

Tvardovsky is much more important as editor of *Novy Mir* and as
an essayist than as a poet. It is significant, moreover, that of all
the Soviet reviews *Novy Mir* is the one that gives least space to
poetry, and that the best poets of to-day rarely appear in it. The
poets it likes best to publish are, for example, M. Aliger,
Smelyakov, A. Prokofyev. *Novy Mir* is the spearhead of the
struggle for the renovation of Soviet literature. This does not,
however, prevent it from being attached to a rather traditional
conception of poetry.

The new generation of poets that has arisen in the last few
years is represented first of all by Evgeni Evtushenko, Evgeni
Vinokurov, and Andrei Voznesensky. We will centre our account
of present-day Soviet poetry on these three names. This limitation
is somewhat arbitrary: the work of other poets, such as Viktor
Bokov, Bella Akhmadulina and Kharabarov, also merits attentive
analysis; but within the frame of this essay it is better to enlarge
in some detail upon two or three leading figures than to present
a fastidious list of names accompanied by a hurried and super-
ficial commentary.

Both Evtushenko and Voznesensky have acquired, in the
imagination of the public, a symbolic value to which the critics
do not fail to draw attention. Viktor Pertsov writes in his article
on 'Poets of the Youth of the World': 'And here are two more
fiery chargers ... whose names occur the most frequently in the
tournaments of our new poetry! Evtushenko and Voznesensky'.[4]
And in a recent critical survey of 'Young Soviet Poetry' the poet
Yaroslav Smelyakov remarks that 'the name of Andrei Voznes-

4. *Oeuvres et Opinions,* January 1962, p. 154.

ensky is almost always pronounced at the same time as that of Evgeni Evtushenko'.[5]

The works of these two poets present many differences, but in the eyes of Soviet youth they symbolize the same demand for creative freedom, the same nonconformity, the same proud, detached attitude to life, the same easy manner. The strictures addressed to both of them by the old Stalinist critics are exactly the same: they are accused of a love of rowdyism, of attracting highbrow publicity by scandalous poems or behaviour, of posing affectedly as aesthetes, of falling back upon decadent mannerisms, etc. The attacks they have to put up with have, of course, a political tendency; but there is also a more practical motive, which can be indicated by two quotations: 'Indeed, what a mass of books of collected poems that no one ever looks at is now piling up on the shelves of bookshops and libraries!'[6] 'What is the explanation, then, of the obvious success of Voznesensky among the younger readers? I have seen an audience of young people acclaim him enthusiastically ... they like to think that Voznesensky is a poet different from the others.'[7] Evtushenko and Voznesensky are read; what they write matters. How can that be accepted with a good grace by the old cart-horses who have grown grey under the harness of the Stalin and Lenin Prizes, and who now write only for catalogues and lists of contents in histories of Soviet literature?

Of the three poets we have cited, it is Voznesensky who, from every point of view, best symbolizes the new generation's poetry. Now 30 years of age, he did not begin to get his poetry published until 1958, whereas Vinokurov and Evtushenko, in fact, began their careers as poets during the Thaw.[8] Up to the present Voznesensky has published only two collections of

5. *Literaturnaya Gazeta*, 9 December 1961.
6. N. Koryavin, 'Why do people write poetry?' *Yunost*, No. 5, 1962, p. 72.
7. Yaroslav Smelyakov, *loc. cit.*
8. An anthology entitled *Poetry during the Battle* appeared in Moscow in 1959, composed of poems about the second world war written by poets of various ages. Among others 'whose troubled youth coincided with those events' (and who wrote their first poetry at the front), it published poems by Evtushenko (who was only eleven in 1944) and Vinokurov (then nineteen, but whose first book of poems appeared in 1956). The poems selected not being dated, we cannot tell when they were composed: but it is certain that Evtushenko did not begin his poetic career at eleven! And the earliest poems that Vinokurov has published date from 1945.

poems: *Mosaic* in Vladimir in 1960, and *Parabola* in Moscow
in 1961. (The latter work was unfortunately subjected to what
Menshutin and Sinyavsky modestly described as 'unjustifiable
corrections' which disfigure it. As always in the USSR, it is pre-
ferable to read an author's productions on first publication in a
periodical.) If Voznesensky is not mentioned in the third volume
of the latest *History of Soviet Literature,* it is not a case of
ostracism, but of his not having yet published anything.
What is significant is that Pasternak is passed over in complete
silence, Akhmatova mentioned three times in passing, Evtushenko three times in passing equally rapidly, and Vinokurov,
fleetingly, once.

Voznesensky himself has pointed out his most interesting contribution to Soviet poetry. At the end of 1961, a collection entitled
My Best Poem appeared in Moscow, edited by Vinokurov,
Gribachev and Pertsov, and subtitled 'poems by Moscow
poets'. The editors had asked each poet himself to choose what
he thought was his best work. Voznesensky chose *Parabolic
Ballad,* his most criticized poem; and although he likes a scandal,
it would be unjust to suppose that he selected this poem for that
reason. *Parabolic Ballad* is a short poetic manifesto, which defines
only one part—externally the most important part—of Voznesensky's own poetic art. As a symbol of artistic activity, he takes
Gauguin, who

> To reach the royal Louvre
> > from Montmarte
> Struck
> > a detour via Java and Sumatra!
> He took off, forgetting the madness of money,
> The cackle of wives, the stuffiness of academies.
> He overcame
> > the earth's force of gravitation.
> The sacrificial priests gaggled o'er their tankards of beer:
> 'The straight line is shorter, the parabola is steeper.
> 'Wouldn't it be better to copy the heavenly tabernacles?'
> While he, he sped away as a roaring rocket
> Through ear-ripping, coat-stripping winds,
> And he entered the Louvre, not through stately portals,
> But as a wrathful parabola
> > piercing the roof. . . .

The poet is the man of the parabola; he must not name things, demonstrate ideas, slip lazily down the slope of logical reasoning or imitate great ancestors ('copy the heavenly tabernacles'), but reveal the hidden face of the stars, forget the conventional truths, suggest unaccustomed relations between beings and things, replace demonstration by oblique, approximate evocation, turn all round the object. The symbol is of no artistic value if it is transparent. What could be stupider than to enter into an art museum by the open portal that is meant for that purpose; a true artist can only enter it by breaking through the ceiling!

For Voznesensky the symbol is no mere literary trick: [9] the question is not how to represent an idea by an object which indirectly points to it, but to evoke those relations between the different aspects of reality that habit screens from us. The poet shows us reality in such a way that its diverse elements are recombined through a *consciousness*. Here, for instance, is how Voznesensky describes a wedding breakfast:

> Where they drink they break
> Cups and mugs on the floor.
> By the lads, underheel,
> Pots are smashed to bits.
> Cups explode into pieces,
> Someone's happiness also
> Is smashed to bits.
>
> And you, in your transparent skimpy skirt
> So young, so white,
> Atremble, as a wine glass trembles
> On the table's edge.
>
> The little smile, like tiny fissures
> Plays round your lips. . . .

For a country in which marriage is a sacred institution, this is a very insolent and uncalled-for picture! Indeed, the desire to

9. As it is in the famous story by Alexander Yashin, *The Levers*, where the battery-receiver symbolizes the poverty of the kolkhoz, the woman teacher hiding herself behind her scarf during the official speech by Tsipichev symbolizes the refusal of the intelligentsia to accept—at least completely—the teaching of the Party, the air made unbreathable by smoke in the secretary's office symbolizes the stifling atmosphere of bureaucratic Russia, etc., etc.

overthrow all the traditional representations of reality brings
Voznesensky's preoccupations rather near the experiments of
the surrealists. He reminds us of these also by the way he asso-
ciates, dissociates, and couples words together. His lines are
caught up in an intoxication with words: he delights in alliterations which break the rhythm of the line by quickening it.
Smełyakov reproaches him for railing at

> The experts reeking
> Of formalin and incense. . . .

simply because 'formalin' and 'incense' (*fimiam*) begin with the
same consonant: but the objection is only partly valid: are not
these essential attributes of the official criticism?—formalin in
which it tries to sterilize youthful talent and the incense it burns
so prodigally to the established writers? Still, it is true that Voznesensky likes playing with words, with their outward forms
irrespective of the immediate content. This playfulness, however,
always tends to create an atmosphere peculiar to his poetry; his
juggling with words and letters is like his juggling with beings
and things.

Thus, when he conjures up 'guests pot-bellied as kettles', it is
because *gruznie* and *grelki* provide a fine alliteration, but also
as detached and disrespectful an image as could be wished. Like
Evtushenko, with less brilliance but more subtlety, Voznesensky
is, in fact, a perfectly disrespectful poet; a number of critics reproach him for his 'impertinences'. Here is one of them, which
shows how Voznesensky can renovate a hackneyed theme, both
in meaning and form. One day he decided to write a poem on
Lenin: there is no more overworked theme in all Soviet literature; the evocation of Vladimir Ilyich always engenders swank,
emphasis, bombast, the grandiloquent pose, tricks—everything
that Lenin himself liked least: 'Lenin lived, lives, and will live
forever!' as the hymn of the Komsomols proclaims. But Voznesensky entitles his poem 'Lenin's Sequoia' [10]

> In the motor-car state of California
> Where the sun itself smells of colophony
> There is a park of giant red-woods. . . .

One already suspects that in a poem about Lenin, the sun smells

10. *Znamya*, 1962, No. 4.

of colophony only because *kanifoliu* has a vague assonance with *Kalifornii*. Voznesensky continues:

> The sheriff, the fly of his trousers undone,
> Steamed up in laborious speech,
> Trudged along to be received by the Mayor:
> 'My Mayor, the shameless rabble
> 'Reach out, leaf and root, for Moscow . . .
> 'Oooo . . .'
> The Mayor swallowed his cigar. Fire! . . .

This off-hand style is combined with great conciseness of form. Voznesensky symbolizes better than anyone some of the deeper tendencies of contemporary Soviet poetry: the rejection of the complacently drawn-out speech, the taste for the elliptical, for the abbreviated, for speed. We find these characteristics again in Evtushenko, in spite of his liking for eloquence, and in Vinokurov. Out of words that telescope one another the image springs naked, without comment.[11] The poet exhibits; he has no time to explain. Hence the contracted, spasmodic, flashing qualities of Voznesensky's poetry:

> Fire in the Architectural Institute!
> Through halls, through blueprints,
> As would an amnesty through gaols—
> Spreads fire. Fire!
>
> Upon the sleepy facade
> Impudently, mischievously,
> Like a red-bottomed gorilla
> Flares up a window! . . .
>
> Farewell, architecture!
> Blaze freely on,
> Cow sheds with cupids,
> Rococo savings banks. . . .
>
> Farewell, age of suburbias.
> Life's a succession of smouldering ruins.
> We are consumed by fire.
> To live is to burn. . . .

11. This exposes Voznesensky to a good deal of criticism, like that of the poet Koryavin in the March 1961 number of *Novy Mir*, protesting that we never know the why and the how of the situations Voznesensky describes.

His detachment and love of ellipsis enable Voznesensky to re-
discover a virtue completely lacking in Soviet literature—
humour:

> And again, looping the loop.
> They tear along all night long
> The same old inveterate
> Motorists and poets. . . .

His horror of 'hurdy-gurdy' leads him to reduce the logical structure of sentences to the minimum:

> Begrimed snouts.
> Camp fire.
>   A stream.
> We are young. We are hungry
> As a legion of imps. . . .

It is here that the tic, the mannerism, the mechanical repetition
of methods is a danger to him. The acceleration of the rhythm,
the multiplication of interjections and the abundance of exclamation marks, sometimes serve only to mask an absence of inspiration. That is what Soviet critics mean when they call
Voznesensky's poetry 'shrill'. But where is the poet who has never
given us the feeling that he caricatures himself? It is unfair,
then, to single out lines like the following in order to reduce
Voznesensky's poetry to a merely clever utilization of methods
which appear new only because Soviet readers and writers have
never really assimilated the art of Mayakovsky:

> Bath-houses! Bath-houses! Doors slam!
> Wenches go jumping into the snow. . . .

Sometimes the machinery revolves in a void: that does not prevent Voznesensky from being the best spokesman for the Soviet
poetry of to-day and tomorrow.

Born in 1933, Evtushenko is the same age as Voznesensky. He
is by far the most widely known in the West: in the USSR itself
his popularity is such that he need not envy Voznesensky's. He
also has a more 'scandalous' reputation. Turned out of the Komsomol at 20 years of age, he has led, with great notoriety, an
amorous life more or less in defiance to the strict norms of 'Soviet'

morals.[12] He likes taking risks, and his poetry is thoroughly 'committed' to topical affairs. Evtushenko takes sides. He is pugnacious, rebellious, insolent, carnivorous—and lucky not to have been born before 1933. The conservative Starikov has accused him of a lack of 'political tact',[13] and the reproach is understandable when we read lines like these:

> You drink to the shades of Verlaine,
> You, with your tightly stuffed bellies.
> You would assassinate all poets
> In order later to recite them. . . .

or again, this passage in the famous *Babi Yar* (a poem which is not included in the latest collection of his poems, *A Gesture*):

> O my Russian people!
> You are really international at heart.
> But the unclean
> Have often loudly taken in vain
> Your most pure name. . . .

As we know, the governing bureaucracy has encouraged Russian chauvinism to the limit, with its inevitable corollary, anti-semitism. We are therefore hardly surprised to read Starikov's exclamation:

Why, then, does the management of a literary journal of our Union allow Evtushenko, at this moment, to attack Lenin's policy of nationalities, by means of associations of ideas and allusions which can only be described as acts of provocation?

To be accused of anti-Leninist provocation is no light matter in the USSR! It shows us that Evtushenko's poetry has nothing in common with 'engagement' as the literary bureaucrats understand it. The poems he writes on Cuba, on Algeria, or on communism, are poles apart from the traditional commissioned works. Evtushenko recently declared to a French journalist: 'I never write to order, and work to no plan of production'.[14] In this he is affirming an independence characteristic of the new generation of Soviet poets as a whole. We can well believe him; this is

12. On several occasions, during a visit to Russia, we heard professors of the University pronounce the name of Evtushenko with horror, as that of 'a monster of immorality'.
13. *Literatura i Zhizn*, 27 September 1961.
14. Interview by K. S. Karol in *L'Express*, 24 May 1962.

one of the elements of his immense success with the young people; they are panting for air, for frankness and sincerity, after the great Stalinist carnival of fear and falsehood. On this point *Babi Yar* is a model, and in the USSR this has been recognized by his adversaries as well as his defenders.

Evtushenko loves to insist upon the *mission*, the *vocation*, of the poet. For him, the poet has a function to discharge in society: he bears within himself a truth that he must communicate to other men; or, rather, he is the spokesman for voices that the poet alone is able to hear:

> Tucked in bed I hear
> The snow storm trying to say something,
> And the tramways in the swish of the snow
> Sadly clanging each its own tale.
>
> Scraps of posters attempting to whisper.
> On the roofs the sheet iron attempting to shout,
> And the water attempting to sing in the pipes,
> And the telephone wires moaning impotently! . . .
>
> There is cause for my vigil this night,
> And to come to the help of them all
> I must become, in duty and in love,
> These trees, these tramways, and these men. . . .

Evtushenko sometimes defines this vocation of the poet in much more restrained and traditional terms:

> I do not want to squander
> My vocation upon trifles,
> But that my verses be
> The very colour of our flag.
>
> Verses so strikingly red
> And their light so solemnly pure
> That the old and the young will say
> 'This is indeed a communist poet.'. . .

As it is, Evtushenko affirms that the poet must be of his time, live with his age, which means that he must renounce the traditional old rubbish so honoured in Soviet art. Such is the theme of his poem *Rockets and Carts*:

> One must not despise the village cart—
> It has done its work.
> But sometimes something jars
> When I meet it in a work of art. . . .

To fulfil his mission, the poet must always try to find means to express, with the utmost possible sincerity, what he himself sees, feels and thinks. Artifice is incompatible with poetry:

> You talk too much, you think all wrong,
> So rarely simple and direct.
> And one is never sure of discovering
> What in you is not you. . . .

'You talk too much': the demand for sincerity implies the rejection of speech-making that we have noted in Voznesensky. The taste for the abbreviated is itself closely linked with the deeper desire to penetrate and depict things and beings as concretely as possible. This double preoccupation does much to account for the enormous popularity of Hemingway's work among the young Soviet intellectuals of today. It is significant that Evtushenko should have dedicated one of his finest poems, *Encounter* (*Yunost*, 1961, No. 4), to the author of *For Whom the Bell Tolls*, and that this poem is winged with an exaltation that is unusual for a poet so conscious of his means and his 'tricks' as Evtushenko:

> With stern, victorious determination
> He walked
>   raising a tidal wave
> Over all the dust of ages
>   that has been faked as 'modern',
> Through all that quasi-antique 'modern'. . . .
>
> The very ground beneath him seemed to give,
> So heavily he trod upon it. . . .
>
> Rough hewn out of some granite crag
> He walked, as one walks through bullets, through ages. . . .

Bella Akhmadulina has also dedicated to the American writer a poem, published in her latest collection of verses, *The Rope*. In a curious antithesis to Evtushenko she writes:

> He walks lightfooted as an Indian,
> He, who knows hunting and love.

Hemingway's dry, short sentences, his love of concrete detail either significant or merely accessory, the astonishing combination of nihilism with feeling for the depth of an existence that is felt, smelt and tasted—all this could not fail to impress the young Soviet writers, in revolt against the traditional treadmill, against the academic lyricism and fulsomeness, the pretentious false simplicity, of the Stalin Prize-winners. In Hemingway they find an example of what they want to do and of the manner in which they tend to feel their existence. Are there not, in Evtushenko, some of the heroic attitudes of Hemingway? But to accuse him of copying the American writer would be as false as to accuse Yuri Kazakov of doing the same in his short stories. Evtushenko and Kazakov are only giving artistic expression, by means similar to Hemingway's, to personal and collective urges that are wholly original.

Though it has greater compass, Evtushenko's lyricism is nevertheless more traditional than Voznesensky's, in content as well as in form. Evtushenko has too much natural eloquence not to be carried away by the very movement of his verse. He constructs his poems out of accumulations of concrete details. But he also loves oratorical effects and crashing cadences. The tone in which he declaims his poem clearly shows his taste for eloquence and sometimes for striking an attitude. Soviet critics often reproach him for 'playing the coquette.' Here, for instance, is a coquettish ending that falls flat, taken from a poem entitled *Moscow Goods Station*:

> Moscow Goods station,
>   I beg you to remember them. . . .
> They go nights without sleep. . . .
> Theirs will be glorious inventions.
> On them depends the fate of the world.
> But meanwhile,
>   for coming to their aid,
> Thank you, Moscow Goods station.
>   Thank you, my dear. . . .

Like Voznesensky, Evtushenko has also written a poem entitled *Marriage,* in which again we find a bride-to-be in tears:

> The bride sheds bitter tears. . . .

But whereas Voznesensky points out, merely by the way, that his young bride

> Has married someone—no, something,

and constructs his poem by juxtaposing a series of logically unrelated images, seen from the outside, Evtushenko lets us know that his young bride is in tears because her husband is going to the front tomorrow:

> Rifle in hand he will go
> Maybe to fall
> Prey to a German bullet. . . .
> Their first, bridal, night
> Is maybe their last. . . .
> The bride weeps bitterly,
> The guests stand in tears. . . .

The evocation is rather banal: more than Voznesensky's, indeed, Evtushenko's poetry is dependent on *the event*; though it is too original to be mere commentary, it is more closely bound to the actual: it is therefore less given to rhythmic and verbal experimentation, and much more ready to draw upon the resources of oratorical rhetoric. Evtushenko writes trenchantly; his poetry often gives the appearance of improvisation, and in the stream of words which sweep away the poet, the good sentiments, the apparent simplicity, the easy coquetry, the reiterations, and the near-misses find their proper place. Evtushenko is not a demanding poet—he easily lets himself be carried away by the inspiration of the moment. The form of his poetry is separable from its content.

His poems sometimes recall Victor Hugo in their oratorical tone and method—in the method, for instance, of accumulations and repetition to accentuate the line. The resemblance to Victor Hugo is not accidental. In some respects Evtushenko does remind us of the young leader of the French romantics; he has the same brio, the same oratory and love of eloquence, the same facility, and, what is more important, the same affirmation of self. Evtushenko has, indeed, written a number of rather complacent love poems . . . but they are incomparably more full-blooded than the triflings of Olga Berggolts or Shchipachev. This affirmation of *self* in lyric poetry makes itself felt at the moment when Soviet literature is emerging from a pseudo-classical period which has points in common with the Napoleonic pseudo-classicism. To try to establish any close comparison between these two periods of world literature would be grotesque, no doubt. But is it not true that Soviet poetry is now taking on several characteristics that resemble those of the European romantic movement: self-affirmation, poems of a biographical character, love of eloquence, the appeal to creative enthusiasm, the development of the love lyric? [15] Of all these qualities Evtushenko is the best incarnation.

Born in 1925 in Bryansk, Evgeni Vinokurov began to write in 1945, but his first booklet of verse, *Poems on Military Service*, was not published until 1956, and was quickly followed by *Blue Sky*. In February 1962, a volume appeared in Moscow entitled *Lyric Poetry*, which contained all his previous booklets of poetry —the two already mentioned, together with *Confessions, The Human Face* and *The Word*, the last of which, a collection of the poems that Vinokurov wrote in 1961, was published separately at the same time. The whole of his work is available in one book of 312 pages,[16] and that of Voznesensky in three booklets. In the first poem of his latest collection, *The Word*, Vinokurov writes:

> The sacred teaching says—
> To speak the word, to build a phrase,
> How simple: open but the mouth
> And, lo, the miracle of words. . . .

These lines by an old pupil of the Gorky Literary Institute, which recall dadaist and surrealist affirmations about the primary importance of spontaneous verbal utterance, stand in complete contradiction to the aesthetic of socialist realism. According to the official ideology of art, the word could never be a spontaneous miracle; it could be of no value except in the service of specific ends.

Vinokurov goes further still:

15. Evtushenko's ideas upon the poet's mission also recall those of Hugo; but these are ideas common enough in Russian literature of the nineteenth century.
16. All references, unless otherwise stated, will be to this volume.

> I know that men consist of words
> Which have entered them,
>   and of a body.
> The word moves. Earth is on fire!
> And the pitchfork transfixes the sky. . . .

Thus, the word is the final reality: it is all-powerful, it keeps the world going. Vinokurov, a poet, vehemently affirms the magic power of the *word*—of the word as the poet uses it, whatever it maye be, not of words intended to project the history of to-morrow upon the poetry of today. He can also write, later on:

> Deep feelings rest on silence.
> Suffering is mute. And so is music. . . .

Here he is not contradicting what he said before, which was an expression of an idea common to all the new poets enjoying their ability to explore the abysses of the word, without restraint or guidance from the ukases of the Politbureau. In the last two lines Vinokurov is simply condemning garrulity and hurdy-gurdy. As he says:

> Then there are words—the eye skips over them.
> Bean pods that are barren. That hold no beans. . . .

So that his words should not be empty, Vinokurov makes them waltz and spin: he, too, wants to give vibrant rhythm to his poem:

> Third gear! Indeed!
> Why crawl? One must tear along! Speed along!
> That the very heart stand still
> Inside my speeding frame!
> That around me, like smoke,
> Drift colours. Whiter—white.
> That my breath rear up
> As a shying horse!
>   Beat the windscreen, wind!
> Beat it! To shivers, to spasms!
> Howl, motor! Not motor, but TNT.
> Third gear!
>   Much too timidly
> Did I tread the earth until now. . . .[17]

17. *The Word*, p. 3. The poem of the same name in the collected *Lyric Poems*, which is also the first in the booklet *The Word*, gives a quite different text.

Voznesensky gives hardly any importance to the subject of a poem: the theme he chooses is first of all a pretext for ascending and descending the scale of his verbal virtuosity. His poetry is not a mere game, but on the loose warp of the theme the lines are woven haphazardly. Evtushenko, more classical, either tells a story (love poems), treats a subject, or affirms an idea (political poems). Vinokurov seems even more traditional; each of his collections is composed of poems written upon a common, general theme: *Poems on Military Service* evokes, as the title indicates, scenes of military life, the central piece of the booklet being a series of short poems grouped under the title *Barracks. Blue Sky* is made up of little nature pictures and of brief sketches (*The Swans; Springtime; Labour*). *Confessions*, a more personal selection, includes love poems and some recollections of childhood and youth—the favourite theme of young Soviet poets. *The Human Face* and *The Word* are more various; here, the different veins of Vinokurov's supple talent mingle together in poems expressive of the writer's need to meditate upon the value of his art.

Vinokurov pays much less attention than Voznesensky to experiments with form; from time to time, it is true, he finds good alliterations:

> *Grust po tebe menya segodnya glozhet*
> *I ya gruschu, i v etom net grekha.*
> (To-day I'm gnawed by a longing for you.
> And I long. And I see no sin in this.)

But these phonetic preoccupations are of secondary importance to him; he is interested above all in *rapidity of rhythm* and exactitude of *concrete detail*. He excels in the evocation of an object, a moment, a memory, a person, in a few words: he does not allow the evocation to extend into description or dissertation; he does not develop it. Like Voznesensky, he leaves part of his poem to the reader's guesswork. Thus, his poem *Adolescence* is made up of a series of details thrown together without much logical connexion:

> Youth is that age
> When you fancy that the world
> Is only a fancy.
> When reality resembles
> A shimmering landscape

> Reflected in some pond outside Moscow.
> The reality seems built of matchsticks—
> Blow on it and it all falls apart.
> Youth is the moment
> When the distance from the heart
> To humanity is the shortest. . . .

No detail follows from the previous one as an amplification of it, as in a poem by Hugo—or by Evtushenko; it is simply added to it; that is why Vinokurov sometimes gives the impression that he is slightly out of breath. It is a method which, in the same piece, mixes such commonplace images as:

> Youth is that age
> When you walk as a recently
> Hatched chick
> Who hasn't yet shaken off
> The shell bits of his infancy. . . .

with fine, new images:

> Youth resembles that
> Indefinite, transient hour
> When blue twilight
> Like water
> Fills the lanes of Arbat. . . .

Vinokurov's qualities are less striking than those of Voznesensky and Evtushenko; his words are less exalted, there is less brio and glitter; he has neither Voznesensky's mastery of words nor the eloquence and lyrical elevation of Evtushenko. He nevertheless occupies an important place in contemporary Soviet poetry. Like Evtushenko, with less noise but certainly with more penetration and sensibility, he has helped to restore a personal quality to lyric poetry, and to bring the 'I' back into poetry.

Besides their individual qualities, the works of Voznesensky, Evtushenko, and Vinokurov present certain common characteristics that we find in other poets.

The young Soviet poets are suspicious of rhetoric, of long speeches, of lofty fluency: as in architecture, this is no time for the gigantic. Addicted to concrete, precise detail, to real things and beings, these young poets are in general writers of short pieces; they outline their themes but do not elaborate them into vast frescoes. To recite names would be superfluous; one has only to open a book of their poetry or no matter which of the reviews, to see their rapid sketches and little pictorial pieces.

Turning away from the mechanical orchestration of the great social themes, these poets are giving more attention than before to the problems of form. V. Soloukhin has written several collections of blank verse: they all love playing with words, multiplying alliterations and assonances. From this point of view we must mention Viktor Bokov. Bokov is the great friend of Voznesensky who, in his *Mosaic*, addressed an affectionate poem to him:

> He goes about—blue-eyed
> His eyes darting like perches,
> Or a window open to the spring . . .
> As unpredictable as the cast of a die,
> Breezy as March. . . .

Bokov, moreover, responded to this homage in his volume *Victor's Springtime*, published a few months after *Mosaic*, with a poem which the critic Chernyakov rightly described as 'arcadian' in tone:[18]

> My darling Andrei! Piper of the cities!
> Caressing my ears with your verses,
> Like love itself you make me young again.
> Oh, how I love you. You, my early leaf-bud
> With its translucent veins! . . .
> . . . the silvery little voice
> Whose every note is so pure. . . .

If Voznesensky pays homage to the work of Viktor Bokov, it is because the two men are very much alike; they share in the exalted tension of the short and dry phrase, in the contempt for outward logical connexions, in the staccato rhythm, in their predilection for tricks and games of sounds, in their sense of humour. Entire poems by Bokov are explainable only by the poet's desire to string together words, quite unpredictable in combination, apparently because they echo one another:

18. *Literaturnaya Gazeta*, 12 May 1962.

> *Otymi solovya ot zaroslei,*
> *Ot rodnovo ruchya s rodnikom.*
> (Part the nightingale from the thickets,
> From its brook, and its source.)

These games are not necessarily gratuitous: for instance, the critical humour in this line is very effective (*Yunost*, 1961, No. 4):

> Breathe in the lily-of-the-valley, not incense. . . .
> (*Ne na ladan, na landysh dyshite.*)

Bokov's talent is more adaptable than Voznesensky's; he readily delights in sparkling trifles (*Yunost*, 1961, No. 7):

> Eyebrows up to the sky.
> Plaits down to the waist.
> She is the girl
> We met in Tallin. . . .
>
> My name has flown
> To me from the sea.
> Ocean winds brought it
> Into my cradle. . . .

He likes to place his poems, generally very short, in a purely imaginary setting:

> The maiden—a cellophane wrapped egret,
> Getting soaked at a tramway stop.
> Importuned by the thin, thin drizzle. . . .
> Steel-clad Don Quixotes hasten to her side. . . .[19]

But whatever style he is cultivating (fantasy, trifles, or political poems), Bokov, like his colleagues, has a very high opinion of the value of poetic creation; which is not the least typical characteristic of this generation:

> When I write I hold in the palm of my hand
> A light sphere—the terrestrial globe. . . .[20]

One must also mention Boris Slutsky, Yuri Pankratov, Kharabarov, Poperechny, and, especially, Bella Akhmadulina (the former wife of Evtushenko) who has just published her first collection of verse, *The Rope*, which includes poems written since 1956.

19. *Literaturnaya Gazeta*, 1 May 1961.
20. *Yunost*, 1961, No. 7.

Akhmadulina's themes are the same as those of other poets of her generation—nature (*April, August, September, December, A winter day, Flowers*) and specifically the distant lands of the USSR (parts of her verse are grouped under the title *From a virgin land notebook* and *From a Siberian notebook*), love poems, poems about objects of modern life (*The automatic camera, The motorcycle*). She adopts an elliptical language, both concise and unexpected.

> I'm changing gears
> In face of the moon and the wind ...
>
> Life is good—as an elephant ...
>
> The hand was breaking
> Against the high piano keys.
> Over it, as in churchyards,
> The grass grows deep ...

She delights, to excess, in rhymes so rich as to become almost puns:

> *Mne nevterpezh, mne nevterpezh.*
> *Mne ne v Tergekh? Mne ne v Tergekh?*
> (I can't bear the delay, can't bear the delay.
> Is it Tergekh I'm going to? Is it Tergekh?)

She loves surprising juxtapositions of words, which becomes almost a mannerism:

> In going red she turned blue
> (*Ona sinela do krasna*)
> One mustn't weep, but swim.
> (*Ne nado plakat, nado plavat*)

—a verse which is based on an assonance of doubtful poetical value.

Her love poems are quite conventional. The best do not rise above these lines, the end of a poem whose only vigour is due to alliteration:

> 'Tis not in pride—'tis in sorrow
> That I bear my head so high. ...
> (*Ya ne iz gordosti—iz goresti*
> *Tak pryamo golovu derzhu*)

Akhmadulina has written very little these last few years. No more than that of her young contemporaries can her poetry deve-

lop except by reaching above the level of elegant, or even brilliant, commentary on subjects, which are bound to appear to us
rather insipid and light.

It is precisely this self-confidence that annoys the Soviet critics,
even some who cannot be counted among the conservatives, such
as Menshutin and Sinyavsky, who write:

Not long ago the 'young' were quiet, modest and respectful. . . .
With the exception, perhaps, of Evtushenko alone, the 'beginners'
tried not to talk at the top of their voices about their private lives.
And now, every poet is uttering pretentious declarations and rowdy
manifestos! The poets have become loud-mouthed, quarrelsome and
impatient.[21]

What Smelyakov likes—though he too cannot be ranged among
the out-and-out conservatives—are the young poets who sensibly
acknowledge, like Vladimir Kostrov, that:

> You, who became my superiors.
> You, of pure eye and of blazing youth,
> My elders, bearing experience and knowledge,
> I believe in you
> And it is from you that I learn how to live. . . .

If it is not the Kostrovs but the Voznesenskys who get the lime-
light, the sole reason, according to Smelyakov, is that the latter
organize their propaganda better. He explains why he does not
much like those rowdy innovators, by attacking, though without
naming it, the *Parabolic Ballad* of Voznesensky:

For example, I do not like the parabola, I like the straight line; I
like poets who cut it short: I like the word to sound clear and firm.
I do not like allusions, I like slogans—of course, bold (?), imaginative
(?) and talented (??) slogans.

If the new generation provoke this reaction among the moderates,
one can imagine what sentiments they must arouse in the
Stalinists. During the appearance in *Yunost* of the novel *The
Ticket to the Stars*, Sobolev surpassed himself in lamentations
over the misguidedness of youth. But such critics have to be pru-
dent: Surkov could not hope to have such an effect to-day as he
had in 1954—the dismissal of Tvardovsky and Panfyorov from

21. *Novy Mir*, No. 1, 1961, p. 288.

their posts as editors-in-chief of *Novy Mir* and *Oktyabr,* after
public denunciation. Recently, a young poet, Robert Rozhdestvensky, got *Literaturnaya Gazeta* to publish a very violent little
note in reply to a poem by Anatoli Kalinin, printed in *Literatura i
Zhizn,* which had attacked a poem of Evtushenko's that Rozhdestvensky, moreover, thought was a bad one! So we can see that
times have changed somewhat.

Since the Pasternak affair, which was a Pyrrhic victory for
them, the conservatives have had to resort to allusion and innuendo. The way Kochetov wrote his last novel *The Obkom Secretary,* may be regarded as a model of the methods used by the
conservatives to ridicule and depreciate the new Soviet poetry.
The Obkom Secretary presents some fifteen characters, of whom
only one is fundamentally negative and remains so to the end—
the modernist poet Ptushkov. Even the woman of bad reputation,
Yuria Pavlovna, comes to a good end, by marrying into the Party;
but Ptushkov does nothing but reveal his meanness and male-
ficence: he is pretentious and stupid; he is an idler who knows
how to do nothing but break hearts, without loving anyone. But
let him be confronted by a true Soviet woman and he crumples
up like a punctured balloon. His new poetry is nothing but a half-
baked mixture of decadent devices that were fashionable in Russia
before the Revolution. Not only is he stupid, pretentious, and a
nobody, he is also cowardly and vicious: the only comprehensible
poem he writes is a satire, *The boyar Vasili Dexter and his faithful following,* in which he ignobly defames the Obkom secretary,
Vasili Denisov, and his friends, who are devoting every minute of
their lives to the Party and the country. The sole reason—suggested though not explicitly stated—why Ptushkov does this, is
evidently his rancour at not having been able to go to bed with the
Obkom secretary's sister-in-law! And despite all this, Ptushkov,
evidently intended as a portrayal of Evtushenko, still remains at
liberty to write.

For all its virulence, this diatribe by Kochetov is weakened by
two circumstances. First, poets who write poems of the sort that
Kochetov likes remain on the shelves of the bookshops, whilst the
productions that he pillories are all the rage among the young
people. And second, the reception given to Kochetov's theses in
literary circles was such that he was not put forward as a candi-

date for election to the board of the Moscow branch of the Union of Writers in April 1962.

In the realm of Soviet poetry, then, socialist realism is now in rags and tatters, although not a single poet has said that he wanted it to be so. The dogma is not denied, nor discussed. It is forgotten.

In fact, during the last few years Soviet poetry has gained the right to exist. That is how the weaknesses and the pliancies that we can discover among the best poets of the new generation are to be understood. Will Soviet poetry hold on to the positions it has won? Will it advance further? Contrary to what one would have thought only four years ago, the answer no longer depends exclusively upon political conditions, but primarily upon the Soviet poets themselves.

To-day two 'schools', without official tags, are openly opposed on the Soviet artistic scene. Of course the 'liberals' do not claim any coherent artistic principles different from socialist realism which could define the 'credo' of a new literary school. The present situation, however, logically leads towards the emergence of literary schools, and these would deepen the divergences which already exist between all those who have now come together only to affirm their right to write more or less what they want.

The fact that a young Soviet poet, Leonid Pashchenko, claims affinity with Mayakovsky, Blok and Khlebnikov, underlines this desire to take up the thread of tradition interrupted by thirty years of Stalinism. It may be rash to suppose that the leadership of the CPSU wishes to return to the policy defined by the famous Central Committee resolution of 1925, inspired by Trotsky, Bukharin, and Lunacharsky. The Soviet leaders cannot yet officially accept artistic polycentrism in the USSR, but their search for a new policy capable of bridging the abyss between the hypertrophied Party apparatus and the passive masses would certainly dissuade them from abandoning (except in case of some serious danger) a policy which leads, more or less gradually, towards the restoration of the 1925 policy. For the new generation of Soviet poets, this is both their opportunity and their responsibility. It also sets limits to their horizon.

10

SOVIET BOOKS, CENSORS AND READERS

Maurice Friedberg

The origins of Soviet control over publishing may be traced back to the prerevolutionary writings of Lenin, particularly his now famous article *Party Organization and Party Literature*. The implications of Lenin's pronouncements on the subject as well as the first instances of the Party's intervention in publishing affairs were discussed in two excellent recent articles by Ernest J. Simmons.[1] While the aim of the present paper is to highlight some of the most recent developments in this area, perhaps a brief summary of earlier events would make the discussion more meaningful.

The Soviet agency charged with censorship duties, the Central Administration for Literary Affairs and Publishing (*Glavlit*) was established by the decree of 6 June 1922.

The law prescribed that one of the two deputy chiefs of *Glavlit* should be a representative of the security police. A law of 1931 redefining the duties of *Glavlit* stated that the agency had been established 'for the carrying out of all kinds of political, ideological, military and economic control of printed matter'. On the basis of this law, secret lists of items (*perechen*) which censors were to prevent from appearing were issued and were frequently revised. . . . To make censorship more strict, it is carried out in two stages: pre-publication censorship guarantees that no undesirable book is published, and post-publication censorship sees to it that the book is published in the approved form and with the censor's corrections.[2]

1. Ernest J. Simmons, 'The Origins of Literary Control', *Survey*, London, No. 36 (April–June 1961), pp. 78–84; *ibid.*, No. 37 (July–September 1961), pp. 60–67.
2. *McGraw–Hill Encyclopedia of Russia and the Soviet Union*, Michael T. Florinsky, ed., New York–Toronto–London, 1961, p. 72. A documented description of day-to-day activities of the Smolensk division of *Glavlit* (in particular some details on the contents of the *perechen*) may be found in Merle Fainsod,

By the decree of the RSFSR Council of People's Commissars of
6 June 1931, *Glavlit* was empowered to exercise similar controls
over 'manuscripts, drawings, paintings, broadcasts, lectures and
exhibits to be printed, made public and disseminated'.[3] It was
also empowered to prepare lists of works whose publication and
dissemination was forbidden. The number of the local *Glavlit*
representative authorizing the publication of each item of
printed matter must, with few exceptions, appear on the last
page of that item by authority of the decree of the same
body of 10 August 1931.[4] The Council's decree of 26 February
1934 established special criteria for the censorship of productions (domestic, exported and imported) of plays, films,
broadcasts, ballets, and even circus acts. Any of these could be
banned for a variety of reasons. Some of these, such as 'propaganda directed against the Soviet system and the dictatorship of
the proletariat', were perhaps understandable, as were also 'di-
vulging of state secrets', 'arousing national and religious fanaticism' and even, perhaps, charges of 'pornography'. Among the
more unusual reasons for banning any of the above were mere
'ideological weakness' (*not* harmfulness!), 'mysticism', and even
anti-artistic character'.[5] The censors were thus not only appointed
guardians of political purity and public morals, but—it seems,
for the first time in history—they were promoted to the position
of judges who were to decide what is and what is not art, and
their verdicts were to be final. On 1 November 1934 a joint decree
of the RSFSR Commissariat of Education, the RSFSR Commissariat of Justice, and the USSR Commissariat of Internal Affairs
(the NKVD) reaffirmed the earlier decrees.[6] Special provision was
now made for the confiscation of banned items (such as films),
which were henceforth not to be returned to their owners; the
ban could not be appealed against.[7] Plays, films, ballets, etc., were
to be reviewed by the censors at least ten days before their official
première. In addition, the management of each show had to reserve for the censors two seats at every performance, not farther
from the stage than the fourth row.[8] Even the technical make-up

Smolensk Under Soviet Rule, Cambridge, Mass.: Harvard University Press, 1958,
pp. 364–77.
3. L. G. Fogelevich, *Osnovnye direktivy i zakonodatelstvo o pechati*, sistema-
ticheskii sbornik, 5th edition, Gosizdat 'Sovetskoe zakonodatelstvo', 1935, p. 110.
4. *Ibid*, p. 112.   5. *Ibid*., p. 121.   6. *Ibid*., pp. 122–23.
7. *Ibid*., p. 123.   8. *Ibid*., p. 125.

of books was to be decided by the censors. *Glavlit* order No. 149 of
11 August 1935 declared war on 'formalistic' (read 'modernistic')
book jackets and bindings.[9]

Errata slips were permitted only for minor typographical errors,
not to exceed ten in number. Otherwise, 'pages must be torn out
or glued in'.[10] Perhaps to encourage the authors themselves to
'update' their own books politically and thus facilitate the censors' work, a decree of the Council of People's Commissars of
17 August 1934 declared that 'revised and corrected editions are
not considered reprints', thus permitting their authors to be rewarded for their vigilance with additional royalties.[11] A regular
feature of the 1930's were also the periodic purges of books and
periodicals in libraries. In fact these were so severe that a leading
Glavlit official issued in 1935 an order to stop 'pilfering' and
'damaging' library collections.[12]

The story of the 'anticosmopolitan' witch-hunts inaugurated
in 1946 with Zhdanov's attacks on the poetess Akhmatova and
the late humorist Zoshchenko is well known and there is no need
to repeat it here.[13] Less known are the instances of the Party's interference in the publication of works by deceased authors. Thus,
for example, on 22 May 1952 the Central Committee ordered
that the publication of a five-volume set of the prerevolutionary
writer M. I. Mikhailov in the city of Chkalov be stopped since the
initial volumes included, among others, his 'politically immature'

---

9. *Ibid.*, p. 117.

10. *Ibid.* The best-known recent example of the treatment of major 'errata'
is the treatment accorded the article on the late secret police chief Beria in the
fifth volume of *Bolshaya sovetskaya entsiklopedia*, originally published in
1950. 'Following Beria's execution as a "traitor" in 1953, subscribers to the
"Encyclopedia" received several replacement pages with following instruc-
tions: "Cut out pages 21 to 24 of volume V, including the full-size portrait and
substitute the enclosed text for them". This new text, which was to replace
Beria's life history and likeness, consisted of a series of illustrations of the
Bering Sea and articles on Auguste de Beriot (a Belgian violinist) and Friedrich
Wilhelm Bergholz (an eighteenth-century courtier at the court of Holstein).'
See Paul L. Horecky, *Libraries and Bibliographic Centers in the Soviet Union*,
Indiana University Publications (Slavic and East European Series, vol. XVI),
1959, p. 156.

11. Fogelevich, *op cit.*, p. 77.

12. Horecky, *op. cit.*, pp. 156–57. See also Fainsod, *op. cit.*

13. The text of the original 14 August 1946 resolution of the Central Committee of the CPSU may be found in *Sovetskaya pechat v dokumentakh*,
Moscow, Gospolitizdat, 1961, p. 94.

and 'artistically immature' writings as well as translations of some 'reactionary' foreign poets.[14]

The 'Thaw' that followed Stalin's death has been characterized by a less rigid application of the censorship laws of the 1930's. The laws themselves, however, have never been rescinded and a return to a stricter observance of their letter and spirit could be accomplished at any time without any publicity or enacting new legislation. Thus, for instance, as in the previous years,

. . . public catalogues, as a rule, record only a selected part of a library's holdings; and centrally-directed discard procedures regulate the elimination of materials which are out of step with the current line. To say that all these devices are more or less agents of thought control is not conjecture but a matter of record supported by a host of Soviet sources. The latest Soviet textbook on bibliography, for one, declares that: 'The bibliography must offer criteria of evaluation and selection . . . must be guided by principles which ensure a correct attitude toward literature, contribute to promoting progressive—and to criticizing reactionary—views and ideas'.[15]

True, in 1956, certain works that had previously been confiscated, were returned to open collection.[16] But book burning, though perhaps on a diminished scale, continues as an integral part of Soviet cultural policies. Thus, in 1957 a Soviet scholar noted that libraries must replace books either because these old books have lost their value, or because they are physically 'worn out'. Fiction 'wears out' most rapidly; technical literature, though it 'becomes outdated due to the progress of science and technology, is kept'. The books that 'grow obsolete' most rapidly—and are, pre-

14. *Ibid.*, pp. 355–56. The problem of textual revisions effected in works of Soviet literature in order to bring them into conformity with current Soviet policies was discussed in two articles by the present writer. See Maurice Friedberg, 'New Editions of Soviet Belles-Lettres: A Study in Politics and Palimpsests', *The American Slavic and East European Review*, Vol. XIII, No. 1 (February 1954), pp. 72–88; also 'Soviet Literature and Retroactive Truth', *Problems of Communism*, Vol. III, No. 1 (January–February 1954), pp. 31–39. On at least one occasion the procedure involved direct intervention by the Central Committee. In its decision entitled 'On Crudest Political Distortions in the Texts of Demyan Bedny's Works' (24 April 1952) two publishing houses were brought to task for reprinting *old* texts of Bedny's propagandistic verse, rather than the new versions, allegedly prepared by the deceased poet himself after his works had been criticized by the Party. The Central Committee ordered that a 'correct' edition of Bedny be published. The text of the Central Committee resolution appears in *O partiinoi i sovetskoi pechati*, Moscow, *Pravda*, 1954, pp. 627–28.

15. Horecky *op. cit.*, p. 155.   16. *Ibid.*, p. 157.

sumably, removed from the bookshelves most frequently—are those dealing with political and socio-economic problems.[17] It is more than likely that Stalin's works, once published in hundreds of millions of copies, are now the chief victims of the book purges. In fact, Stalin's works are even retroactively eradicated from book publishing statistics which now use a new category in their break-down—'founders of Marxism-Leninism'[18]—which is a convenient way to bypass Stalin. However the 'Thaw' did have a definite impact on the quantity of political literature printed. In 1946 books dealing with political subjects constituted over one third of the total book output; in 1956 they accounted for only 14.3 per cent. The decline was no less impressive in absolute figures: 209,600,000 copies in 1953, and 158,700,000 in 1956. As the Soviet researcher put it:

The lower output of political literature was influenced by the CPSU's campaign against survivals of the cult of personality.[19]

In 1950 the average printing per title in the category 'Marxism-Leninism' was 62,300 copies; in 1956 it was 23,000. In contrast, the printings of *belles-lettres* rose from 34,300 per title in 1950 to 43,400 in 1956.[20] Yet in spite of this, there is ample evidence that the mass of readers feels that the amount of 'political' books produced is still far too great. Thus, while 'political' books constitute approximately eight per cent of all copies printed, they account for fifteen to twenty per cent of all *unsold* books. In public libraries, 'political' books constitute slightly less than one quarter of all books, but only some ten per cent of those on loan. An average 'political' book is taken out less often than once a year, or two times less frequently than the average for all books. In the countryside the demand for 'political' books is even smaller; an average 'political' book is borrowed from a public library only once in two years.[21] On the other hand, there is a

---

17. N. I. Buzlyakov, *Voprosy planirovania pechati v SSSR*, Moscow, Gosizdat 'Iskusstvo', 1957, pp. 23–24.

18. *Ibid.*, p. 98.

19. *Ibid.*, p. 52. It should be stressed that Soviet figures on book production are far less impressive than they appear at first glance. Unlike in the West, in the USSR a 'book' is any item of four pages or more sewn or glued together (*ibid.*, p. 82, footnote). The oft-repeated Soviet claims to world primacy in book production should be evaluated with this point in mind.

20. *Ibid.*, p. 94.   21. *Ibid.*, p. 53.

great shortage of juvenile books which comprise eight to nine per cent of the monetary value of all books, but only two to three per cent of the unsold books.[22] There is also an acute shortage of multi-volume editions of the Russian classics and of certain Soviet writers.[23] Most of the *belles-lettres* that cannot be sold are the 'masterpieces' of Stalinist socialist realism.[24] In the libraries, *belles-lettres* constitute thirty to forty per cent of all the books on the shelves, but fifty to sixty per cent of books borrowed by readers.[25] A 1959 article divulged such surprising facts as that:

Works of many of the Russian classics who brought to our literature world fame, who constitute the eternal treasure of our literature, cannot be purchased for years and years.[26]

Thus for example, not a single Chekhov play could be had for approximately six years.[27] Also in 1959 a reader from Tashkent pleaded with the publishers to bring out a long list of authors— all Russian and foreign classics with the exception of Forsh, Tynyanov and Shishkov, authors of historical novels and thus hardly 'typical' practitioners of socialist realism.[28]

The publishers, eager to make a profit, and sensing a more relaxed political atmosphere, obliged. In connexion with the centennial of Chekhov's birth in 1960, for example, they planned to bring out a total of 2,250,000 copies of his works.[29] Readers were supplied with large amounts of translated Western literature, for the most part classics, but also with some significant works of modern European and American writers.[30] Many of

22. *Ibid.*, pp. 55, 57.   23. *Ibid.*, pp. 38, 55–56.

24. In 1950–55 unsold *belles-lettres* constituted some twenty-five per cent of all unsold books, but of this number approximately forty per cent were books printed before 1954. See *ibid.*, p. 55.

25. *Ibid.*, pp. 54–55.

26. T. Shestakovskaya, 'O stikhakh, prose i ob isdatelstvakh', *Sovetskaya knizhnaya torgovlya*, No. 6 (June 1959), p. 18. *Sovetskaya knizhnaya torgovlya* will hereafter be abbreviated as *SKT*.   27. *Ibid.*

28. L. Babayev, 'Golosa podpischikov', *SKT*, No. 7 (July 1959), p. 41.

29. *SKT*, No. 1 (January 1960), p. 21.

30. However, no original editions of Western European and American books can be purchased in Soviet bookstores, though it appears that some books from the 'people's democracies' are being sold. On the other hand, when foreign ships are in Soviet harbours an effort is being made to sell Soviet books to foreign sailors. For a report from Odessa see G. Chiznik, 'Knigi stran sotsializma', *SKT*, No. 8 (August 1959), p. 19. The agency importing books from 'people's democracies', *Knigoimport*, was organized in 1956, i.e. toward the end of the 'thaw' (*SKT*, No 2, February 1958, p. 47).

204   *Maurice Friedberg*

the early Soviet writers who had been 'unpersons' during the latter period of Stalin's life have now been 'rehabilitated' and their works republished.

Certain works of Soviet writers of the older generation which have not been republished for many years, even though their authors were in 'good standing' with the authorities, were also brought out during the 'Thaw'. Much new Soviet writing, some of it daringly unorthodox, was allowed to appear in print.[31]

No attempt will be made here to discuss the overt and covert methods whereby erring Soviet writers were to be brought to reason.[32] We shall limit ourselves to a consideration of ideological pressures brought to bear on bookselling and book publishing agencies by the Party in an effort to arrest the liberal trends of the 'Thaw'. As so often happens in the USSR, the degree of the danger was disclosed only *after* measures were taken to cope with it. Some of the perils the Party had to contend with have already been referred to earlier. They seem to fall into six categories:

(a) Lack of interest in 'political' books, such as the 'classics of Marxism-Leninism', texts of Party decrees, speeches by Soviet leaders, etc., as demonstrated by their poor sales and lack of demand in libraries.

(b) Apathy with regard to 'good' and 'useful' books by contemporary Soviet writers, as manifested by their comparatively small printings, '30,000 or, rarely, 100,000 copies'.[33]

(c) Excessive interest in relatively apolitical Soviet *belles-lettres*, including Soviet 'whodunits' by such authors as Shpanov and Val. Ivanov.[34] A bookstore in Nivosibirsk, for one, sold, during the first three quarters of 1958, some three million roubles worth of

31. For a lucid discussion of this subject see George Gibian, *Interval of Freedom*, Minneapolis, University of Minnesota Press, 1960.

32. The condensed text of Khrushchev's 1957 speech to writers, composers, and sculptors appears in *Sovetskaya pechat* . . . , 1961, pp. 383–413; his speech of 22 May 1959 at the Third Writers' Congress, *ibid.*, pp. 444–70; and his speech of 17 July 1960 delivered at the meeting with 'representatives of the intelligentsia' *ibid.*, pp. 503–21.

33. Speech by deputy chairman of the RSFSR Union of Soviet Writers, S. V. Sartakov, *SKT*, No. 9. (September 1960), p. 51. Sartakov dismissed possible protests with this remark: 'You may object: such is the readers' demand. But first of all, *readers may and should be influenced*' (*ibid.*, italics added).

34. 'Chto skazali o nashei rabote poet, pisatel i kompozitor', *SKT*, No. 7 (July 1959), p. 19. Again the same authoritarian comment: '*One must not bow to the so-called readers' demand. This demand must be correctly created*' (*ibid.*, italics added).

fiction over and above the plan: most of these books were apolitical 'adventure' books.[35] The danger was even evident in the armed forces. Thus it was reported with some concern:

Not enough attention is devoted to dissemination of military and political books: one also observes a passion for 'The Library of Military Adventures' which includes many books of inferior ideological and artistic value.[36]

(d) Unusually high degree of demand for nineteenth-century Russian classics which in the late 1950's, together with translations of foreign literature, constituted over half the copies of all *belles-lettres* published in the Soviet Union.[37] This demand probably became particularly apparent after the decree of the Ministry of Culture of 19 December 1956 abolishing restrictions in the number of subscriptions to be accepted for 'certain' multi-volume editions.[38]

(e) Alarmingly high interest in translated Western literature of the past and present. Thus, Conan Doyle's tales of Sherlock Holmes were printed between 1956 and 1957 in 1,500,000 copies.[39] Works of E. M. Remarque were sold in 3,000,000 copies.[40] Half a million copies of *A Thousand and One Nights* were printed in the provincial city of Kishinev, where the publishers also brought out large quantities of books by George Sand and by the nineteenth-century Polish novelist Boleslaw Prus.[41] There were also complaints about excessive infatuation with the works of Alexandre Dumas (père), etc.[42]

(f) The tendency of book publishers to publish, and of individual bookstores to trade, only in items that are easy to sell. As a result, provincial publishers tend simply to republish books that

35. On the other hand, the same bookstore did not order a single copy of such 'important' books as *Revisionism: the Chief Danger* and *Against Contemporary Revisionism*. L. Titova and V. Tyutyukin, 'Plany vypolnyayutsya, a chitabeli bez knig', *SKT*, No. 5 (May 1959), p. 17.

36. A. Karev, 'Knigi prinyaty na vooruzhenie', *SKT*, No. 11 (November 1958), p. 35. The author recommended closer co-operation with the army's political officers. (*ibid.*, p. 39). Similar complaints were voiced by B. Reznikov, 'Knigu—voinu' *SKT*, No 2 (February 1958), p. 9.

37. Sartakov, *SKT*, No. 9 (September 1960), pp. 51–52.

38. *SKT*, No. 8 (August 1957), p. 26.

39. *Sovetskaya pechat* . . . , 1961, pp. 360–62.

40. Sartakov, *op. cit.*, p. 51.

41. G. Gurevich, 'O zakupkakh mestnykh izdanii', *SKT*, No. 5 (May 1959), pp. 20–22.   42. Sartakov, *op. cit.*

have already been brought out—and sold out—in Moscow.[43] One bookstore, eager to increase its profits, began to sell fashion magazines; it made more money on them than on all the books it sold.[44] Other bookstores even sell pictures and frames to fulfil their sales quotas, etc.[45]

The Central Committee of the C.P.S.U. showed its profound concern over this state of affairs by adapting a series of resolutions between 1958 and 1960.

On 11 February 1958 it ordered Soviet newspapers not to use too many photographs because this practice '. . . is a result of harmful influences of the Western bourgeois press and results in the fact that individual issues often become empty, apolitical, illustrated editions catering to philistine tastes.' [46]

On 5 April 1958 it warned publishers of translations from Western authors against bringing out worthless books merely because they are a good source of revenue. Authors mentioned included Conan Doyle and Alexandre Dumas. The Central Committee upbraided publishers for failure to append introductions to editions of the more 'harmful' Western writers, such as the four-volume set of Upton Sinclair, whose 'latest views require merciless criticism'. The Central Committee decided that henceforth its own Department of Propaganda and the Department of Culture will co-ordinate all publishing of foreign authors and will also see to it that the works of these authors be given proper ideological evaluation in book reviews.[47]

On 4 September 1958 the Central Committee decided that some multi-volume editions (presumably those of the Russian classics) are printed in too many copies and the publishers have failed 'to consider whether these editions ought to be given mass dissemination'. Again, the Central Committee took it upon itself to decide in the future how many copies to print.[48]

On 9 September 1958 the mass-circulation illustrated magazine

43. A. Koryakin and S. Khanin, 'Pochemu knigi lezhat na skladakh?' *SKT*, No. 6 (June 1957), pp. 18–19; also G. Shaidurov, 'Obsuzhdaem tekhnicheskie plany', *ibid.*, p. 20.

44. D. Kuzovenko, 'Rassuzhdenia i deistvitelnost', *SKT*, No. 6 (June 1958), pp. 54–56.   45. Gurevich, *op. cit.*

46. *Sovetskaya pechat* . . . , 1961, pp. 286–87.   47. *Ibid.*, pp. 360–62.

48. *Ibid.*, pp. 294–95. It is possible that the Central Committee was having second thoughts about the large printings of such 'reactionary' authors as Leskov (eleven volumes, 350,000 copies per volume) and Dostoevsky (ten volumes, 300,000 copies each).

Ogonyok was chastised for printing too many photographs of life abroad, as well as publishing detective stories, such as L. Ovalov's *The Bronze Button*.[49]

On 31 March 1959 the Central Committee criticized the Academy of Sciences:

1. [The Central Committee] notes that the Department of Language and Literature of the USSR Academy of Sciences committed a crude mistake by having published in 20,000 copies the 65th volume of *Literaturnoye nasledstvo*, 'New light on Mayakovsky'. The book includes materials which distort the image of the outstanding Soviet poet. Correspondence of a profoundly intimate nature and of no scholarly interest was made public. Other materials, tendentiously selected in the book, give an incorrect picture of the poet who was allegedly in conflict with Soviet conditions, which echoes the slanderous fabrications of foreign revisionists about Mayakovsky. The reactionary foreign press is making use of the book 'New light on Mayakovsky' for purposes of anti-Soviet propaganda. The contents of the book have caused indignation among the Soviet public.

*   *   *

4. The editorial board of the journal *Kommunist* is to publish an article on the state of literary scholarship, with particular emphasis on incorrect tendencies in the study of the work of V. Mayakovsky.[50]

In spite of the fact that the 1958 resolution placed the work of the Foreign Literature Publishing House under direct control of the Central Committee, the publishing house came under fire again in the Central Committee's resolution of 4 June 1959. The Party's grievances were similar to those voiced a year before: too many 'harmful' authors, lack of good introductions which would explain to the Soviet reader what is true and valuable in a particular book and what is false and objectionable. The only fiction writer involved was Somerset Maugham. The others were historians, scholars and public figures: D. Fuller (*The Second World War*), Thomas Finletter (*Power and Politics*), and D.

49. *Sovetskaya pechat* . . . . , 1961, pp. 112–14.
50. *Ibid.*, p. 300. The reference to 'reactionary press' was probably directed primarily at the American paperback, Vladimir Mayakovsky, *The Bedbug and Selected Poetry*, edited and introduced by Patricia Blake, New York: Meridian Books, 1960. Miss Blake's selection and introduction have been attacked in the Soviet press.

Smith (*The Military Doctrine of the United States*). This time
the objectives of the Soviet publishers of foreign books were
clearly defined:

The chief tasks of the Foreign Literature Publishing House are to
be the publication in Russian of the following:

(a) Political, scientific and technical works as well as *belles-lettres* of
    Socialist countries which shed light on problems of political, eco-
    nomic and cultural development, on the international Communist
    and labour movements, on the struggle for national liberation in
    colonial and dependent countries.
(b) Books written by members of fraternal Communist and labour
    parties of capitalist countries, which shed light on the struggle of
    the toilers for their rights and social progress, and also of litera-
    ture depicting the decay of the capitalist system, unmasking con-
    tradictions within the capitalist camp.
(c) Literature of foreign progressive organizations and individuals,
    public and political figures who struggle against the preparation
    of a new world war, for a peaceful solution of international prob-
    lems, for a ban on atomic and thermonuclear weapons, for a
    widening of business contacts with our country, and for a peaceful
    coexistence of the two socio-economic systems.
(d) Works of bourgeois authors dealing with philosophy, history,
    economics, diplomacy, and law. *Such books are to be published in
    limited printings: passages of no scholarly or practical interest are
    to be deleted from them; and they are to be supplied with lengthy
    introductions and annotations.*[51]

On 6 January 1960 the Central Committee chastised the youth
magazine *Smena* for insufficient militancy in combating alien
'bourgeois' ideas among Soviet youth, and for poor taste in the
magazine's make-up.[52]

On 29 January 1960 Soviet television was upbraided for insufficient concern with ideological problems.[53]

And, finally, on 31 May 1960 the Central Committee accused
the entire book trade of lack of political vigilance and of merely
catering to the tastes of its customers:

Many book trading organizations order books without considering
the interests of the buyers, basing their decisions on commercial considerations. They are insufficiently enterprising in pushing timely

51. *Sovetskaya pechat* . . . , 1961, p. 368. Italics added.
52. *Ibid.*, p. 126.   53. *Ibid.*, pp. 135–41.

literature, in particular political books and modern *belles-lettres* and at the same time place large orders for translations of certain foreign writers which have no artistic merit.[54]

[Book trading organizations are to] see to it that in all large population centres the following be on sale: classics of Marxism-Leninism, materials of congresses and plenums of the Central Committee of C.P.S.U., and also political and socio-economic literature aimed at the mass of readers.[55]

The accusations were partly unfounded. For some time now Soviet book trading agencies, perhaps sensing the changed political atmosphere, have been trying to 'push' propaganda books. Full-page advertisements on the inside back covers of *Soviet Book Trade* have been urging bookshops to order books, postcards, and even postage stamps dealing with ideological and military problems as well as atheism. Such advertisements were featured in the August, October, and November issues in 1959 and in the January, March, and May issues of 1960. And an editorial in the December issue of 1959 stressed that 'it is extremely important that the bookseller himself be interested first and foremost in current political literature'.[56]

As was to be expected, the response of book trading organizations was swift. The June 1960 issue featured already one article urging that bookstores 'create' demand for 'political' books,[57] and one demanded that orders for 'political' books (presumably, unlike those for other types of reading matter) be accepted 'without limitations'.[58] The August 1960 issue of the journal featured an article by the chief of the All-Union Book Trading organization urging—by an interesting twist in logic—that Soviet people be supplied with books they *really need* and not those that *merely sell well*.[59] The same issue contained an article promising an annual minimum of five new books on problems of atheism and anti-religious propaganda.[60] The November 1960 issue featured

54. *Ibid.*, p. 314.   55. *SKT*, No. 7 (July 1960), p. 2.
56. 'Torgovat kazhdoi knigoi', *SKT*, No. 12 (December 1959), p. 3.
57. S. Kugel, 'K voprosu o metodike izuchenia sprosa na obshchestvenno-politicheskuyu literaturu', *SKT*, No. 6 (June 1960), pp. 6–7.
58. S. Kopchenov, 'Nuzhen li spetsializirovanny magazin politicheskoi knigi?' *ibid.*, pp. 8–9.
59. T. Barashkov, 'Boyevaya programma sovetskikh knizhnikov', *SKT*, No. 8 (August 1960), pp. 1–4.
60. V. Boyarskii, 'Ateisticheskaya nauchno-populyarnaya kniga', *ibid.*, pp. 34–35.

an article dealing with advertising techniques which might be used to promote the sales of 'political' books.[61] Several articles of similar nature appeared in the December issue.[62]

The new ideological offensive in the book trade was even felt among the *bukinisty*, the second-hand book dealers who have, for years, led a precarious existence in the USSR. In 1959 *Soviet Book Trade* carried an appeal for the expansion of this form of book trade, though, to be sure, with the reservation that only 'experienced' people enter the field so as to prevent the dissemination of '. . . rubbish, ideologically harmful (!) and obsolete literature'.[63] A year later the journal printed an article complaining that second-hand dealers refuse to purchase any old political books (for reasons that need not be explained) or even technical books, and are interested in acquiring only most recent editions of fiction.[64]

The Central Committee's dissatisfaction with the book trade's alleged slackness in the dissemination of 'political' books was also reflected in the closing of the journal *Chto chitat* (What to Read) and the founding of a new one, *V mire knig* (In the World of Books).[65]

The 1958–60 decrees of the Central Commitee of C.P.S.U. with their demands for a greater degree of ideological militancy, are to some extent, reminiscent of the events of 1946 and their aftermath. Events of recent years, however, lack the intransigent fanaticism of the early postwar years.

No books really 'harmful' to the Soviet system can possibly appear in the USSR under present conditions of highly efficient censorship. The Soviet reader has merely an opportunity to choose from an assortment—a much wider one since Stalin's death—of 'useful' and 'harmless' books. There is a constant pressure on librarians, bookstore managers, and travelling book salesmen to see to it that the Soviet citizenry read fewer 'harmless' and 'useless' books, and instead develop a taste for 'useful' works, whether in the form of fiction or non-fiction.

61. A. Marin, 'V tsentr vnimanyia—politicheskuyu literaturu', *SKT*, No. 11 (November 1960), pp. 22–24.

62. *SKT*, No. 12 (December 1960), pp. 11–20.

63. A. Samartsi, 'Segodnya i zavtra bukinisticheskoi knigi', *SKT*, No. 5 (May 1959), pp. 24–25.

64. A. Sukhanov, 'Bukinisticheskaya kniga v zagone', *SKT*, No. 7 (July 1960), p. 27.   65. *SKT*, No. 7 (July 1960), p. 17.

11

CONFLICT AND CHANGE IN SOVIET LITERATURE

Max Hayward

During the last three years, since the Third Writers' Congress in May 1959, the general pattern of development in post-Stalin literature has become fairly clear. This seems, therefore, to be the moment to attempt a review of the present state of affairs, of which one can perhaps speak with more confidence than at any time during the ten years since Stalin's death. The main object of this essay is to examine the new relations between the Party and the writers, and to speculate on the wider implications of the changes that have taken place.

In the years since Stalin's death the relationship between the Party and the writers has been fluctuating and ambiguous, but on the whole, despite occasional alarming setbacks, developments have been remarkably beneficial to literature, and one is justified in being cautiously optimistic. One may say that at the present stage the Party has arrived at a position of compromise which allows both itself and the writers more room for manoeuvre—in practice, if not in theory—than at any time since the middle Twenties. If it did not involve a grave loss of face through the explicit admission of past errors and the removal from the record of the Central Committee decree of 1946, the Party could to-day reissue its famous resolution of 1925 as an adequate expression of its present *de facto* policy vis-à-vis literature and the arts.

The painfully slow evolution of this policy over the last decade has followed a course which, as one can see in retrospect, was dependent on obscure quarrels in the highest inner councils of the Party, and also of course on the international situation, notably in 1956. I shall review the main stages briefly.

The sense of liberation which followed Stalin's death, combined with 'panic and disarray' among Stalin's heirs, made

possible the first attempts, in cautious and Aesopian language, to
challenge the Party's self-arrogated right to control literature.
The whole fabric of orthodox literary theory and practice was
implicitly questioned in the famous articles of the *Novy Mir*
group at the end of 1953 and the beginning of 1954. To a large
extent this first Thaw was a genuine attempt from below to dis-
mantle Stalinist literary orthodoxy, but looking back on it one
cannot escape the feeling that it was to a certain extent licensed
or even inspired by some of the panic-stricken legatees of Stalin's
power. There is reasonable circumstantial evidence to suggest
that the main subject of contention in the so-called collective
leadership in the first few years after his death was the question
as to who should get the credit for exposing the misdeeds of the
late dictator, and thus secure popular backing for himself. It
seems quite likely that the first Thaw may have been sanctioned
by Beria or Malenkov as an attempt to curry favour with the
intelligentsia. It is possible that the reaction against the first
Thaw during 1954 was due to other members of the presidium
who were acting not so much out of conviction as out of the desire
to prevent certain of their colleagues from jumping the gun on
the exposure of Stalin. This much one may judge from the fact
that the reaction was a comparatively mild one, and that the
strictures on Pomerantsev, Ehrenburg, and others were far from
intimidating. Indeed at the Second Writers' Congress in December 1954, despite rather unconvincing expressions of repentance
for their outspokenness earlier in the year, some of the offending
writers still voiced cautiously-worded pleas for a more reasonable
approach to literary problems. It was clear that the die-hards—
the people who are now commonly referred to as the 'dogmatists'—were still overwhelmingly strong, and could count on
decisive political support at the top. At this Congress, however,
we find the first clear evidence of the existence of two camps in
literature, and as one could see from the behaviour of Konstantin Simonov, who scurried from one to the other, their relative
strength evidently depended on some configuration in the Party
presidium about which it would be idle to speculate, and of
which it would be wrong to think crudely in terms of pro- or
anti-Stalinism. It was perhaps more a question of the tempo and
tactics of modifying the late dictator's policy.
    In the two years after the Second Writers' Congress there was

an uneasy truce between the two camps, with little apparent change in the balance between them. After the twentieth CPSU congress there was a clear shift in favour of the liberals, who were of course inevitably joined by a horde of opportunists. In the extraordinary spate of writing which followed the congress, the foundations of socialist realism were virtually demolished, and there were novels, poems, and plays which in practice wiped out the specious distinction between socialist realism and critical realism. The most significant event in 1956, whose far-reaching implications I shall discuss later, was the attempt by the group of writers associated with the almanac *Literary Moscow* to set up a quasi-autonomous organization of *Moscow* writers outside the Party-controlled Union of Soviet Writers.[1] At the time this could easily have led to the establishment of a centre of intellectual disaffection on the lines of the Petoefi circle in Budapest. Although it would hardly have been allowed to develop this far—that is, to the point of making the explosive contact with the workers which was so remarkable in Hungary—there were nevertheless real fears of such a possibility, as one may judge from certain passages in Kochetov's *Brothers Ershov*.

At the time of the Hungarian revolution, as we know, Khrushchev not unnaturally panicked over the consequences of his own actions, and desperately tried to put a stop to the process of liberalization. He now gave decisive political support to the diehards among the writers. There was the famous meeting in a *dacha* near Moscow in 1957, at which Khrushchev admonished the writers in violent terms to adhere strictly to the principles of socialist realism, and never to forget that they were servants of the Party. There was evident official backing for Kochetov's scurrilous anti-intellectual pastiche, with its denunciation of those Soviet writers initially responsible for the Thaw and its sinister implication that they would have been morally responsible for a Hungarian-type crisis in the Soviet Union. The lesson of the novel was that 'revisionism' is potential treachery, and that hence the

1. It was probably this move to escape Party control altogether that N. Gribachev was referring to at the twenty-second Party congress when he said: '. . . a few years ago our literature was in a very hectic state, because a small group of writers took the crude bait of the Western fishers of men. At that time there were demands, sometimes even from communists, for a revision of the Party line in literature, and the liquidation of its influence on literature. . . .'

intellectuals must be kept firmly under the control of the 'proletariat,' i.e. of the Party leadership. Another measure, which was
only belatedly put into effect in December 1958, when its constituent congress was held, was the creation of the Union of
Writers of the RSFSR. This was dominated by reactionaries, such
as its president, L. Sobolev, who made quite a career out of baiting
'revisionists' in the difficult months after Hungary. It was clearly
designed as an answer to the attempted move by the *Literary
Moscow* group. The idea was to reduce the cohesiveness of the rebellious writers concentrated in the metropolitan centres of Moscow and Leningrad by diluting them with a mass of tractable
provincials, who were far too thinly spread and far too out of
touch with the new mood in the capitals to be affected by the
changed atmosphere. The tone of the constituent congress of the
Union of Writers of the RSFSR was well characterized by the
vicious attacks of several speakers on Pasternak. One of them
added a new charge, namely, that of 'corrupting youth'. He
alleged that two young poets, Pankratov and Kharabarov, students of the Moscow Literary Institute, had fallen under the spell
of Pasternak, made 'secret' visits to his *dacha*, written verse in
imitation of him, hung his portrait in the Institute hostel and—
horribile dictu—circulated a manuscript copy of *Dr. Zhivago*.
For these heinous offences, he said, they had undergone their deserved punishment: expulsion from the Komsomol.

At the time all this looked far more serious than it in fact was,
and there was much talk in the West of a complete reversion to
Stalinist methods. There was a tendency to underestimate
Khrushchev's abiding commitment to reform and his need to
manoeuvre in the face of powerful opposition from the 'anti-
party group'. We perhaps also overlooked the fairly obvious point
that you can't have Stalinism without Stalin.

In any case, during the next two years or so the Party gradually
got over its panic about Hungary, and Khrushchev was able to
improve his position in the presidium. He also proved capable of
learning an important lesson from the aftermath of events in
Poland and Hungary, namely, that the granting of somewhat
greater licence to writers and artists (he may, too, have profited
here from the Yugoslav experience) does not necessarily threaten
the stability of a dictatorial regime. On the contrary, to allow
writers to practise their art without undue interference and with-

out imposing on them absurd and largely unfulfillable demands may even contribute to the stability of the regime in post-Stalinist conditions. 1956 showed that the pent-up frustration of writers and artists is bound to take a political direction. As became particularly clear in Poland, they are less likely to cause trouble if they are allowed a certain latitude as artists. At any rate, by early 1959 Khrushchev felt confident enough to allow a further relaxation, and now, furthermore, in terms which for the first time indicated some willingness to countenance a partial abdication of the Party's hitherto sacred prerogative to 'control' the work of writers and artists. He did this in his address to the Third Congress of Soviet Writers in May 1959.

I shall dwell on this Congress and various circumstances connected with it, because it seems to me to have marked a turning-point; its momentous implications were obscured by an apparent dullness of the proceedings, from which in fact they were only saved by Khrushchev's speech. In contrast to the Second Congress, which was alive with the tension and exhilaration of the Thaw, the Third Congress, at least as far as the main proceedings were concerned, was for the most part uncontroversial and even somehow somnambulant. Ehrenburg attended only on the last day, and then did not speak. Sholokhov did not turn up at all for reasons of a personal nature. All other writers of note who took the floor were somewhat lethargic—perhaps under the influence of Surkov's monumentally tedious opening speech—and left the field to docile provincials and sycophantic fraternal delegates from abroad. This lack of excitement in the proceedings was certainly the result of deliberate restraint on the part of the 'progressive' writers, who probably did not regard the Congress as a very serious forum anyway. One may surmise that the reasons for this restraint were twofold: (a) Most people knew through the grapevine that the Congress would be addressed towards the end by Khrushchev, and there was probably an instinctive feeling that any sharp controversy, or any attempts to settle accounts with the dogmatists on this occasion might put him in a bad humour and thus upset the chances of his reversing the post-Hungary trend; and, (b) it was in any case much easier to express 'progressive' opinions in journals such as *Novy Mir* and and *Literary Gazette* than on a pompous official occasion in the presence of Party and government representatives. Just before and during the Congress, for example, each of these journals published articles which flatly contradicted the Party line on literature, and reiterated in much stronger terms what Pomerantsev had said in *On Sincerity in Literature* in 1953. The first of these articles was Ehrenburg's intriguing parable *On Rereading Chekhov*. Written in the same Aesopian manner as his *Lessons of Stendhal* published the previous year, this reappraisal of Chekhov amounted, through skilful choice of quotation for comment, to a point-by-point demolition of the theory of socialist realism. For example, the key concept of *partiinost* was implicitly dismissed in the phrase 'in the eyes of Chekhov the highest arbiter was conscience'. Here Ehrenburg mentioned Chekhov's quarrel with his close friend Suvorin over the Dreyfus affair, and also his resignation from the Academy of Sciences in 1903 after the government had annulled Gorky's election. Both these examples were, needless to say, very pointed in view of Pasternak's expulsion from the Union of Writers. The socialist realist demand for positive heroes and happy endings was laughed out of court by a quotation from Chekhov's remarks about a bad novel by Sienkiewicz: 'The purpose of the novel is to lull the bourgeoisie in its golden dreams: be true to your wife, pray with her according to the prayer book, earn money, love sport, and your well-being is assured in both this and the next world. The bourgeoisie loves so-called positive heroes and novels with a happy ending because they soothe it with the thought that one may make a fortune and yet preserve one's innocence.' Ehrenburg's comment on these words is: 'Chekhov hated the spiritual smugness, the greed and inhumanity of that world which he called "bourgeois".' (N.B. The quotation marks are Ehrenburg's.) Perhaps the most extraordinary thing in the article is Ehrenburg's remarks on another central idea of socialist realism, namely *ideinost*, i.e. the enforced commitment to official Party views. 'All words are elastic. Sometimes a man is called immoral because his accusers have a different moral code. Sometimes a work, the idea of which conflicts with the ideology of the critics, is branded as "idea-less" [*bezideiny*]. The liberals in *Russkaya Mysl* called Chekhov "unprincipled" [*besprintsipny*] because his principles did not coincide with theirs.' One interesting implication of the Ehrenburg article was that writers under the tsarist regime had certain essential privileges—such as the possibility of conscientious objection—which are still denied them under the Soviet regime.

Konstantin Paustovsky, writing in *Literary Gazette,* made some of the same points in a more direct fashion. It was an unusually long article, occupying about half a page—a very liberal allotment considering that the article contradicted the official line of the Congress. One cannot help feeling that Paustovsky was chosen as the spokesman of an influential group of progressive writers who preferred, for the reasons I have already suggested, not to air their views at the Congress itself. The choice of Paustovsky for this role was a defiant gesture in itself. He had several times in the past compromised himself by outbursts in public against official literary policy, notably at a discussion of Dudintsev's novel three years previously. The publication of Paustovsky's article would scarcely have been possible without the removal of Kochetov, now the chief spokesman of the reactionaries, as editor of the strategic *Literary Gazette* and his replacement by a moderate, S. S. Smirnov. This appointment was certainly a signal to the progressives that the Congress would go in their favour, and it was no doubt very demoralizing to the opposite camp.

It was Khrushchev who, whether wittingly or not, tipped the scales against the latter. The only thing that could have saved them would have been an intervention by him on their behalf, and they must have sensed, even if they had not been informed beforehand, that they could no longer expect any decisive support from this quarter, as they had in the year after Hungary. Their only hope was a declaration by Khushchev that they were the guardians of Party truth in matters of literature, that they were entitled to defend their argument by appeal to higher authority, and, if necessary, by censorship and other coercive methods. Their ideas are far too outworn and their arguments far too weak and contradictory to be upheld by any other means than by the silencing of their opponents. They knew perfectly well that they did not stand a chance in free competition. Khrushchev did not of course call for free literary debate, but he did condemn the only methods by which the dogmatists can in the long run survive. What is fascinating about his speech is its latent ambiguity. On the one hand, he trotted out many of the familiar

clichés of a Zhdanovist type: the educational function of literature as the Party's handmaiden, the primacy of the idea of *partiinost*, and the need for positive characters. Interestingly, however, he did not enunciate the latter as a principle, but rather
defended it as something that had been too severely criticized.
It was almost as though he was saying that positive characters
are not such a bad thing after all. In the same way he was
curiously defensive in a passage in which he said one should not
be too hard on those writers who in the past had given too rosy a
description of reality (the famous 'varnishers'). But the main
thing is that all this was given as his opinion, rather than as an
oracular judgement which could be used as a final argument to
crush opponents. There was a note of sincerity about Khrushchev's remarks at the beginning of his speech in which he dis-
claimed with mock diffidence his competence as a judge of literary affairs.

What really disarmed the dogmatists in Khrushchev's speech
was his insistence on tolerance. He repeatedly stressed the need
to allow writers, particularly the younger writers, to find their
own way and to learn from their mistakes. In one of his typical
metaphors he said, 'In order to learn to swim you have to jump
into the water and try your strength. . . . Let young writers develop their talents in their own way (*sobstvennymi silami*).' The
dogmatists must also have been very discouraged by his quotation of the old Russian saying: 'One must not hit a man when he
is down.' This refusal on the part of Khrushchev to be authoritative in matters of literature, and his insistence on tolerance,
was in great contrast to his tone at the *dacha* party in 1957, when
he provided the doctrinaires with excellent, unambiguous quotations in their fight against 'revisionism'. The present speech was
very much more useful to the progressives, who could now
effectively silence a die-hard by saying, for instance, 'as Nikita
Sergeyevich said in his speech to the Third Writers' Congress,
"In order to learn how to swim one must be allowed to jump into
the water".' The overall impression gained from Khrushchev's
speech was that his main concern was not so much that writers
should be ideologically pure as that they should keep the peace
and not trouble the government with their interminable
squabbles. To achieve this end he even appeared willing to relin-
quish to a certain extent his *ex cathedra* prerogative to control

literature in the name of the Party, leaving literary matters to the corporate judgement of the writers themselves. This on condition that they achieved what he called 'consolidation', by which he apparently meant that the different factions should coexist peacefully, if not amicably. The most important passage in his speech, which must clearly have been understood by the majority of his audience as a hint of some relaxation of Party control, was the following: 'You will ask: what guarantee is there against mistakes? It is difficult to give guarantees, because a writer, if he is a real Soviet writer, makes mistakes not consciously, not intentionally, but for such reasons as inadequate knowledge of life, incorrect premises, etc. In order to prevent this, one must remember that writers live in society, reflect the life of society, that their work must be guided by the criticism of society and that they must take account of this criticism. . . . Again you may say: "Criticize us, control us. If a work is incorrect do not print it", but you know it is not easy to decide right away what to print and what not to print. The easiest thing would be to print nothing, and then there would be no mistakes . . . but that would be stupid. Therefore, comrades, do not burden the government with the solution of such questions. Decide them for yourselves in a comradely fashion.'

This grant of relative autonomy to the writers was accompanied by guarantees that there would be no return to the intolerable phenomena associated with the 'cult of personality', and the progressives immediately availed themselves of it in order to strengthen their representation in the secretariat of the Writers' Union. The board of the Union met the day after the Congress ended and elected Fedin instead of Surkov as the new secretary-general. Surkov remained in the secretariat, but he now had to contend with two new colleagues, Tvardovsky and Panfyorov, both of whom he had victimized in 1954 when he succeeded in having them dismissed from their editorial posts (*Novy Mir* and *Oktyabr* respectively), to which they returned only in the better climate of the first half of 1956. This new board gave some guarantee of moderation, and though not a decisive victory for the progressives it meant that the die-hards had lost their commanding position. Fedin has proved to be an excellent exponent of the policy of 'consolidation'.

The last three years have seen a steady growth in the influence

of the progressives and a corresponding decline in the prestige
and power of the die-hards. The extent to which matters im-
proved after the Congress is best demonstrated by the extraordinary sequel to the story of the delinquent young poets who were
denounced at the constituent congress of the Union of Writers
of the RSFSR in 1958. In August 1959 *Kazakhstanskaya Pravda*
announced in fulsome terms the arrival in Tashkent of the 'two
well-known young Moscow poets', Pankratov and Kharabarov,
who had come there on a travel warrant issued by the Central
Committee of the Komsomol, and had honoured the editorial
board of the paper with a visit. The announcement was accompanied by two specimens of their work. Kharabarov's poem was
entitled *On an untrodden path*. It is a moving appeal for the right
to go one's own way, and it is quite clear that the 'untrodden
path' was the path which two years previously had led Kharabarov to Pasternak's *dacha* in Peredelkino and later to his expulsion from the Komsomol.

Another remarkable example of the extent to which the third
Writers' Congress cleared the atmosphere was an interview given
by Ehrenburg to a correspondent of *Literature and Life* in which
he made an unprecedented appeal for 'solidarity' among the
writers. He obviously had in mind something different from
Khrushchev's 'consolidation'; 'In the very difficult times of the
Eighties Chekhov spoke of the solidarity of the writers of that
generation. Is it not time to give serious thought to the question
of solidarity among writers in our Soviet epoch? Savage attacks
on young writers, cliquishness, and novels in which authors settle
accounts with their fellow writers (i.e. Kochetov's *Brothers
Ershov*, M.H.) would be incompatible with such solidarity.'

The emergence of two camps in literature and the apparent
reluctance of the Party to arbitrate between them creates a novel
situation in Soviet society. It is interesing that there has been no
parallel development of Party control over the historians and
philosophers, as far as one can judge from reading *Questions of
Philosophy* and *Questions of History*. This is mainly, no doubt,
because these fields are so directly concerned with the basic myth-
ology of the Soviet regime that any free discussion here, uncontrolled by the Party, would raise grave doubts as to the legitimacy
of the official ideology which is, however, in any case being under-

mined by much of the new writing. The main question is: why
does the Party acquiesce in this situation? It is self-evident that
ultimately the power and authority of a totalitarian regime rests
on its self-arrogated right to arbitrate in all cultural and social
matters and to impose clear-cut decisions in matters of doctrine.
That the Party is at present either unwilling or unable to intervene in the literary dispute and apparently stands helplessly on
the sidelines, condoning the rapid decline of the most ardent
champions of its totalitarian authority, is, I think, not due only
to the strength and courage of the progressives. Obviously the
Party could still intervene if it wished, and Khrushchev must
understand as well as anybody the logic of the present situation
and its dangers in terms of the erosion of Party authority. His
dilemma is that, once he has committed himself to de-Stalinization, not only can he not afford to antagonize that majority
element among the intelligentsia which shares his reforming
zeal (and which would, of course, go much farther and faster if it
were not apprehensive about jeopardizing the gains already
made), but he is even forced into a sort of tacit alliance with them
against those many middle-aged *apparatchiki* in the country who,
having almost literally achieved their positions over the dead
bodies of their colleagues in the Stalin era, are temperamentally
incapable of accepting the consequences of the exposure of Stalin
and thus admitting their own moral bankruptcy. Kochetov has
emerged as the spokesman of these people, who might now well
form the most serious opposition to Khrushchev's policy. It is
not so much that they hanker after Stalin as that they are nostalgic for a new master who would allow them to play the role of
faithful watchdogs. Khrushchev has gravely disappointed them,
and their mood is best summed up in a brilliant passage in
Abram Tertz's *The Trial Begins:*

The Master was dead.
The town seemed empty as a desert. You felt like sitting on your
haunches, lifting up your head and howling like a homeless dog.
Dogs who have lost their masters stray about the earth and sniff
the air in anguish. They never bark, they only growl. They keep their
tails between their legs, or if they do wag them, they look as if they
were crying.
They wait, they are for ever waiting, gazing, longing. 'Come! Come

and feed me! Come and kick me! Beat me as much as you like (but
not too hard, if you please). Only come!' . . .
     Already, you can hear a whine here and there.
     'Let's live in freedom and enjoy ourselves, like wolves.'

If Khrushchev does not let them off the leash at which they are
straining so hard they might indeed become wolves, and he must
be aware of this. In the meantime, the role assigned to them
is of a rather different order. The Party has clearly decided
on a more sophisticated way of controlling the literary situation
by a system of checks and balances. In order to prevent the progressives from going too far, the die-hards are kept in being as a
permanent reminder that the present trend is not irreversible.
     The proceedings at the twenty-second CPSU congress in Octo-
ber 1961 showed that Khrushchev is even willing to allow the
issue to be debated in a forum which for decades has brooked no
difference of opinion. Indeed, the literary situation is the first
issue ever to be debated in a real way at a party congress since
Stalin's advent to power. The debate was veiled and there was no
overt name-calling, but the contrast between the speeches of
Kochetov and Tvardovsky, as spokesmen of the two camps, was
clear enough.
     Kochetov spoke on the last day of the congress, having evi-
dently obtained permission to reply to Tvardovsky's eloquent
appeal on behalf of the liberals. It is significant that Kochetov
was the only speaker on this last day who did not welcome in
prescribed ritualistic fashion the decision, announced the previous day, to remove Stalin's body from the mausoleum. Tvardovsky had begun his speech by welcoming what he called the
'spiritual regeneration and liberation from certain restraints'
which had taken place in the period after the twentieth congress.
As a token of this liberation he mentioned the rehabilitation and
restoration to Soviet literature of those many writers whose names
had been erased from the record as the result of the 'cult of personality', but, he said, none of this had been achieved without
a struggle, and not everybody understood the 'serious and highly
complicated ideological changes' which resulted from the
twentieth congress; and in a clear reference to such people as
Kochetov he warned his listeners that 'we still encounter certain
residual forms of . . . previous habits of thought and of literary

practice in the way in which our realities are depicted'. Despite all improvements since the twentieth congress, literature had not yet been able to take full advantage of the favourable conditions created by it, and it had often not 'followed the party in being bold and truthful'. There was still too much 'reticence, and a lack of living depth and truth'. This continuing lack of truth implied lack of trust in the Soviet reader. Tvardovsky then went on to make the subtle suggestion that, since one of the functions of literature was to assist the Party in re-educating man, writers of the old school were in effect cheating the Party as well. Writers who took their materials from the newspapers and Party documents were compared with *kolkhozniks* who met their compulsory state deliveries of meat by buying it in the shops. It is noteworthy that not once in his speech did Tvardovsky use the term socialist realism or *partiinost*.

In his reply to Tvardovsky, Kochetov, employing a device which is now characteristic of the literary die-hards, quoted some of those remarks in Khrushchev's speech to the third Writers' Congress which appear to be favourable to the Zhdanovist treatment of literary problems. He quoted, for instance, Khrushchev's remark that the writers should educate people primarily by *positive* examples in life. He noted with satisfaction that there had indeed been some books in recent years which laid the main emphasis on 'positive heroes', and he picked out for special mention only such writers as Bubennov, Karavayeva and Gonchar, who were notorious under Stalin for their abject conformity, and whom Tvardovsky certainly had in mind in speaking of those who had failed to draw any consequences from the twentieth congress. Later on, Kochetov gave a list of approved poets, such as Mykola Bazhan and Maxim Rylsky, who are also distinguished only by their resistance to the 'wind of change'.

Having noted these 'successes', Kochetov went on to denounce those who in recent years had tried to introduce into Soviet literature the 'truth' for which Tvardovsky appealed in his address to the congress. Kochetov replied to Tvardovsky's expression of satisfaction about the rehabilitation of writers liquidated under Stalin with the following sarcastic reference to Ehrenburg: 'There are still . . . morose compilers of memoirs who look to the past or the present day rather than to the future and who, because of their distorted vision, with zeal worthy of a better cause rake around in their very fuddled memories in order to drag out into the light of day mouldering literary corpses and present them as something still capable of living.' He then referred to young poets of the type of Evtushenko in the following terms: 'We also have some poetic, as well as prosaic, chickens who have still scarcely lost their yellow down, but who are desperately anxious to be thought of as fierce fighting cocks.' The most astonishing passage in Kochetov's speech was the one in which, in total contradiction to the spirit of the congress, he called for a purge of the leadership of the Union of Writers: 'It must be said in all frankness that the congress should have been told about the state of our literary affairs by the leadership of the Union of Writers, but this leadership . . . to put it in military language has, as you can see yourselves, lost its combative spirit and is in need of a radical regrouping. Yet it would have had a lot to report, if it had not consigned to oblivion the main questions of our ideological and creative life.'

This was an outburst of despair which can only have brought further encouragement for the liberals. Kochetov was patently out of tune with the general mood and indeed, according to eyewitness reports, he was constantly interrupted and heckled from the floor with shouts of 'Enough!' and 'Shut up!' If Kochetov still has some protection, it is probably, as I have suggested, mainly because of the value of his rearguard action as a check on the progressive writers. It must be assumed also that he has some political support in the higher councils. This is the only possible explanation of his appointment to the editorship of *Oktyabr* at the end of 1961, and of the fact that he was awarded the Order of Lenin on his fiftieth birthday. There has, however, been no significant intervention from above in the controversy about his new novel *The Obkom Secretary*, which was scathingly attacked in the *Literary Gazette* and *Novy Mir* as an apologia for Stalin, and weakly defended in *Sovetskaya Rossiya, Partiinaya Zhizn* and *Kommunist*.

The affair of Evtushenko's *Babi Yar* was also striking evidence of the division in the ranks of the Soviet writers and of the Party's unwillingness to commit itself to either side. The reactions in *Literature and Life* to Evtushenko's vehement denunciation of Russian anti-Semitism were an ominous expression of the ugly Great Russian chauvinism that characterizes the neo-

Stalinists. (It is significant that a current term for them in Moscow is *chernosotentsy*.) It was wrongly assumed by some observers in the West that these reactions were officially inspired. In fact, however, it seems as though the authorities were less distressed by Evtushenko's poem than by the embarrassing display of scarcely veiled anti-Semitism which it provoked. It was an encouraging sign of the relative lack of influence of the neo-Stalinists that, while no sanctions were applied to Evtushenko, the editor of *Literature and Life* was dismissed for having published the disgraceful outburst of Markov and Starikov. From all this and much similar evidence it would seem that the Party continues to lean to a neutrality which is favourable to the progressives.

In recent months the struggle has gone a stage further. Before the twenty-second congress the conflict was mainly a verbal one, and was conducted in a somewhat veiled way, by innuendo and anonymous aspersion in the pages of the various journals controlled by the two factions. At the moment, however, it looks as though there is a fight to control strategic institutions.

On 4 and 5 April 1962, there was a meeting of the Moscow branch of the Union of Writers, at which the liberals used the weapon of the vote against the dogmatists. So far we know of this extraordinary event only through a dispatch from Tatu, the Moscow correspondent of *Le Monde*. The meeting was announced in the *Literary Gazette* of 5 April, and an account was promised in a forthcoming number of the paper, but I have failed to trace it.

It was a question of appointing a new board of the Moscow branch of the Union. There were seventy-six candidates, of whom only sixty-eight were elected by secret ballot. A number of the leading dogmatists were not even put up for these elections: Kochetov, Gribachev (the editor of the export journal *Soviet Union*) who made a speech at the twenty-second congress much in the spirit of Kochetov's, and Sofronov, the editor of *Ogonyok*. Two others, Abalkin, the head of the literary section of *Pravda*, and Leonid Sobolev, the President of the Union of Writers of the RSFSR, were actually voted off the board. On the other hand, three well-known progressives were voted on to it. These were

Evtushenko, his friend Andrei Voznesensky, and the critic
Maryamov, who mercilessly dissected Kochetov's novel in *Novy
Mir* at the beginning of the year.

As far as one knows, this may be the first occasion for many
years on which a vote in the Soviet Union has really been used
to express the will of the majority, and it is obviously a precedent
of momentous importance.

Another interesting sign of the times was a meeting of the
board of the Union of Writers of the RSFSR held in Rostov-on-
Don on 13 May. One has the impression from reading accounts
of this 'Forum of the Writers of the South' that the reactionaries
who control this organization might well have been shouted
down if they had held their meeting in Moscow. They evidently
felt much more at ease down on the Don, not too far away from
their patron, Sholokhov, who did not, however, honour them
with his presence. It is a nice irony that the Union of Writers of
the RSFSR, which was originally created in 1958 in order to
neutralize the Moscow writers by means of an invasion from the
provinces, must now apparently slink out of the capital to hold
a meeting.

There was open talk at the meeting about the intolerable
atmosphere in Moscow. One of the speakers, Semyon Babayevsky (the author of that egregious Stalinist novel, *Cavalier of the
Golden Star*) talked darkly about attempts in Moscow to deprive
their organization of its wheels (*snyat kolyosa s nashego pravlen-
ia*) and hence to slow down the advance of Soviet literature into
the communist future. Another speaker, Anatoli Kalinin,[2]
assured the gathering that they would never allow this to happen,
and gave his audience cold comfort by saying that it was only
in Moscow that one found all the disturbing new trends such as
'modernism' and enthusiasm for Western styles. There were the
usual innuendoes about Evtushenko and other young writers,
and there were rather pathetic attempts to discount their influence. They were written off as ephemeral phenomena who confuse lasting glory with cheap and transient popularity. In his
closing remarks, for instance, Sobolev compared them with a
certain Air Force mechanic who, in dreaming of the fame of the

2. This speaker also made a personal attack on Evtushenko, and was rebuked
by Evtushenko's friend, Robert Rozhdestvensky, in *Literary Gazette* a few
weeks later.

legendary Herostratus, had illicitly flown a plane over his aero-
drome and performed all kinds of stunts for half an hour only
to be rewarded for his pains by twenty-four hours' confinement
to barracks. Sobolev also scorned the idea of the wheels being
taken off 'progressive' Soviet literature because, as he said, it is not
a cart but a much more efficient vehicle equipped with ball-bear-
ings. There is a clear reference here to Evtushenko's poem entitled
Rockets and Carts, in which he contrasts the technology of the
age of sputniks with the obsolete literature and art of socialist
realism.

I should like to conclude with a few reflections on the importance of all these developments for the Soviet regime and Soviet
society as a whole. As I have said, literature is the only field of
Soviet cultural or social activity in which overt differences of an
ideological nature are allowed to manifest themselves. Whether
the reasons I have suggested are right or wrong, the fact itself is
indisputable. Though perhaps the Party is for the time being
able to manipulate the situation to its own short-term political
advantage, it has willy-nilly allowed literature to become a forum
—the only one so far—in which certain ideological alternatives
may to a certain extent be openly ventilated. As we saw, this
happened even at the last Party congress. By tolerating this
fissiparious trend, the Party is inevitably preparing the ground
for a formidable challenge to the legitimacy of its rule, and the
credentials by which it claims to have the right to control all
aspects of life in the country.

With their vastly extended freedom of expression, it is unlikely that the writers will rest content with a purely passive role
in society. Freedom is useless and even frustrating if it cannot be
used to promote social and political change. What we may en-
visage as a first step is a renewal of the demand first voiced in
1956 by the *Literary Moscow* group for an autonomous writers'
organization. The tactics this time, as we can see from the results
of the elections to the board of the Moscow branch of the Union
of Writers, appear to be the infiltration of existing organizations.
If this were achieved, it would be a major breach in the totalitarian structure. How far the Party is aware of this possibility, and
the extent to which it would go in trying to put a stop to it, remains to be seen.

If the mood expressed in the following passage from the latest instalment of Ehrenburg's memoirs—which includes a well-nigh incredible defence of the Spanish anarchists during the Spanish Civil War—becomes predominant among the Soviet intelligentsia, then the Party has indeed every reason to be disturbed about the maintenance of its authority: '*Communismo libertario*—"free communism". All the anarchists spoke about this and nearly all of them believed in it. They tried to prove—and they made their point well—that there can be no communism without freedom. . . . In an old notebook I have found the words of a French author (I don't remember who) from whom I copied out these words: "The unfortunate thing about a despotism is not that it does not love people, but that it loves them too much and trusts them too little".'

INDEX